Child Sexual Abuse

Family Life Series

Edited by Martin Richards, Ann Oakley, Christina Hardyment and Jackie Burgoyne.

Published

Janet Finch, *Family, Obligations and Social Change*
Philip Pacey, *Family Art*
Jean La Fontaine, *Child Sexual Abuse*

Forthcoming

David Clark and Douglas Haldane, *Wedlocked?*
Miriam David, *Mum's the Word: Relations between Families and Schools*
Lydia Morris, *The Household and the Labour Market*
Ann Phoenix, *Young Mothers*

Child Sexual Abuse

JEAN LA FONTAINE

Polity Press

Copyright © Jean La Fontaine 1990

First published 1990 by Polity Press
in association with Basil Blackwell

Editorial office:
Polity Press
65 Bridge Street
Cambridge CB2 1UR, UK

Marketing and production:
Basil Blackwell Ltd
108 Cowley Road, Oxford OX4 1JF, UK

Basil Blackwell Inc.
3 Cambridge Center
Cambridge, MA 02142, USA

ISBN 0 7456 0560 5
ISBN 0 7456 0561 3 (pbk)

British Library Cataloguing in Publication Data
A CIP catalogue record for this book is available from the British Library.

Library of Congress Cataloging in Publication Data
A CIP catalogue record for this book is available from the Library of Congress.

Typeset in 10 on 12pt Sabon
by Hope Services (Abingdon) Ltd.
Printed in Great Britain by
T. J. Press, Padstow, Cornwall.

Contents

Preface		vii
Introduction		1
1	The Nature of the Problem	20
2	The Extent of the Problem	44
3	The Victims	71
4	The Offenders	99
5	Natural and Unnatural Fathers	126
6	Brothers and Sisters	156
7	Sexual Abuse at Home	183
8	What Can Be Done?	208
Bibliography		235
Index		243

Preface

This book, like many others, owes its existence to various people besides its author. To begin with, the research on which it is largely based was financed by the Economic and Social Research Council; I am glad to be able to acknowledge their support here. Without the hospitality and friendly help of the staff of the hospital in London where I studied cases of incest and sexual abuse, there would have been no project. I owe them a special debt of gratitude for putting up with an extra, untrained person about the place, whose questions were often irrelevant to their concerns and sometimes impertinent. They taught me a great deal. In the general tradition of anthropologists studying people who may feel disturbed by what they have to say, I have not identified the hospital, in order to protect the anonymity of the patients. This means, unfortunately, that I cannot thank the staff of the child sexual abuse unit by name as I would wish to do, as they are well enough known for their names to identify the hospital. I hope they realize, however, that this work would have been impossible without them, and so it is, in part, their book.

The British Broadcasting Company gave me permission to use the results of two surveys they undertook for the programme ChildWatch. I am very grateful to them and to Sarah Caplin, Ritchie Cogan, Rachel Carter and Robin McCron in particular. Part of the royalties of the book go to ChildLine, a confidential and free helpline for children, that was set up by Esther Rantzen in response to what the surveys discovered. The idea of the book was first suggested to me by Dr Martin Richards, of the Child Development Group of the University of Cambridge, with whom I have discussed many of the issues as they arose. I also had help from Richard Johnson of the Incest Crisis Line, members of the Essex social services and Sue Burrell in the social work department of the Maudsley Hospital, to all of whom I send thanks. I got much encouragement from my discussions with them and also with Joe Gorry, whose study of cases of incest reported to the police provided a different perspective. His help, like that of Amanda Sackur, Richard Rathbone and other friends and colleagues who read drafts and suggested amendments or further reading, was invaluable, but the responsibility for the book's final form is mine. But I owe a real debt of gratitude to Ann Bone who took on the task of knocking my manuscript into shape and did it a great deal of good.

My family and friends put up with hearing more than they wanted to know perhaps about the cases I was studying and helped me cope with my feelings about what had happened. The research disturbed me more than I had anticipated and I could not have done without their support. I am lucky to have had them to rely on and thank them all very much. One aim of this book is to bring some clarity into the debate about the sexual abuse of children. If it helps to ensure a more enlightened effort to help the victims, it will have achieved its purpose.

J. S. La Fontaine
Southwark

Introduction: The Cleveland Affair

These screaming headlines are part of the public storm which developed in Britain in June and July 1987 over what came to be known as 'the Cleveland affair'. It came to public notice that what appeared to be an unprecedented number of children in Cleveland County had been diagnosed, largely by two doctors in Middlesborough General Hospital, as having been sexually abused. Many of them were taken from their parents into care. The implication of this action by the social services was that at best their parents had failed to protect them, at worst the children had been abused by their fathers and stepfathers. The public reacted with shock and disbelief. Newspapers and television programmes represented these events in the most dramatic and partisan terms: parents were represented as the innocent victims of unnecessary and repressive state action; one particular paediatrician, Dr Marietta Higgs, and a senior social worker, Mrs Sue Richardson, both specialists in the field of the sexual abuse of children, were attacked as prime causes of the suffering inflicted on both parents and children, and their refusal to comment signally failed to calm the uproar. There was a general division into attackers and defenders of these central figures and heated debates took place in public forums and, no doubt, among individuals.

The matter finally reached Parliament. On 9 July 1987 the Government announced a statutory inquiry into the matter. It was chaired by Lord Justice (Elizabeth) Butler-Sloss and lasted 74 days, the report being finally presented to the Secretary of State for Social Services on 6 June 1988 and to Parliament in July 1988. Throughout the year there was continued public debate about the issues involved, which was characterized by extraordinarily high levels of emotion. At one stage, for example, a local Member of Parliament, Mr Stuart Bell, was reported in two national newspapers as having said of the actions of the social services: 'There is a clear parallel with the earlier activities of another body which carried the initials SS.'

How can we explain the extraordinary furore which the events in Cleveland provoked? There is a level at which it is a matter of dissecting the coincidence of pressures of work, misunderstandings, failures in communication, differences of opinion and personal antagonisms which combined into an explosive mixture. This was done, with clarity and fairness by the Inquiry into Child Abuse in Cleveland (the Cleveland Report). Criticism of individuals and institutions there was, but it was equitably distributed and (mostly) moderate. At this level, reading the report, one must conclude that the Cleveland affair was an unfortunate coincidence of many different problems and conflicts, no single one of which would have warranted more than an average amount of concern; in conjunction they constituted a crisis.

The events in Cleveland were not the first intimation that the British public had been given of the existence of the problem of the sexual abuse of children. Concern about it among therapists and child protection workers had been growing since the late 1970s but their concern made no general impact. The first reports of research on children's sexual abuse attracted little public notice or concern. The publication in the press of details of a number of shocking cases of the treatment of young children gave no indication that the problem was other than rare. (In those cases, ironically, there was widespread anger at the failure of members of the social services to remove the children from their parents in time to save their lives.) The social services lacked staff who were trained to cope with cases of sexual abuse and were generally slow to turn their attention to it. A friend with 15 years service as a magistrate recalled that the bulk of the child-care cases with which he had had to deal over that time concerned parental violence. Cases of sexual abuse had only recently begun to come to his court, largely through police action.

Public attention began to be aroused by a number of television programmes on the subject of sexual abuse. The most widespread publicity had been given to the issue of all forms of the abuse of children in 1986, the year before the Cleveland crisis, by the BBC. The popular programme *That's Life* presented by Esther Rantzen, which had established a reputation as a consumers' watchdog, was extending its scope more widely by adding social problems, such as the use of drugs, to its remit. In 1986 it announced a major investigation into all forms of the abuse of children. Esther Rantzen called for volunteers to give information by filling in a postal questionnaire on the subject; the majority of those who responded were women and girls who had been victims of sexual abuse. On the basis of preliminary conclusions drawn from this information, a national survey to establish the prevalence of abuse was carried out. It established that a large number of the nation's adults had been subjected, as children, to abuse of all sorts, much of it sexual. The programme based on this research, ChildWatch, went out on 30 October 1986 in two parts; it was watched by an estimated 16.5 million people.[1]

The shock to the public given by the disclosure of what had been happening in Cleveland was thus not the revelation of the existence of sexual abuse of children but the apparent scale of the problem, the fact that the social services were taking action over cases referred to them and the implications of this for a number of other issues. Between February and July of 1987, 125 children from 57 families in Cleveland had been diagnosed as having been sexually abused.[2] It was an unprecedented number which was straining the available facilities to the limits. Sixty-seven children became wards of court and a further 27 were the subject of place-of-safety orders which removed them from their parents into the care of the local authorities. Few people thought to point out that the numbers which were seen as so overwhelming represented less than three per thousand children under 16 per year.

The diagnosis of this number of children in a short space of time undoubtedly caused practical problems. There were not enough foster placements or vacancies in children's homes to accommodate the children and many of them were placed in the children's ward of the local hospital, Middlesborough General Hospital. Normal medical routines were disrupted and there were formal protests from some of the staff. Doctors and social workers were working long hours under pressure, which resulted in delays in examining children and in providing information to parents and others.

The crisis reached the public through the complaints of parents who came together to protest against the allegations of sexual abuse and to take legal action to obtain the return of their children. A national parents' support group, Parents Against Injustice (PAIN), formed originally to support parents accused of battering their children, was contacted and became involved in supporting the parents. An employee of the Cleveland social services and part-time priest, the Reverend Michael Wright, became co-ordinator of the Cleveland Parents Support Group. In making their complaints public, their most important supporter was one of the local Members of Parliament to whom some parents appealed, Mr Stuart Bell. He raised the matter in Parliament and his speech was widely reported using the most immoderate terms. Massive media coverage of events publicized the conflict, which spread to involve, not only the social services and parents, but also the police and a number of administrators and doctors in the health authority, officers of the British Paediatric Association as well as lawyers and the courts. Stuart Bell and the Reverend Michael Wright, and Dr Irvine, a police surgeon, gave interviews on television and there were claims that there had been serious misdiagnoses.

Reactions were sharply divided between horrified acceptance that the problem was much greater than had been suspected, and hostile disbelief, apparently the majority view. As the report of the inquiry pointed out: 'There is an emotional element from which no one is immune, the effect of which may be manifested in various ways.'[3] During the height of the publicity surrounding these events, highly emotive charges of sacrificing children and families to further their own careers and allegations of conspiracy were made against Dr Higgs and Sue Richardson. The report is categorical in denying the truth of these, stating: 'From all the evidence before the Inquiry, oral and written statements, minutes of meetings, correspondence, there has not been a shred of evidence to support any collusion, conspiracy, bad faith or impropriety.'[4] In addition, it became clear that the aims of the police (to obtain reliable evidence leading to convictions) were different from those of the social services (to fulfil their statutory duty to protect children at risk);

neither understood the other's aims and individuals in those organizations had not merely ceased to co-operate but were in open conflict. The parents were angry, hurt and shocked at what they saw as their powerlessness in the face of accusations they could not refute and state action they could not influence. The majority of the public, particularly those who were parents themselves, could sympathize with their portrayal of their situation and there began to be a general acceptance of the view that the problem had been much exaggerated. The media portrayal of the issues was largely sympathetic to the parents. The possibility that some parents might be misleading in their accounts or even untruthful was hardly ever mentioned in public, although during the inquiry some of them were found to be so.[5] The doctors and social workers at the centre of the dispute were adamant that they had been pursuing their statutory duty of caring for children; they explained the apparent rise in diagnoses as the effect of the recent appointment of specialists in the sexual abuse of children, so that fewer cases were missed, and as the result of the backlog of cases where there had been suspicion which was then brought to the newly appointed specialists. Figures given to the inquiry by Cleveland social services indicate that few of the children were not the subject of earlier concern and that they had been referred in a variety of ways.

The conflict appeared to centre on a controversial physical indicator of anal sexual abuse used by the two doctors in the centre of the storm, anal dilatation or reflex anal relaxation. The term refers to a condition of the sphincter closing the anus, which under certain conditions may open reflexively. While it seems to be agreed that it should give rise to suspicion of sexual abuse, it is not conclusive evidence of it; nor is it a test of anal sexual abuse as it was sometimes inaccurately called. Research to determine the other conditions under which it might appear or discover whether it occurs in non-abused individuals seems yet to be done. However, as the report took pains to point out: 'in only 18 cases out of 121 cases was it [anal dilatation] the sole physical sign and in *no* case was it the sole ground for the diagnosis' (my emphasis).[6] Yet the focus of interest seemed to narrow to the reliability or otherwise of reflex anal dilatation as an indicator of sexual abuse. It was argued on behalf of the parents that the same physical signs could be produced by chronic constipation; second opinions were sought specifically to refute the original diagnoses.

The two doctors were, in most cases, examining children who had been referred to them because of the suspicions of individuals in other agencies. The doctors were not the source of these anxieties; nor did they link their confirmations that there had been sexual abuse to the accusation of parents, as was made out. On the other hand, the social services appear not to have considered the possibility that some children had been abused by adults outside their homes. However, the various parties were usually represented as being either supporters or opponents of Dr Higgs. Even the publication of the report of my research, which had been completed before the Cleveland crisis came to light, was covered by one paper under the headline: Report Supports Higgs.

Several parents took legal action to challenge the orders making their children wards of court and succeeded in getting them returned home. This was taken as 'proof' of their innocence rather than the weakness of the case for wardship. In removing the order for wardship, at least one judge made highly critical remarks which indicated total disbelief in the social services' case. The cases where the diagnosis had been shown to be accurate received little or no publicity. One mother reported to the inquiry that although she had believed the diagnosis and subsequently discovered that her husband, unknown to her, had an earlier conviction for sexual offences against a child, her view was not accepted by Stuart Bell, who believed her husband's denial and was not prepared to listen to her. The views of the Cleveland Parents Support Group were reported as though they were representative of all parents. As the parents were not identified in descriptions of cases, it is possible that the same few cases figured in several accounts.

When the report of the inquiry was published it dealt out criticism in a mainly even-handed way, making it clear that no individuals were solely to blame for the crisis, which was the product of a number of contributory factors. The over-reliance of the paediatricians on the validity of the critical test was balanced by the description of the police surgeons as over-emotional and unprofessional. The strongest criticism was reserved for Stuart Bell and two police surgeons who had allowed their feelings to colour their actions. Detailed refutations of Stuart Bell's allegations were provided and the report's final comment was: 'We were sad that he was unable, in the light of the further knowledge that he clearly had, to withdraw or modify allegations which could not be substantiated.'[7]

However, to understand the significance of the public uproar about what happened in Cleveland and the spending of large sums of public money on a judicial inquiry, chaired by a High Court judge, one has to consider the specific social context of the time. The Cleveland affair must be seen in the context of earlier revelations in the media that parents can and do damage their children, physically and sexually; these culminated in the ChildWatch programme, broadcast less than a year before the crisis in Cleveland became public knowledge. It appeared to release a wave of protest against the idea that such things could happen, which had probably been building up for some time before the events in Cleveland. The backlash against the intervention by social workers was supported by the changing social climate of the late eighties: the Government's action to decrease state expenditure and welfare commitments, together with their more *laissez-faire* market approach tallied with the greater emphasis being placed on 'traditional' values. Parents were seen as wrongly accused and children as having been removed from their homes unjustly. As Stuart Bell and his supporters seemed to see it: 'the family' was under attack.

The publication of the inquiry report did not end the public controversy. The health authority concerned transferred the two doctors to other duties pending its own inquiry but refused to censure or dismiss them, despite concerted efforts to make them do so. During the early months of 1989 the issue continued to be debated in the newspapers; some colleagues of the two doctors, provoked by the length and vehemence of the campaign against them, published a letter in support of their actions, which in turn provoked a reaction. Clearly the debate about whether children are used as sexual objects by adults and, if so, what should be done about it will continue.

A number of important social and moral issues were raised by the Cleveland crisis, quite apart from questions to do with the degree of responsibility for the crisis to be attributed to any single individual. The conflicts provoked by the Cleveland affair were questions of fundamental moral values. British society is not homogeneous and its members may hold a range of values which differ from or contradict one another. Most of the time they coexist as different interpretations of events but on occasions they induce serious conflicts of opinion. I shall outline the most important areas of concern here; they will need to be discussed again in the body of the book.

THE TRADITIONAL FAMILY: PARENTAL AUTHORITY AND THE INDEPENDENCE OF THE FAMILY   Without doubt, the major issue explicitly raised by the Cleveland affair was the question of parental authority and rights. While there were complaints, which seem to have been justified in some cases, about the manner in which children had been taken into care, the main issue was what rights parents could claim over their children against the state, represented by social services. The use of the term 'parents' implies that husband and wife form a single unit, with a common viewpoint and purpose, as in British society it is believed that they should. But in some cases the husbands and wives were not in agreement. One woman was relieved when her daughter was taken into care, since she believed the diagnosis and was afraid that her husband would remove the child from home. Too often it seemed that it was really paternal rights over children which were at issue and the conflict of interests between fathers and mothers when children may be at risk of abuse was ignored.

'FREEDOM' AND STATE INTERFERENCE   A related issue is the question of the autonomy of 'the family' and its freedom from interference by agents of the state. There is an irreconcilable conflict here: if children are to be protected, then the agency which protects them on behalf of society must have the power to intervene against any threat to them. If there is no power of intervention, then there is no means of protecting children. If the possibility of children being damaged by the people normally responsible for them, their parents, is admitted, the protection of children and the complete autonomy of the family are incompatible objectives. It is not surprising therefore that those who were most concerned with parental rights and individual freedom were motivated to deny the existence of sexual abuse of children altogether.

CHILDREN'S RIGHTS   The question of children's rights was less often raised, although it is implicated in the issue of child protection. The Cleveland affair demonstrated extremely clearly how the interests of children may be submerged in the conflict between adults. As

Lord Justice Butler-Sloss remarked: 'It was perhaps inevitable that during the crisis in Cleveland attention was largely focussed upon the adults, both parents and professionals, and their interpretation of the experiences of the children involved. The crisis came to public gaze as a result of complaints of adults suspected of committing acts of sexual abuse. The voices of the children were not heard.'[8] The inquiry tried not to fall into the same trap and took evidence in private from any children who wished to speak. This evidence is presented in the first chapter of the report, the rest of it is described as 'the events and the responses of the adults [which] from time to time may appear to be entirely centred upon adult perceptions and concerns, and the arguments which surrounded them seemed to have little to do with the problems of the children themselves'.[9]

While the Cleveland parents evidently considered that they were the appropriate interpreters of their children's wishes, in some cases where a child had been sexually abused and had not told its parents, or where the abuser was himself a parent, this clearly could not be the case. This is recognized in the recommendations of the inquiry where it is suggested that a child should be represented by the Official Solicitor. Legal recognition of the separate rights of children may conflict with parental authority and the control parents exercise over their children. A report in the *Guardian* newspaper of reactions to a proposal that children be entitled to attend case conferences which would decide their future is interesting in this respect. While social workers envisaged that it would cause them difficulties and were not enthusiastic, the strongest opposition to the proposal came from the representatives of Parents against Injustice, who were adamantly opposed to the whole idea because they considered that a child's presence at a case conference to decide its future would undermine parental authority. Parental rights, in this instance, seemed to deny children the right to a voice in decisions about their future. A majority of members of British society probably considers the nature of parenthood a sufficient guarantee that children will be protected. When there is evidence that children have been seriously mistreated by their parents, as happened not long before the events at Cleveland in the much publicized case of Kimberley Carlisle,[10] this comfortable assumption can no longer pass without question. If all parents without exception did actually protect their children from mistreatment, and specifically from sexual abuse, there would be no reason to write this book.

ISSUES OF GENDER   The Report of the Inquiry into Child Abuse in Cleveland revealed an interesting, though not surprising, pattern in the distribution of individuals on one or the other side of the dispute. Prominent among those who threw doubt on the diagnoses and supported the parents' claim to innocence were men in positions of authority such as Stuart Bell, the Reverend Michael Wright and Dr Irvine, the police surgeon whose views strongly influenced the actions of the police. These three men were prime movers in encouraging resistance to the idea that sexual abuse had occurred. Stuart Bell in particular was very emotional in his appeals on behalf of the parents and in claiming that there was a general attack on the family. The story he told most often was that of a man whose wife, he alleged, had been 'brainwashed' into believing the accusation against him. The diagnosis made by Dr Marietta Higgs and the defection of his wife were somehow combined as the cause of his 'tragedy'. In this case, there was a strong presumption of the man's guilt (see the case referred to on page 6), although people's names were, quite properly, not reported, and tragedy seems hardly an appropriate word though it might have been used with justice for his daughter's situation. The point here is that Stuart Bell seems to have unquestioningly sided with the man concerned. A very one-sided programme made by Tyne Tees Television used a similar story to demonstrate the suffering caused by interfering in family life. It would appear that the strongest supporters of parental authority and the autonomy of family life are men and particularly men of some authority.

The chief women in the public presentation of the Cleveland conflict were the paediatrician Dr Marietta Higgs and Sue Richardson, the child abuse consultant appointed by the social services. Interestingly enough the colleague of Dr Higgs, Dr Geoffrey Wyatt, who was responsible for examining a third of the children, received far less and much less criticial publicity, and the same was true of Mr Bishop, the Director of Social Services. Dr Jane Wynne was often referred to as a proponent of the 'anal dilatation test'; in fact the article describing reflex anal dilation for which she was known was written jointly with Dr Christopher Hobbs.[11] He received much less publicity. In many ways the media presented the Cleveland crisis not merely as one of Parents versus the State but as Men against Women. In one of his speeches, Stuart Bell made a reference to the witch trials in Salem; he seems to have been referring to pressure put on young people to make false accusations. The analogy of a witch-hunt was more appropriately applied to much of the media representation which, at some points during the summer of 1987, did seem to be pursuing a campaign against professional women as threats to paternal authority, rather than reporting matters of public interest.

It could be said that women are more likely to be prepared to believe that sexual abuse does happen and also to put the protection of children above the rights of parents, and that men are more likely to refuse to accept the reality of sexual abuse. This is intelligible when one realizes that it is largely men who are accused of sexual abuse and men whose parental authority is undermined by such accusations. However, the portrayal of the Cleveland crisis as a war between the sexes would be an oversimplification. Dr Wyatt, Dr Higgs's male colleague, appears to have been convinced by some of his cases that sexual abuse may underlie a failure to thrive; he said: 'I felt that I was not doing my best for the children and that I had better correct that.'[12] Clearly he must count as being a committed supporter of the idea that children's welfare must take first priority. In the opposite 'parental rights' camp was a woman, Dr Raine Roberts; she was one of the police surgeons who refused to accept Dr Higgs's diagnoses. Her mind had been made up by an experience that made her strongly oppose the view that anal dilatation might be an indicator of sexual abuse. It was remarked that 'her criticisms were couched in strong and emotive language including strong personal criticism of Dr Higgs'.[13] She seems to have been motivated more by her opposition to Dr Higgs than a concern with family rights. Another woman, the director of PAIN, which encouraged the Cleveland Parents Support Group, was Mrs Amphlett. She produced an expert witness, Dr R. Underwager, whose view clearly supported the idea that children may be pressured into false accusations.[14] (The question of false accusations is discussed in chapter 3 below.) One of Mrs Amphlett's main points was that 'There was not sufficient emphasis on the child within the family setting. Until child abuse was established the emphasis on [sic] our society should be on the protection and preservation of family life.'[15] Her views put her clearly among supporters of 'the family', the opponents of the social services.

Despite there being no clear-cut opposition between men and women on the issue of whether the protection of children should take precedence over the authority of parents, the alignments are suggestive. At the very least they show the necessity of considering not merely 'parents' but mothers and fathers in discussing cases of the sexual abuse of children. They also indicate that domestic authority is a significant issue to men, a topic that will be taken up later in the book.

INSTITUTIONAL CONFLICT   One element of the Cleveland crisis was the conflict between various organizations, and between individuals within those organizations. The police were concerned to obtain evidence which would lead to the conviction of an abuser; where there was no such evidence they were inclined to behave as though there had been no abuse. They were thus able to sympathize with parents who felt they had been wrongly accused and even give them advice. They did not recognize that for the social services and others responsible for the protection of children, the objectives were defined quite differently and that suspicion was a sufficient reason to act. The social services for their part did not understand the police emphasis on evidence. Both organizations seemed concerned to ensure that a case remained under their control and found co-operative work very difficult. This state of affairs is by no means unusual where cases of the sexual abuse of children are concerned, although this book will not discuss it. A number of case-files in the hospital where I worked indicated similar conflicts, although on a smaller scale and without benefit (or otherwise) of press publicity. Research in the United States and Britain,[16] has shown how this is a product of conflicting institutional aims and of the tendency for individuals to become emotionally involved and identified with the perspectives of one or other member of the family. Thus, as has already been remarked, inquiry after inquiry into the abuse of individual children or a group of children like those in the Cleveland cases called for better inter-agency co-operation. It seems all too likely that in many cases this will fail.

However, it is worth noting that in Cleveland relations between the paediatricians, social workers and the police seemed perfectly adequate to ensure co-operation in cases of the physical abuse of children;[17] it was only where the question of sexual abuse and, in particular, in cases where there was alleged to have been anal abuse that co-operation turned into conflict. Yet, in the early years of the discovery of the battered baby syndrome, there were disputes similar to the one which arose in Cleveland between the police and social workers. It seems that disputes over the management of cases of the sexual abuse of children have as much to do with the common refusal to believe these revelations as with the failure of inter-agency communication and co-operation. Indeed, there is a danger that inter-agency communication may become an end in itself and obscure the aims that co-operation is designed to further.

The Research Basis for the Book

The emphasis of the book is on research, partly because I have an academic training and background, but additionally because it provides information and perspective which should be helpful to those who have the difficult responsibility of taking charge of these cases. There is a dearth of such research which is published in a form available to the general public. The lack of reliable information on the prevalence of the sexual abuse of children was referred to by Lord Justice Butler-Sloss in her Report of the Inquiry into Child Abuse in Cleveland. More research has been done in the United States than in this country but it is unwise to expect that social problems will be the same in two rather different countries. Much remains to be done before there is enough information on the sexual abuse of children in Britain to give an account of its nature and extent, but the research that is available has been little publicized. Much writing on the topic is designed to prove that the issue must be treated seriously and resources provided to deal with it. Some adults who have suffered sexual abuse in childhood have written of their experiences. Experts on dealing with the victims have given accounts of their work, or illustrated their views with material from case histories. Unfortunately, social scientists, for a variety of reasons, have largely ignored the problem. There is a serious lack of discussion of what is known and of its significance for our understanding of society.

This book is based on two different types of research material: my own intensive study of cases in the Department of Psychological

Medicine in a London hospital (the CSA Unit), and the two surveys, a volunteer postal survey and a nationally-representative one, carried out for the BBC programme ChildWatch.[18] The hospital was chosen initially because of the existence of a special unit treating cases of children who had been sexually abused, which ensured that it received a number of cases of incest, the subject I had intended to study. In addition the method of treatment used was group therapy, which seemed likely to produce information on the family and general circumstances of the patients. Where patients are treated by psychotherapy on an individual basis, less attention is paid to other members of the family and there is correspondingly little information on them. As a social anthropologist I was interested in the family as a whole; in the hospital special unit, I would be able to study all the members of the household and others who were involved. This indeed proved to be the case, although there was often only a rather scanty report to work on. In particular the social workers who provided the information seemed very little interested in the financial and social circumstances of the family and the kinds of work that the adults did.

Almost immediately it became obvious that to limit the inquiry to incest was unjustified. Reading the files to discover whether a particular case involved incest as well as sexual abuse, the similarity between the cases of incest and the others struck me immediately. Looking more carefully, I could find no major differences in the age of the victims, duration of the abuse or the use of violence in cases where the perpetrator was closely related and those in which he was not. I therefore enlarged the study to include all the cases of the sexual abuse of children during a predetermined period.

I read all the files of cases which were referred to the department after the special unit to deal with sexual abuse was set up in the autumn of 1980, until the end of 1984, supplementing this information with videotapes of interviews the staff had conducted and of therapy sessions, where these were available. Whenever the staff had time, which was not often, I discussed cases with them. I also attended two series of about ten sessions each of group therapy for parents of abused children as a participant observer. Virtually all the men were the perpetrators of the sexual abuse. This last experience was very valuable in giving me some insight into the attitudes and ideas surrounding the whole problem.

The limitations of this study lay in the fact that the CSA Unit sample, or hospital cases as I shall also call them, was not representative and therefore conclusions based on them could not be generalized to the country as a whole. The hospital was a local hospital for the London borough in which it was situated, but it was also a specialist centre which accepted referrals from all over the country, particularly from counties close to London. It was clear that not all cases were referred in the same way and I tried to get some idea of the pattern of referrals but with only partial success. In one county, Essex, the authorities were extremely helpful and provided me with details of all the cases on their registers for two years so that I could see what proportion of cases were referred and what kind of cases. I had hoped to compare this with similar information from the Borough of Southwark but unfortunately the plan ultimately collapsed under the difficulties of obtaining departmental co-operation. What I learned from Essex leads me to suppose that the cases in the CSA Unit, as it was referred to in the hospital, were likely to involve more 'difficult' cases and those in which the abuse had either been very serious or the damage long-lasting. A certain proportion of the cases, particularly in the early part of the period under study, were cases in which it was not clear whether there had been abuse or, if so, who was the perpetrator of it.

The BBC surveys provide a very different type of information. The first consisted of a questionnaire sent to 2,530 adults who wrote to the BBC for one. I call this the postal or volunteer survey. Ninety per cent of them said that they had suffered some form of sexual abuse as a child. The questionnaire included a blank space for informants to write in whatever they liked and this provided valuable data on the course of sexual abuse. Most of them were adults, remembering what it had been like; some of them were recalling incidents over fifty years ago, but some were much younger, and all the accounts tallied with material in the children's case histories. However, conclusions from this source of information cannot be used to generalize for Britain as a whole since the respondents selected themselves and they are clearly not a representative sample of the whole population.[19]

In order to be able to assess the numbers of adults who have been abused, the BBC carried out another survey, referred to as the national, or representative survey, in 1986. Great care was taken to

ensure that the sample represented the general population in terms
of class composition, age, sex and where they lived. Urban and
rural areas were included and the survey was tested twice
beforehand to ensure that the questionnaire which was to be used
by interviewers presented no difficulties. Two thousand and forty-
one adults over 16 were interviewed about their childhood
experiences and any abuse they suffered, including sexual abuse.
The interviewers were also asked to note on each form whether
they thought the person interviewed might have been abused but
was not revealing it. It is important to note that the questionnaires
of 71 people, more than the total number who revealed sexual
abuse, were marked in this way. This material forms the basis of
any generalizations that can be made about Great Britain as a
whole.

The two types of material complement each other very well. The
hospital cases are those of children and the information about them
was rather similar to that obtained in the questionnaire, but each
also provided detailed material on different aspects of the problem:
the hospital cases included discussions of what had happened, how
the case came to light and the consequences of disclosing the abuse,
while the volunteer survey included accounts of the victim's
memories of how they felt about it, in response to questions which
could not be asked of the children. Any bias towards the more
serious or dubious cases in both these sets of data could be checked
against the national survey, which provides a broad overview of the
problem as a whole – although in some respects its results were
rather disappointingly unclear and it was weak in other ways, as
the discussion in chapter 2 will show. In addition, there is research
on various aspects of children's sexual abuse from the United States
and, though it is rather sparse, in this country. This provides
additional comparisons which can be used to evaluate the
conclusions drawn from either of the two main sources of material.
I shall use these from time to time.

The book starts with a discussion of the social significance of the
problem, which begins, of necessity, with a review of the different
definitions of sexual abuse that may be used. The range of meanings
that have been given to the phrase 'child sexual abuse' and to
'incest', which is often confused with it, have obscured many
issues and provoked needless debate. The chapter following then
considers what is known about the extent of the problem, showing

how different definitions and types of research material alter the picture. Chapters 3 and 4 concentrate on the individuals centrally concerned: the victims and the offenders. This shows that the position of children relative to adults makes them vulnerable to sexual exploitation and that opportunities for this are produced by the way in which children are incorporated into the social life of adults, without, however, being visible as social beings.

Yet it is clear that explanations based on this approach fail to deal with a number of the questions that are asked and that one must consider sexual abuse in the context of particular relationships. Since more children are abused in their own homes than outside them, chapters 5 and 6 consider the main types of offender in the home: fathers, stepfathers and brothers. They deal with a number of accepted but unjustifiable assumptions about these relationships in order to show that the way in which they are envisaged ignores the actualities of physical power, social superiority and conflicts of interest. In examining them the relevance of considering other persons who are not implicated in the sexual abuse but are inextricably involved in the problems it causes is made apparent. The parts that mothers and other children may play lead to a consideration, in chapter 7, of the whole family. This raises the question of whether family relationships or the organization of households provide the best context in which to consider sexual abuse; it is the conclusion of the chapter that in fixing our attention on the family, much of significance may be missed. The practical questions of what can and should be done to ensure that children can grow up free of the serious damage to their future that sexual abuse represents, or, more realistically, what should be done when sexual abuse does occur, are reserved for the final chapter when the reader should have a better understanding of the difficulties. Protecting children against sexual abuse is not a simple matter and there are no easy solutions. The aim of the book is to present its complexities in an intelligible manner, not to simplify the issues into any form of crusade.

Some people who work with sexually abused children or who are themselves survivors of sexual abuse might claim that research on the subject is a form of academic voyeurism, and no substitute for more action on behalf of victims. To them I would respond that action that is informed by research is likely to be both better and more effective than measures taken in ignorance of the true dimensions of the problem. None of the real names of the people referred to in particular cases have been used.

This book is intended as a contribution to general understanding and is not written to propose a particular course of action. I endeavour to maintain an objective attitude to the data, but I am unable to be entirely neutral. My sympathies are engaged. I was angered and appalled when I read about what children, sometimes quite small children, had had to suffer: the physical injuries, the despair and the nightmares represent personal tragedies which should not be tolerated in any society.

Notes

1 N. Koshal, 'An Audience Analysis on ChildWatch', BBC Broadcasting Research, Information Section, 1986, unpublished.

2 The figure of 200 in the headline above was an exaggeration, entirely characteristic of some reporting.

3 Lord Justice E. Butler-Sloss, *Report of the Inquiry into Child Abuse in Cleveland 1987* (Cleveland Report) (HMSO, London, 1988), p. 11, paragraph 36.

4 Ibid., p. 83, paragraph 4.188.

5 Ibid., p. 168, paragraph 9.3.30.

6 Ibid., p. 165, paragraph 9.3.22, point 1(b).

7 Ibid., p. 168, paragraph 9.3.30.

8 Ibid., p. 25, paragraph 1.1.

9 Ibid., p. 25, paragraph 1.6.

10 The trial of her mother and stepfather for treating this little girl with appalling cruelty, which eventually killed her, was reported in May 1987.

11 C. Hobbs and J. Wynne, 'Buggery in childhood – a common syndrome in child abuse', *The Lancet*, 3 (1986).

12 Cleveland Report, p. 147, paragraph 8.9.12.

13 Ibid., p. 201, paragraph 11.65.

14 Ibid., p. 162, paragraph 9.2.9.

15 Ibid., p. 162, paragraph 9.2.

16 D. Finkelhor, *Child Sexual Abuse: New Theory and Research* (Free Press, New York, 1984), pp. 205–15; T. Furniss, 'Mutual influence and interlocking professional–family processes in the treatment of child sexual abuse and incest', *Child Abuse and Neglect*, 7 (1983), pp. 210–23.

17 Cleveland Report, p. 13, paragraph 4.

18 A sample (600) of the postal questionnaires were given me to use as well as copies of the questionnaires from the national survey that referred to sexual abuse. All names had been removed from the questionnaires before I saw them and where I have quoted from the postal questionnaires (as epigraphs for example) I have sometimes changed some characteristics to ensure they are not identifiable. I also had tables prepared by the BBC and three unpublished reports on the surveys. I have not referred to them every time I have used them in the text, so as not to spatter the page with even more reference markers, but they are to be found in the bibliography.

19 Chapter 3 below deals with the usefulness and limitations of different ways of collecting material.

1 The Nature of the Problem

The recognition of sexual abuse is entirely dependent on the individual's inherent willingness to accept that the phenomenon actually exists.

Dr Suzanne Sgroi, 'Kids with clap'

It is difficult to think clearly about the sexual abuse of children because it implicates deep-seated assumptions about the nature of human beings, about parenthood and the family. The ideas involved are rarely questioned because they are accepted as fundamental truths about the world, rather than beliefs which can be changed. Any threat to them arouses strong emotions. People do not believe that 'normal' adults will want to have sex with a child or, worse, that they will actually do so. They are particularly unwilling to accept that some parents may do this, as there is a general belief in a maternal or paternal 'instinct' to care for and protect children. Men or women who hurt or mistreat children may be referred to as 'unnatural', 'inhuman' or as 'monsters' or 'animals', which implies that fully human beings do not do such things.

In all societies there are commonly accepted ideas about sexuality, human reproduction and the relations between parents and children but they are not the same everywhere. The fact that the content of them varies from one society to another shows that they are not immutable truths, 'facts of life', but products of particular cultures or social arrangements. This does not mean, however, that these notions are lightly held or easily changed; on the contrary they are unquestioningly accepted and firmly believed. The sexual abuse of children implicitly challenges many of these fundamental assumptions: about sexuality, about parenthood, about children and their relations with adults. The attempt to do something about the problem raises in turn questions about the nature of the family and the proper relations between the family and the wider society or the institutions of the state. The strong emotions felt by adults who are faced with the fact of child sexual abuse are produced by its implications for all these issues. This chapter will try to set out the main concerns but they will need to be raised again in subsequent chapters.

Sex with Children

The idea of sexual activity, particularly intercourse, with a child arouses the deepest concern, even outrage, among all but a tiny minority. What most people consider normal sexual activity is in fact shaped by convention and custom, which differ from place to place. In Britain, heterosexual vaginal intercourse is what is thought to be normal by the majority, while homosexuality, though tolerated, is still considered by many people to be abnormal in the sense that it is a deviation from what is expected or seen as 'natural'. There are differing opinions about particular sexual practices, such as anal intercourse, which is still, formally, illegal even when practised by husband and wife. Individual views may range from considering variations on the 'reproductive' sexual act to be normal sexual activity to labelling them abnormal or even perverted.

Sexual activities with children, however, are almost universally condemned as a violation of what is normal sexual behaviour; the possibility arouses feelings of disgust and horror. 'Child molesters' as they are often called are reviled in the strongest terms. The strongest punishments are called for; people who declare themselves against capital punishment may say that it should be retained for those who sexually abuse, hurt and kill children. It is widely known in Britain that those who are imprisoned for such offences risk serious harm from other prisoners if it becomes known what their offences were;[1] their danger is recognized in a prison rule allowing them to choose segregation for their own safety. These people are seen as less than human, even by those who have themselves been convicted of serious crimes.

It would not be accurate to imply that this horror of sexual activity with a child is universal among adults in British or American society. Child pornography is produced and widely sold in Western societies, even where it is illegal to do so. No one knows how many people buy it. Formerly, members of the British Paedophile Information Exchange, an organization which is now banned, argued publicly that children have a right to a sexual life and that early sex is educational. It is argued by this minority that children under 16 are able to give their consent to sexual acts and should be entitled to do so. There are some who argue that the repression of children's sexual nature does more harm than sexual activities between adults and children.

The argument that children should be allowed to engage in sexual activity with each other and with adults rests on the discovery that sexual feelings and desires do not suddenly spring into being at puberty. The question of how early young people should be permitted to engage in sexual activities is difficult to decide; there is no agreement about when children should begin their sexual lives, or whether it is harmful for them to start too young. However, such activities are not generally called sexual abuse, a term reserved for sexual activities between a child and an adult. There is a general consensus that this is very wrong and there is good evidence which supports it. There are a few adults who say that they do not feel damaged by having had sexual contacts with adults when they were children, but this is usually in surveys where nothing more is known about the circumstances. There is much more evidence that children are damaged by such activities, however mild and gentle the perpetrator of them. Their long-term mental health, their capacity to form lasting relationships and their ability to act as effective parents may all be distorted by the experience.

Legal Offences

The sexual abuse of a child is not specified as such in the British criminal law concerning sexual offences, although the behaviour concerned may involve one or more of a number of criminal offences. The most serious is that which forbids sexual intercourse with a minor, that is a child under the age at which he or she is considered old enough to give their consent to it. An important issue in the controversy surrounding the sexual abuse of children is whether or not they could be said to be willing partners in the sexual activities, but the law is unequivocal: the ability to give consent depends on age. For girls, this age is 16 but if a child is younger than 13 this is a separate offence carrying a heavier penalty, including the possibility of life imprisonment. Where a boy is concerned there is no lower age limit for heterosexual intercourse except that in law a boy under 14 is deemed incapable of it. Where homosexual intercourse is concerned, it is an offence when one partner is under 21, since he is not considered legally capable of consenting to such a relationship before that age. These offences refer to sexual intercourse, which must be proved to have taken place if the accused is to be convicted; the criminal offences of indecent assault or gross indecency with a child refer to sexual acts other than full intercourse. They carry lesser penalties than incest, discussed below, or unlawful sexual intercourse.

The graver offences are much more difficult to prove in court. Although medical evidence may show that intercourse has taken place, there may be no evidence except the child's statement to identify the offender. A child's evidence is not allowed to stand without corroboration so that, as Tranter and Vizard remark, there is the anomaly that although the accused is innocent unless proved guilty, a child is deemed to be lying unless proved otherwise.[2] Thus even if a man is thought by the police to have committed a serious offence, if the evidence is not strong enough to stand up in court he may be charged with a lesser one, or not charged at all. Men may be charged with more than one offence in respect of activities with one child and be convicted on one or all of them. These practices all affect the nature of criminal statistics, as the next chapter will show.

Incest

Great confusion has been caused by the tendency of some writers and journalists to use the terms 'incest' and 'child sexual abuse' interchangeably. The meanings of the two terms do overlap but not completely; the words also have different connotations and evoke very different attitudes. Incest commonly refers to intercourse rather than other forms of sexual behaviour; it is heterosexual and defined by the relationship that already exists between offender and victim rather than by their relative maturity. Incest thus refers to sexual relations between certain types of relatives rather than to sexual activities between adult and child. However, like the term 'child sexual abuse', 'incest' can be used with a variety of meanings. There are three main sources for the differing definitions of the term: there are dictionary definitions which rely heavily on literary evidence; there is the meaning given it in the criminal law; and there are the common understandings of most people. The three are not entirely consistent with one another.

To many people incest is linked with the idea of prohibited marriage and some dictionaries support this view. Thus the Shorter Oxford Dictionary (1982 edition) defines incest as 'The crime of sexual intercourse or cohabitation between persons related within the degrees within which marriage is forbidden'. As far as the English law is concerned, this definition is not exact. There are relatives, like uncle and niece for example, who may not marry but sexual relations between them are not incest in English law although many people may think they are. The author of *The Woman Book of Love and Sex* includes a discussion of sex between uncles and nieces in a section on incest.[3] The usage seems somewhat different in the United States: in her excellent survey in San Francisco Diana Russell uses the term to refer to sexual abuse by any relative, 'no matter how distant the relationship'.[4] This seems to give the word a meaning which ignores the implication that close kin are involved. It would be inappropriate in considering Great Britain because in this country the closeness of relatives is usually as much a part of the definition of incest as the ban on sexual relations.

Others would define incest as sex within the family; the inclusion of adopted children in the law against incest as though they were genetic offspring seems to support this interpretation. However, the law also forbids sexual relations between a man and his granddaughter, who are not usually thought of as members of the same family in its primary sense, although they are of course closely related. As we have already seen, uncles and aunts, whom many would consider just as closely related as grandparents, are not included in the list of relatives with whom sexual relations are banned. So incest in this second sense does not fit with the law punishing incest either.

Incest in the law as it affects England, Wales and Northern Ireland derives from the 1908 Punishment of Incest Act. This defines incest as the crime of sexual intercourse between people related as grandparent/grandchild,[5] parent/child and brother/sister. Adopted children and parents were added when legal adoption was introduced. Until 1857 incest had been a religious offence, dealt with in the ecclesiastical courts, except for a short period from 1650 until the restoration of the monarchy in 1666, when the law passed by the Commonwealth government making death the penalty for incest was in force. After 1857 when marriage and domestic matters were removed from the jurisdiction of the ecclesiastical courts, incest was not subject to any secular law and there was no penalty.[6]

The law on incest in Scotland is very much older, having been passed in 1567. It is also rather different in its provisions. Incest is defined in it in a similar way, as sexual intercourse between designated relatives, but the list includes many persons not included in the 1908 Act. As well as grandparents and grandchildren, parents and children, and brothers and sisters, including half-siblings, the Scots law includes uncles and aunts, nephews and nieces and a range of step-relations: step grandparent/step-grandchild, and step-parent/step-child. Certain relations by marriage other than those of a step-relation are also included: they are parent-in-law and child's spouse, and grandparent-in-law and grandchild's spouse. On the other hand, some relations which figure in the law for the rest of Great Britain are not included in the Scots law. No relations which are not based on legal marriage are covered; thus in Scotland, if a man sleeps with his step-daughter he may be charged with incest, if he sleeps with his illegitimate daughter he is not committing incest, although the act is still against the law if she is under age. In England the opposite would be the case.

Common usage may not exactly coincide with either the law or dictionary definitions. It is probable that most people would consider that sexual activities between a parent and child were incestuous, whether they included sexual intercourse or not; but the law defines incest as sexual intercourse. The result of this is that there may be sexual abuse of a child by a parent, a brother or a grandparent which is not incest as far as the law is concerned, simply because the full act of intercourse has not occurred. In this book I shall use the term incest in its English legal sense of intercourse between the categories of kin defined by law because it is clearer than referring to 'sex in the family' and more accurate than defining incest as related to marriage prohibitions. 'Incestuous abuse' will mean sexual activities with the same relatives but will refer to behaviour which stops short of vaginal intercourse. However, incestuous abuse covers oral and anal intercourse which do not constitute incest in law.

General reactions to the idea of incest are varied. In general it is (wrongly) considered a curious habit of peoples who are either of low status or culturally different (and hence considered inferior). It may be associated with remote and 'backward' areas, like the Fens, Ireland or urban slums. Peoples of non-British cultural origin may also be suspected of practising incest. A senior policewoman once asked me if it were true that in some societies incest is considered 'normal'. Other policemen have told me that working in the Fens always produces teasing by colleagues about the amount of incest they must have to deal with. This mythology even affects some medical practitioners and therapists; thus Lukianowicz, on the basis of evidence which has subsequently been discredited, concludes that incest is culturally normal in Ireland.[7]

Alternatively, incest is associated with overcrowding, hence as afflicting the poor. In this connection it is worth noting the common ideas in the allocation of public housing that children other than babies should not share a bedroom with their parents and that brothers and sisters over ten should sleep in separate rooms. Ignorance and low intelligence may also be thought to be associated with incest, with the implication tht such people do not understand the rules forbidding these sexual activities or, in the language of earlier writings, that they were 'degenerate' and uncivilized. Finally, criminals and alcoholics may be suspected of incest and, although there are rational reasons for both these associations, the ease with which they are accepted and the manner in which the association is taken as obvious indicates a much more fundamental association of incest with, on the one hand, deviant behaviour and, on the other, animal-like, uninhibited instincts. Thus any allegation of alcoholism in an offender is not subjected to rigorous testing but is accepted at face-value, often middle-class face value. Criminal behaviour, particularly by young abusers, may be seen as symptomatic of a failure of training in respect for social rules; incest, like stealing cars or other anti-social behaviour, is evidence that the individual is not a normal member of society.

These associations with incest are very like the beliefs found in many other societies that incest is the practice of evil or anti-social beings; witches who may also be said to be cannibals are quite commonly said to commit incest. In short, in many societies incest is linked with behaviour which is thought wrong or unnatural by that community and is thought to be common among marginal communities who are odd in some other way. However, anthropologists have not yet discovered any society in which incest is 'normal', in the sense that it is either acceptable or so common that it is the norm. The general view is that 'It doesn't happen here, among people like us.' Hence those who are wealthy, educated or in respected positions are rarely suspected of incest. One of the arguments which was used in court to obtain the return home of some Cleveland children was that their parents were respectable and well-off, providing a comfortable home for the children. The implication was clear: such parents could not be committing incest. As the next chapter will show, this is not true: incest occurs at all levels of society.

The different forms of incest provoke rather different reactions in the public generally. Incest between parents and children is regarded as unthinkable, by which most people mean that it could not, and does not, happen among 'normal' people. There is great resistance to believing the evidence to the contrary. Brother/sister (sibling) incest is generally regarded with much less horror than incest between generations. It is widely thought that a certain amount of sexual experimentation may go on between young brothers and sisters. This is seen as childish and short-lived, hardly to be counted as 'incest'. The courts treat it much more leniently[8] and there have even been proposals to remove incest between consenting adult brother and sister from the list of sexual crimes in the Sexual Offences Act. In fact sibling incest may be seen in a rather romantic light; the chance meeting of a brother and sister brought up separately and not knowing each other's identity is the common idea of what such cases are like. Such circumstances could only be very rare and the incest which may occur in even rarer cases is seen more as a tragic love affair than an offence. From time to time, stories in newspapers about couples who resemble this stereotype confirm the belief and help to maintain it.[9] We know less about sibling incest than about any other types of incest or sexual abuse but what evidence there is suggests that the reality is not like the romantic myths (see chapter 5).

Unlike the sexual abuse of children, the idea of incest arouses no strong emotions: it is a distant and curious practice, not characteristic of known people, and therefore of little concern, mildly titillating perhaps but nothing to get excited about. The traditional but still current definition of incest as sexual intercourse between people who are forbidden to marry implies that it concerns mature people, and so glosses over the possibility that the victim of incest may be a child. This may be a reason why it raises no powerful feelings. In no known human society is sexual activity entirely unregulated. All societies place restrictions on their members which, among other rules, prohibit sexual relations between certain kinds of people. These may not all be relatives, but some of them always are. These rules banning sexual intercourse between related people are referred to as the incest taboo, although it is often a case of several taboos, since in other societies there may be more than one offence, each called by a different term[10] and regarded in a different light. In virtually all societies the relatives who may not have sexual relations include parents and children, brothers and sisters. An important, but often neglected point is that the incest taboo(s) in any particular society, including our own, always cover more relatives than just these most closely related people.

In all societies, too, there are regulations which cover which people may or may not marry. Some of them are negative rules, defining who may *not* marry but some societies lay down who may, or even who *must*, marry one another. Thus many peoples consider it proper to marry a close cousin or other relative and in some places to marry someone unrelated would be morally wrong. These marriage rules are obviously related to rules regulating sexual relationships but they are not identical. Since in all societies marriage implies the birth of children, it would not be likely that people would be allowed to marry someone they were prohibited from sleeping with, although in former times children might be married off by their parents for political reasons. These formal marriages were not consummated until years later. But it is not uncommon to find that there are people who are not marriageable but with whom sexual relations would not be considered incestuous. An example from modern English society until comparatively recently was the case of step-parent and step-child.

The Christian Church considers sexual relations outside marriage to be sinful so that sexual prohibitions in Christian societies are explicit in referring to all relatives who were forbidden to marry. The prohibitions used to be quite extensive, extending to second cousins; this is still the case as far as the Catholic Church in Poland is concerned and for the Greek Orthodox communities in the Eastern Mediterranean, although the restrictions are not identical in the two cases. Some marriages with cousins did occur but a dispensation from the Church had to be obtained for them. In England the 1650 Act shows that the ban also used to extend to many people related by previous marriages: in-laws and step-relations, as it does in the Scottish Act passed a hundred years earlier. None of these were what we would now call 'blood relations', but in former times there was no great emphasis on the biological or genetic relationship between relatives and more on their social bonds. (Even today the English language makes no formal distinction between a sister of one's mother or father who is genetically related and an uncle's wife who is an in-law: the term aunt refers to both.)

The nineteenth century and the early part of the twentieth saw many changes in the British marriage rules. Most of these removed prohibitions on marriages with people already related by marriage. One of these, the ban on a man's marriage with his dead wife's sister, provoked a protracted parliamentary controversy. Wolfram, who provides a detailed discussion of it, points out that 'It took 65 years, 46 sessions of debate, 18 successful second readings in the House of Commons to effect this piece of legislation, and in the meantime there had been annual leaders in *The Times* on the subject, pamphlets in their hundreds, a Marriage Law Defence Association and a Marriage Law Defence Union.'[11] Opponents of the reform based their position partly on the argument that if marriage were allowed with one relative in law then the whole principle of relationship in marriage would be eroded. In addition they used arguments which were very similar to those which were later to be used in discussions of the function of the incest taboo: that the possibility of marriage and sexual relations between related people altered their relationship and their relations with others. Thus the possibility of a man marrying his wife's sister would not only alter the relationship between brother-in-law and sister-in-law but damage that between the sisters themselves, introducing jealousy and sexual rivalry into a relationship which ought to be the source of warm loyalty and ready help for both.

In arguing that permission to marry the dead wife's sister would erode all prohibitions on marriage between those related as in-laws the opponents of reform proved to be right. The idea that marriage should only be banned between people who were related genetically gradually established itself, together with a growing general distinction between people 'related by blood' and those who were 'connected by marriage'. Even so the identification of these two types of relationship as equally close survived into this century. Until the reform of the Divorce Law in 1923, one of the very restricted grounds on which a woman might divorce her husband was incestuous adultery, which meant adultery with *her* sister. The most recent step in this process occurred in 1986 when a Bill was passed permitting a step-parent and step-child, when they have not lived together in the same household as parent and child, to marry.

The modern legal rules in Britain restricting marriage between related people cover a different, wider range of people from the law against incest, although public attitudes still tend to associate them together. Many people would probably feel that a love affair between uncle and niece is incestuous, since they may not marry. Yet as long as the niece is over the age of consent they are not doing anything unlawful, although they may be the subject of disapproving gossip if they live together as man and wife. Other people are not too sure what relatives are referred to by the term incest. In his study of cases of incest reported to the London Metropolitan Police, Gorry found that a number of cases were wrongly reported as incest; the people involved were related in ways that meant the law on incest did not apply to them.[12]

Many of the varied, often inconsistent, ideas about family and sexual relationships which are held by people today have a long history in the intellectual life of their society. They are intimately connected with the theories of human nature and society which have developed in discussion and speculation over a long period. Long before the birth of the intellectual disciplines now known as the social sciences, scholars had speculated about the origins of social arrangements and the variations that they showed in different parts of the world. Marriage, the recognition of parentage and patterns of family life were important elements in these discussions. However, it was the incest taboo rather than incest which attracted these early thinkers and this has changed very little over the three hundred years since the early remarks on this subject with which this chapter began.

Theories of the Incest Taboo

The history of theories on the incest taboo usually presents them as a progression of ideas, each invalidating earlier views and improving on them in the ideal manner of scientific discovery, but there are several issues which have reappeared in a variety of guises over the long period that people have studied human societies. The most important of these concerns the nature of the ban itself. Is it the result of human intelligence, a rule which reflects the divide separating humanity from the rest of animal species? Or is it merely the effect of evolutionary processes which have discriminated in favour of those groups who restricted their mate selection? These two conflicting views depend on opposite assumptions about the nature of human beings, which are usually not amenable to argument. On the one hand are those who assert the fundamental differences between human beings and other species; they argue that language, culture and the formulation of social rules are unique to humanity. Those who take the opposite view underline the similarities between human beings and other animals and hold that the distinctive features of human societies rest on biological traits that have slowly evolved and which are similar to the characteristics of related social animals. Each position carries certain implications for ideas about parenthood, sibling relations and the nature of 'the family'. While theories of the incest taboo have developed over time the underlying division into these two intellectual camps persists.

Most nineteenth-century scholars believed that the incest taboo was the result of a recognition of the biological disadvantages of inbreeding or the positive advantages of outbreeding. In their view it was this knowledge which led to progress in the organization of domestic life, lifting human beings out of an original 'animal' state of promiscuity in which the parentage of children could not be known. Monogamous marriage and the nuclear family were accepted as the most recent stage in social developments by men who, in general, believed that social progress followed technological advances that reflected developments in human thought and knowledge. In such theories about the development of human society from an original savage state, the incest taboo represented both an advance in human understanding and an improvement in society.

Another theory associated with the name of E. B. Tylor was that it was the positive advantages of making alliances with others through marrying their women and giving them sisters and daughters in exchange which underlay the rules against incest.[13] His theory postulated a social rather than a biological advantage to marrying out; his theory aimed to explain the incest taboo by reference to marriage rules, for like his contemporaries he assumed the rules relating to sex and to marriage were the same. At that time, as the brief history of changes in these laws given above showed, there was much less difference between the two. Both these theories showed human beings as subjected to restrictions of their instincts for the general good, and as characterized by an intelligence which reflected on and controlled the natural world, including themselves.

There are difficulties with this approach as its opponents pointed out. If early humanity was promiscuous how would they have known who was or was not a close relative in order to prevent them sleeping together or marrying? Could early man have had a true appreciation of the connection between inbreeding and defective children? The critics argued that the hypothesis that the earliest stage of human society lacked any regulation of mating was pure speculation, and unscientific. In that, of course, they were quite right.

Those who disagreed with the view that the incest taboo was a discovery of the dangers of inbreeding argued that, as Sir James Frazer, the famous author of *The Golden Bough*, put it: 'blind savages blindly obeyed the impulse of great evolutionary forces.'[14] In their view the incest taboo was a recognition of practices which had evolved through the mechanism of the survival of the fittest; it had not been consciously developed. A more developed theory of this type was put forward somewhat later by the Swedish anthropologist Edward Westermarck, in opposition to Freud, whose views he contested over many years. Westermarck argued that 'there is a remarkable absence of erotic feeling between persons living very closely together from childhood . . . Persons who have been living closely together from childhood are as a rule near relatives. Hence their aversion to sexual relations with one another displays itself in customs and in law as a prohibition of intercourse between near kin.'[15] Westermarck's ideas were strongly criticized and did not gain general acceptance then. It was pointed out, for example, that his theory did not account for the ban on sexual relations between persons who were not brought up together, such as a parent and child, or for the horror felt in many societies at the idea that the taboo might be broken. Recently, however, his work has been taken up again by scholars propounding a theory that there is a natural tendency among many animal species, including the human, not to inbreed. His work represented a development of Frazer's idea that the incest taboo is innate rather than a social rule, the result of centuries of evolution.

Westermarck's opponent, Freud, like the scholars who were his predecessors, saw the incest taboo as a restriction on human desires; he asserted that attempts to explain it as 'natural' were 'preposterous'. Freud explained the origin of the incest taboo as the primal recognition of the destructiveness of sexual competition between a man and his sons. His ideas were cast in the form of a fable about the father killed (and eaten) by his sons out of resentment of his authority over them and his monopoly of sexual rights in their mother and sisters. Subsequently the sons in remorse imposed the incest taboo on themselves. This sketch of the origins of the incest taboo was thrown out in the course of a discussion of totemism in which he equated members of simple societies, children and neurotics.[16] His ideas got short shrift from anthropologists who demolished his view of the origins of the incest taboo as pure speculation and attacked his inaccurate depiction of members of simple societies.

If Freud's theories won no acceptance among students of social life, his work has been an immensely powerful influence on general thinking. His earliest work proposed an explanation of what was then known as hysteria (what laymen would probably now call neurotic or disturbed behaviour). He claimed it was the result of early sexual trauma and he certainly had access to published information on the rape and battering of children in Paris, where he worked for a time. However, he was later persuaded to view the accounts given him by his patients of sexual experiences with fathers and step-fathers as fantasies rather than memories. His later characterization of incestuous feelings emphasizes the strength of children's desires for their parents, the boy's for his mother and the girl's for her father, for it is these emotions which give rise to the 'fantasies'. The existence of adults who engage in sexual activities with children is implicitly denied. The belief that is now so widely held that children 'fantasize' and so their allegations of sexual abuse cannot be accepted must be attributed to the great influence Freud has had on general thinking. So too, in a rather different way, the idea that children are to blame for their own abuse, that they are seductive and encourage sexual approaches may be an unwarranted conclusion drawn from his arguments that children are sexual beings, rather than the innocents of Christian doctrine, and that they have strong possessive feelings towards the parent of the opposite sex.

Recently there has been the beginnings of a reaction against Freud's ideas, with the exposure of his radical change of mind about both the data from his patients and the French forensic evidence that was available to him. The scattered indications from earlier times of adults engaging in sexual relations with children could be ignored but the modern evidence is too strong to allow people to continue to believe that children's accounts of their sexual experiences are fantasies; the idea has been abandoned, particularly among those who are experienced in treating the victims of sexual abuse. Yet his influence is still strong, both on contemporary scholars and in general thinking.

By the middle of the twentieth century, there had been two important changes which affected thinking about human societies. First, a great deal more detailed and careful information about societies outside Western Europe had been collected. Secondly, there had been a reaction against the whole cast of earlier thinking which, in concentrating on producing a hypothetical scheme for the evolution of societies and cultures, had too often relied on pure speculation rather than historical evidence. In reaction, those who studied the incest taboo were concerned to show its effect in maintaining social life, its function rather than its origin. The functionalists as they came to be called took up another old idea and refurbished it. Their general approach was that the structure of the family depended on reserving sexual relations to the adult couple. Incest, in this view, would undermine the whole structure of the family which depended on the authority of parents and the obedience of children. The superiority of parents was considered to be derived from their biological and social maturity but was also believed to be essential to the fulfilment of their roles as rearers and teachers of their offspring. The subordination of children was related to the physical dependence of human infants and the long period of maturation characteristic of our species, but was equally necessary to enable them to become fully adult social beings. Thus the inequality of the parent–child relationship was seen as based in human biological nature; it was the inevitable concomitant of the difference in maturity. However, since maturity in the human species involves learning as well as mere physical growth, the relationship of parents and children was more than merely biological; it was the means by which culture was transmitted from generation to generation. This relationship was capable of being undermined or disrupted. The incest taboo was a social rule which acted as protection against the disruption of the vital social relationship between parent and child.

This anthropological view, which has persisted with little serious reconsideration, reveals, quite unintentionally, what these students of social life thought characterized any relationship based on sexual association. The emphasis on its disruptive potential is by no means incompatible with the Freudian view. Competition and rivalry, jealousy and instability of affection were its main features. Underlying these emotions there lay the assumption that sexual partners were equals. By implication it was the equality of sexual partners or sexual competitors which was dangerous to the structure of the family. A man who engaged in sexual relations with his daughter was thought to lose his authority over her, that is his right to command her obedience; he was reduced to her level, or she was raised to his. Similarly, rivals were equals so that incest, it was argued, would destroy a man's authority over his sons, changing their relationship. The model of sexual relationships they were using, as the French sociologist Durkheim had earlier made clear,[17] was that of pre-marital courtship. The mental picture created is of individuals free of social constraints engaging in choosing partners. The disapproved aspects of sexuality – rape, paedophilia and homosexuality – were ignored.

This scenario is clearly related to the Western ideal of sexual relations as indistinguishable from marriage; marriage is the sanctification of a sexual relationship which is based on personal and mutual choice among equals. In this view the instability of mutual sexual attraction in private relationships between individuals is ultimately transformed by marriage into a public and lasting conjugal partnership which is the first step in creating a new family. Family relationships are assumed to be based in nature, to be long-lasting and ordered.

There are several other assumptions underlying this approach which will need to be unravelled one by one. First of all the ideal of 'the family' as a natural unit on which all social life is based has to be considered. In attempts to understand both incest and the sexual abuse of children the assumption that a man and a woman live together to share the care and support of their offspring is usually taken for granted, as it is more generally. In many societies this is not the case. While in all societies there is some recognition that children have two parents, the relationships between them and their children vary considerably; living in the same house is not an invariable part of them. Among the Hopi of the south-western United States, for example, traditionally most adult men and women lived in households composed of brothers and sisters rather than married couples. Children lived with their mothers, so that the wives and children of Hopi men lived under the care of their mother's brothers and great-uncles. In parts of Highland New Guinea, men slept and ate in a men's house together with the initiated boys of the village; women lived in small huts with their young children and the domesticated pigs which belonged to their husbands. In Africa, several generations, including married couples, may live together. In considering the range of human social arrangements it becomes clear that there is no 'natural' unit, if by unit one means a set of people who habitually live and eat together. Even in Western societies actual households often do not follow the ideal pattern: death and divorce separate the original couple and many households contain people who are not members of 'the family' in the narrow sense.

Today there are several approaches to understanding the incest taboo and it has lost much of its significance in anthropological debate. The first view denies that the incest taboo is universal. It points to the fact that sexual prohibitions, including those against homosexuality, adultery or rape, are very variable. While in most societies they include all the people whom we think of as members of one family, this fact is misleading. First the rules are often characterized in very different ways: sexual relations with a parent may be seen as a different offence from sexual relations with a brother or sister. Secondly, the strongest prohibitions often include a wide range of other relations, some of whom may be more strongly tabooed than close relatives. Thirdly, the sense of horror or outrage which we think of as associated with the crime of incest does not seem to occur in some societies, who merely think incest foolish or are indifferent to the idea. Finally, the family as we think of it, a small nuclear unit living in a single household, does not exist in many societies outside the West. It is far more common for households to be larger, sometimes with more than one wife and their children or three generations living together. Relations between the members of these households differ from those expected in the family households of Western societies. From this point of view, the notion that the incest taboo is universal and hence has to be explained as an aspect of human nature is a figment of the imagination of those scholars who saw all societies through the eyes of their own. The incest taboo is not universal and there is thus nothing to be explained. To scholars holding these views there is greater interest to be found in studying whole systems of relationships than in the incest taboo.

Others, following Schneider, have argued that the incest taboo is an idea which symbolizes how certain relationships should be conducted.[18] Other prohibitions, on eating with or speaking to certain relatives or in-laws, may be viewed in much the same manner as the incest taboo. What is important to him and to those who think like him is to explore the meaning of incest in each particular society and consider what it stands for there. Only when we have done this will we begin to understand what these sexual prohibitions are. Both these approaches ignore the question of whether the incest taboo is broken or not. Like all other anthropologists before them, those who use them have concentrated on comparing taboos rather than considering whether they are effective. Freud, if he had stuck to his earlier thesis, might have revolutionized thinking on the incest taboo by producing evidence that incest had damaged many of his middle-class patients, but the idea was too shocking to be entertained in the society of his day; it was transformed and the foundation of psychoanalysis was laid.

However, the old idea that the incest taboo is a natural aversion to sexual relations with close kin, whether for biological reasons or through the evolution of habits of outbreeding, is not dead. The new mixed discipline of sociobiology has brought back, with various degrees of sophistication, ideas like those of Frazer and Westermarck. One theory in particular, which refurbishes Westermarck's theory of 'familiarity breeds contempt', is extremely relevant to our view of brother–sister sexual relations and will be discussed in more detail in chapter 5. The others need not be discussed in detail here save to note that they assume that incest does not occur and that sexual relations, which they equate with the breeding systems of animals, take place only between mature individuals of opposite sex. Although clothed in modern language, they are views more akin to those of the nineteenth-century scholars, with their failure to distinguish between sex and marriage, than to the more recent theories they oppose so strenuously.

In general, anthropology has been of little assistance in understanding either incest or the sexual abuse of children. A very few anthropologists have recorded cases of incest that came to their notice but the lack of information about incest or the sexual abuse of children is striking. One scholar has gone as far as to characterize the profession's assumption that the incest taboo was not broken and its lack of interest in evidence to the contrary as a 'denial of incest'.[19] He is not the first to complain of anthropology in this way. Many of the ideas that were developed by nineteenth-century scholars have by now become part of the general thinking of a wider public. Many people are convinced that the incest taboo is an inviolable rule that prevents inbreeding and marriages that are 'too close'. They do not consider that it refers to a ban on sex between adults and the children they live with. But the evidence of the sexual abuse of children that has been provided in the last few years challenges all these comfortable assumptions. Most disturbing of all, it raises the question of whether parental love can be relied on to protect children from harm.

A History of Growing Concern?

Public concern over the sexual abuse of children is a relatively recent phenomenon. Sexual abuse was not even mentioned in Department of Health and Social Security circulars until 1980, as the authors of one of the earliest surveys of the problem in Britain pointed out.[20] It is only comparatively recently that the general public in Britain has begun to realize that, far from being an extremely rare phenomenon, the sexual abuse of children is much more widespread. In the United States this realization came about ten years earlier than it did in Britain. Even so an American textbook of psychiatry published in 1975 estimated the number of cases as one in a million, whereas today no one would produce an estimate that was not a matter of numbers per hundred.[21] By the end of the seventies there was considerable publicity given to what had been discovered to be a serious social problem; in the United States, according to Finkelhor, 'Between 1977 and 1978 almost every national magazine had run a story highlighting the horrors of children's sexual abuse . . . in record-breaking time it obtained the passage of protective legislation nationally and in 35 states'.[22] From the point of view of the public, it was a new and appalling social problem. Finkelhor suggests that it had become so largely as the result of the growth of two popular campaigns: the feminist movement, and that for the protection of children, which had highlighted their vulnerability in the privacy of domestic life. The earlier discovery that children and babies might be physically hurt or even killed by their parents also contributed to the recognition of their sexual abuse.

Something similar seems to have happened in Britain. Although child specialists here had been alerted by what was happening in the United States, and the first survey to detect incidence was carried out between 1977 and 1978,[23] public awareness has only recently reached the stage that it had reached there in the late seventies. The rest of Western Europe is at an earlier stage still, although a German study of incest offenders published in 1968 implied that many of the victims had been children.[24]

Yet despite the neglect of incest as a subject of study, concern over incest and the sexual abuse of children is not new in England or elsewhere in Western society. Reports on cases of sexual abuse go back to before the turn of the century. In 1878 Tardieu described post-mortem findings of the sexual abuse of children;[25] Masson has shown convincingly that Freud based his early view that sexual trauma was the source of adult neurosis not only on the accounts of his patients but on this material.[26] There has also been concern about child prostitution at certain periods, but as a social problem the sexual abuse of children has tended to come to public notice only intermittently. In Britain the Punishment of Incest Act passed by Parliament in 1908 was in part a response to concern about the sexual abuse of children and the pressure of the newly-formed National Society for the Protection and Care of Children for measures to be taken against it.[27] Since the passage of the Incest Act a variety of other laws have been passed preventing sexual relations with children who are under the age of consent.[28] Perhaps the public came to assume that the passage of such laws had solved the problem. For whatever reason, it appears to have been assumed, even among specialists, that the sexual abuse of children was confined to rare acts committed by perverts.

The most recent recognition of the sexual abuse of children was preceded by concern with their physical abuse. The phenomenon of 'baby-battering' was revealed in the 1960s; the term for it came from an original paper by Kempe and his colleagues in 1962.[29] Concerns over the difficulties of diagnosis, of drawing a line between behaviour that deviates to a lesser or greater degree from the ideal or the expected and that which threatens a child's welfare or even its life, which were discussed then, resemble the issues being aired with respect to sexual abuse twenty years later. There was a similar reluctance to believe that parents could inflict injuries on their children and a parallel debate over children's rights and the freedom of parents to bring children up without too much supervision and interference from the state. There were public controversies over the diagnoses in particular cases which show many parallels to the debate over anal dilatation as an indicator of sexual abuse. It is probable that the general acceptance that some parents may beat their children, torture or even kill them has hastened acceptance of the existence of sexual abusers of children, particularly among social workers and other child protection workers who deal with it.

What is Sexual Abuse?

Despite general agreement about the undesirability of sex between adults and children, there is no such consensus as to what is meant by 'sexual abuse'. Although there has been public discussion of it in Britain and the United States for several years and furious controversy over what has actually happened in particular cases, any close scrutiny makes it obvious that the label, like that of incest with which it is often confused, is used in different ways by different people. The absence of agreed meanings for these and other terms used in the debate about the problem has added to the arguments surrounding the various issues, generating more emotional heat without shedding much more light of understanding on the problems. This makes it essential to make clear how the terms are to be used in this book.

The sexual abuse of children refers primarily to the activities of adults who use children for their sexual gratification. This meaning is common to all uses of the phrase 'child sexual abuse' which appears more and more frequently in the press and on television and radio. When it comes to specifying what behaviour is considered abusive, there are differences. The term is commonly used in the media without making it clear what sense is intended. This adds considerable confusion to the debate because, as we shall see in the next chapter, the meaning given to this term can affect the findings of research and give very different impressions of the nature and scale of the problem. 'Sexual abuse' refers to bodily contact of all sorts: fondling, genital stimulation, oral and/or anal intercourse as well as vaginal intercourse. But some people may extend the meaning to include suggestive behaviour, sexual innuendo or exhibitionism ('flashing'). Two of the studies which will be considered in the next chapter use sexual abuse with this wider meaning. Such behaviour is included because it concerns adult sexual behaviour which involves a child and these events are undoubtedly unpleasant and may have damaging emotional consequences. To many people they seem less serious than and rather different from the other sexual activities which are referred to in the phrase. What is more important, there is no evidence that they may lead to the more serious kind of sexual abuse, whereas even mild touching may be the beginning of an involvement which is much more damaging. In what follows, and throughout the book, the sexual abuse of children will mean adult or sexual activities involving bodily contact with a child or adolescent for the gratification of the adult. 'Child sexual abuse' in this definition involves two main features: it is an adult activity and it involves a child as victim. The definitions of offender and victim depend on their ages and not on their relationship.

Where Britain is concerned, the problem of the sexual abuse of children exploded into the public domain through the events at Cleveland in 1987. Although the report of the Statutory Inquiry did something to calm the atmosphere of anger and confusion, the need for information was made abundantly clear. Lord Justice Butler-Sloss in her report referred on more than one occasion to the lack of reliable data on the prevalence of the problem. There is information but much of it can be misleading unless it is seen in context and looked at in detail. This assessment, which will be the task of the next chapter, requires consideration of the ways in which figures are produced: the definition of the subject, the methods of collecting the raw data and the factors which might enhance or diminish the accuracy of the final results.

Notes

1 Howard League for Penal Reform, *Unlawful Sex: Offences, Victims and Offenders in the Criminal Justice System of England and Wales*, report of a Howard League working party (1985), pp. 45–6.
2 M. Tranter and E. Vizard, 'The professional network and management of disclosure', in A. Bentovim et al. (eds), *Child Sexual Abuse within the Family* (Wright, London, 1988), p. 147.
3 D. Sanders, *The Woman Book of Love and Sex* (Sphere, London, 1985), pp. 176–7.
4 D. E. H. Russell, *The Secret Trauma: Incest in the Lives of Girls and Women* (Basic Books, New York, 1986).
5 Grandmothers are not in fact mentioned in either the 1908 law against incest or in marriage prohibitions; presumably it was considered unthinkable that a woman and her grandson should either commit incest or want to marry. Technically therefore there is no penalty against either.
6 S. Wolfram, *In-laws and Outlaws: Kinship and Marriage in England* (Croom Helm, London and Sydney, 1986).
7 N. Lukianowicz, 'Incest', *British Journal of Psychiatry*, 120 (1972), pp. 301–13.
8 V. Bailey and S. McCabe, 'Reforming the law of incest', *Criminal Law Review* (1979), pp. 749–64.
9 *South London Press*, 30 September 1986; *Observer*, 4 August 1974 and 2 November 1975.
10 J. Goody, 'A comparative approach to incest and adultery', *British Journal of Sociology*, 7 (1956).
11 Wolfram, *In-laws and Outlaws*.

12 P. J. Gorry, 'Incest – the Offence and Police Investigation', M. Phil. thesis in Criminology, University of Cambridge, 1986.

13 E. B. Tylor, 'On a method of investigating the development of institutions: applied to laws of marriage and descent', *Journal of the Royal Anthropological Institute*, 18 (1889), pp. 245–69.

14 J. G. Frazer, *Totemism and Exogamy* (Macmillan, London, 1910), p. 169.

15 F. Westermarck, *The History of Human Marriage* (Macmillan, London, 1921, first published 1894).

16 S. Freud, *Totem and Taboo* (W. W. Norton, New York, 1950).

17 E. Durkheim, *Incest: The Nature and Origin of the Taboo* (Lyle Stuart, New York, 1963 trans., first published 1898).

18 D. M. Schneider, 'The meaning of incest', *Journal of the Polynesian Society*, 85 (1976), pp. 149–69.

19 W. Arens, *The Original Sin: Incest and its Meaning* (Oxford University Press, Oxford, 1986). The last chapter of this book considers what one might expect in other societies but the debate must remain largely speculative until there is more evidence.

20 M. Tranter and E. Vizard, 'Recognition and assessment of child sexual abuse', in Bentovim et al. (eds), *Child Sexual Abuse*.

21 D. J. Henderson, 'Incest', in A. M. Freedman, H. I. Kaplan and B. J. Sadock (eds), *Comprehensive Textbook of Psychiatry* (Williams and Wilkins, Baltimore, 1975), p. 1532, quoted in J. Herman, *Father–Daughter Incest* (Harvard University Press, Cambridge, Mass. and London, 1981).

22 Finkelhor, *Child Sexual Abuse*.

23 P. B. Mrazek, M. Lynch and A. Bentovim, 'Recognition of child sexual abuse in the United Kingdom', in P. B. Mrazek and C. H. Kempe (eds), *Sexually Abused Children and Their Families* (Pergamon, Oxford, 1981).

24 H. Maisch, *Incest* (Andre Deutsch, London, 1973 trans., first published 1968).

25 A. Tardieu, *Étude médico-légale sur les attentats au moeurs* (Ballière et fils, Paris and London, 1878).

26 P. M. Masson, *Freud: The Assault on Truth* (Faber and Faber, London, 1984).

27 S. Wolfram, 'Eugenics and the Punishment of Incest Act 1908', *Criminal Law Review* (1983), pp. 508–18.

28 They were consolidated in the Sexual Offences Act of 1956.

29 C. H. Kempe, F. N. Silverman, B. F. Steele, W. Droegmueller and H. K. Silver, 'The battered child syndrome', *Journal of the American Medical Association*, 18 (1962), pp. 17–24.

2 The Extent of the Problem

... now I realise that I wasn't alone in my torment.

Woman, aged about 40, Great Yarmouth

... it is only the past six years when people have talked openly about child abuse that I've realised it was not my fault and that I was not the only one it ever happened to. If only I'd felt like I do now 30 years ago how [much] better my life would have been.

Woman, aged about 50, Hemel Hempstead

Once a social problem has been given as much nation-wide publicity as recent events have given to the sexual abuse of children in Britain, there is widespread concern about the extent of it. The public wants to know how many children are affected, and whether the numbers can be expected to increase. A variety of figures which purport to give the answers to these questions are quoted in the media but the differences between them fuel public debate and controversy rather than providing a firm basis of information. Estimates of the proportion of the adult population that have been abused in childhood range from 3 per cent[1] to 54 per cent.[2] Low estimates of the extent of abuse may be used to argue that the problem has been much exaggerated, while the higher ones serve to confirm the opposite view. People with firm convictions on either side of the argument greet new estimates with various degrees of credulity or scepticism or attack the figures presented by others as inaccurate. As most of the research is vulnerable to criticism, it is fairly easy to undermine either case. The result is that the uncommitted public becomes thoroughly confused and there is a general search for 'accurate information' on which to base conclusions, or a demand to know the 'true' rate.

The need for better information is not merely that it might settle a public and increasingly acrimonious argument about what is happening to children. There are also very practical concerns involved. If social service departments are to provide the staff and resources to cope with sexually abused children, then what resources will they need? Moreover, if it can be shown that a large proportion of parents are unable to see that their children are not abused in this way, or even that they themselves are to blame for the abuse, should legislation be enacted to protect the vulnerable individuals who are our future citizens? On the other hand, are the child protection agencies over-reacting and diagnosing unharmed children as abused in a moral panic that is unjustified? Do the social services have too many powers and parents too few? Accurate data are essential both to our general understanding and to the determination of policy, although for reasons that have already been outlined, it seems clear that the debate is also a moral one about the nature of parenthood and the proper relations between 'the family' and 'the state'. Such questions too cannot be resolved without an attempt to understand the complex nature of what is happening.

The Problems of Research

The search for 'the truth' about child sexual abuse is somewhat misguided because, as this chapter will try to show, figures depend very much on the way in which they are produced: they are affected by the definition of abuse but they are also affected by the sources of information and the methods of research that are used. The difficulties of establishing anything like an accurate assessment are seldom given serious consideration and they are formidable. The characteristics of the problem itself present barriers to research: sexual abuse is a crime that can be kept entirely secret. Many victims of it are unwilling or unable to talk, for many different reasons – fear, shame, guilt and the quite justifiable feeling that they may not be believed or that, if believed, they will be seen as somehow tainted by the experience. Its exposure disturbs widely held and deeply felt convictions. Many people would prefer not to know or not to tell what they know. Others, impelled by their outrage at what happens to the victims and at society's failure to protect its most vulnerable members, may emphasize the most shocking cases and the most inflated figures to try and arouse public concern. It is a subject in which few people can be entirely neutral.

However, it is also essential to provide an understanding of what research can or cannot do in order to prevent the problem being buried in a mass of over-simplified assertions. It is possible to give only approximate answers to the questions which are being posed, and the 'true' rate will probably never be known, but the general pattern is clear. Moreover, the recognition of a serious social problem need not depend on the percentage of those affected being exact to the last decimal point.

Information on the sexual abuse of children in Great Britain is obtained in a number of different ways. Most of the results are presented as figures which have a quite unjustified air of reliability. There is a general acceptance of figures as being more 'scientific' than other kinds of information, which may be quite misleading. Quantified information, displayed as tables or statistics, is only as reliable as the means used to produce it. As this chapter and chapter 4 will show, the processes of retrieving or discovering information about the sexual abuse of children affect the final result; they introduce bias. By 'bias' I do not mean an intentional distortion of the evidence but a slant which prevents the results of research accurately reflecting the object of study. Generalizations which are based on these results may, quite unintentionally, be misleading. The consequences can be unfortunate and disturbing.

Rates of Sexual Abuse

Two kinds of rates of sexual abuse are often confused. A prevalence rate is a figure for the numbers of people who have been affected over their whole childhood, usually presented in the form: X out of 100 individuals have been abused in childhood. But this does not mean that X number of children are being abused *now*. The abuse to X adults happened at some point in their first 18 years of life, which is what is normally meant by 'childhood'; children now are at various stages of this. For ethical reasons, children are not made the objects of survey, so that a survey of problems relating to children must ask adults to recall their own childhood. The information obtained refers to events scattered over a period from immediately before the date of the survey to soon after the birth-date of the oldest – that will be over 75 years before, when social conditions were very different. Death reduces the numbers of older people who are available to the survey so that the numbers of older people answering the questions are not representative of their generation but merely of those of it who have survived. Moreover it seems probable that older people are much less likely to answer questions on subjects like sexual abuse, since they grew up at a time when such subjects were unmentionable, particularly to a total stranger. The higher rate of recorded abuse found in some surveys among those in their early twenties may be the product of their willingness to talk and of the fact that a little distance from the events enables them to do so. A national survey is only a rough guide to the contemporary prevalence of the sexual abuse of children and a poor guide to whether it is increasing.

The numbers of children affected over a single period, usually given as a year, is an incidence rate. This can be obtained either by extrapolation from a prevalence rate or from figures obtained from other sources; either of these methods may introduce significant bias in the results. Another method of assessing an incidence rate, which is highly suspect because it needs far more detailed information than is usually available, is to count the average number of incidents of abuse in known cases, multiply them by the number of cases and produce an annual total of events of sexual abuse. This is extremely misleading because it assumes, first that a few cases can represent all those occurring in the nation as a whole and secondly that it is possible to be sure how many incidents of abuse have taken place in each case; neither of these assumptions is justified. All three rates may be confused with one another in discussions of the extent of the problem. Incidence and prevalence rates are not related in any simple way. Most figures that are collected are prevalence rates and even if incidence rates are calculated from them they may contain sources of serious inaccuracy. The differences between various prevalence or incidence rates are, however, not merely a matter of greater or lesser accuracy. Figures are not necessarily 'right' or 'wrong'. Rates which purport to give the prevalence of the sexual abuse of children may, in fact, be measuring rather different things and be subject to different kinds of bias or error. It is often impossible to compare the figures derived from different sources.

Some Available Sources of Information

The collection of figures obtained for a variety of other purposes, which may be referred to as research, provides information that is useful in the absence of research specifically designed to analyse the problem, but which also has serious limitations. The sexual abuse of children concerns a number of government departments, voluntary agencies and experts such as child specialists, both medically and psychologically trained, who make records of cases in the course of their work. Much of this information is published. Some of these organizations deal with the victims, others with the offenders. The Home Office publishes figures which result from the processes of law, from the police and the courts: these are figures of reported offences, offences tried in the courts and convictions. The social services report the numbers of children on their 'at risk' registers. Organizations concerned with the victims of abuse, such as the Incest Crisis Line, incest survivors' groups, the National Society for the Prevention of Cruelty to Children (NSPCC) and departments of psychological medicine all collect figures relating to the cases they deal with. Individual practitioners may also publish studies based on cases they have treated.

Allegations of children's sexual abuse may also be made in a number of contexts where they are less likely to be recorded. Doctors, voluntary agencies working with families, workers in refuges for wives, rape crisis centres, family conciliation services and solicitors dealing with custody disputes may also have allegations made to them. In Britain, unlike the United States, there is no statutory obligation to report these cases; although they may be referred to the social services or to therapists, there are indications that many, perhaps most, are not. There is thus an unknown number of cases which are disclosed but not included in the published records.

The material collected by the various institutions is, not surprisingly, influenced by their aims and activities. Each one approaches the problem from a slightly different angle and their aims affect the nature of the information available to them. The major source of information on offenders would appear to be the Home Office crime statistics. The figures of reported offences, numbers of prosecutions and of convictions are published regularly. However criminal statistics do not give a clear indication of the incidence of the sexual abuse of children, as a brief consideration of them will show.

The figures of recorded sexual offences and convictions in England and Wales for 1983 are given in Table 1. Three categories of offence, gross indecency with a child, unlawful sexual intercourse with a girl under 16 and unlawful sexual intercourse with a girl under 13, appear to refer to the sexual abuse of children. Further analysis of crime figures shows that children may be the victims of the other categories as well, so that to show annual figures of sexual offences against children an unknown number of other offences must be added. A study of 1973 statistics showed that nearly 70 per cent of indecent assaults on females (by far the commonest sexual offence) involved children and nearly a third of the incidents of rape.[3] This is not new: of some 2,000 victims of sexual crimes examined by a police surgeon over a period from 1927 to 1954, over half were girls under 13.[4] There appears to be no comparable research on the offences involving males to indicate how many of the victims are children. In addition, these particular figures cannot

TABLE 1   Sexual offences in England and Wales in 1983

Offence	Reported		Convicted	
	No.	% of total[a]	No.	% of total[a]
Indecent assault on female	10,833	53.1	2,226	34.3
Unlawful sexual intercourse (girl under 16)	2,773	13.6	419	6.3
Indecent assault on male	2,178	10.7	616	9.3
Indecency between males	1,362	6.7	1,145	17.3
Rape	1,334	6.5	402	6.1
Buggery	588	2.9	209	3.2
Gross indecency with a child	511	2.5	231	3.5
Unlawful sexual intercourse (girl under 13)	254	1.2	71	1.1
Incest	243	1.2	100	1.5
Procuration	161	0.8	329	5.0
Abduction	81	0.4	17	0.3

[a] Bigamy, which cannot involve a child, has been removed from the list as published. Percentages are proportions of the total including bigamy.
Source: Home Office, *Statistical Bulletin* 5/84.

tell us how many *individuals* commit sexual offences against children, as the records are concerned with offences not offenders. One person may be charged with more than one offence and thus appear more than once in the figures; the victim in each offence may be the same or different. More commonly, a perpetrator of sexual abuse is charged with an offence against only one of the children he has abused, either for lack of evidence in the other cases or because they are not disclosed to the police. Where a man is being charged with an offence against a child with whom he lived, it is only rarely that he is even asked about other victims. There is anecdotal evidence that it is not uncommon for abusers to have victimized over a hundred victims in the course of their sexual careers.[5]

There are many fewer convictions than reports, and this is particularly true of cases in which the victims are children. However, one cannot conclude from that that those who are not prosecuted or not convicted were all wrongly accused. Some are cautioned and since a caution is only given to an offender who admits an offence, those cautioned are guilty by definition.[6] The legal authorities are concerned to secure convictions but cases involving sexual offences against children are very often difficult to prove in court because of the ruling that forbids the conviction of an adult on the uncorroborated evidence of a child. Although the members of the police force may believe a report from a child, the evidence to prosecute the more serious charges of incest, rape or buggery may depend largely or entirely on the child's statement and therefore be inadmissible in court. As a result many cases are not prosecuted. In many cases which are prosecuted and which depend on admissions by the perpetrator, the offender may only agree to plead guilty to a lesser charge.[7] In his study of cases of incest reported to the Metropolitan Police, Gorry states that prosecutions are unlikely where either the accused or the victim is mentally unstable, or in cases of brother/sister incest or in contested cases where the victim was under 12 years old. Under pressure from her/his parents, the child may deny the allegation or be unwilling to testify in court. He goes on to comment: 'If the perpetrator adamantly denies the incest allegation, and there is very little corroborative evidence a prosecution is unlikely.'[8] Even if a prosecution results, there may not be a conviction. An adult's word is more easily believed than that of a child; even if there is corroborative evidence it may not convince jury or judge that the case has been made. This too does not necessarily mean that the accusation was false. A child may break down in court under cross-examination and be unable to give evidence or may retract it under pressure. I observed a court case where the victim, a 12-year-old girl, withdrew her evidence in court to the obvious consternation of prosecuting counsel. There were statements before the court from the girl and from her mother who, in her statement, claimed that she had come home from work to find her husband and daughter in bed together. But the girl's mother also withdrew her evidence. The hospital cases contained a number of similar stories.

Thus while the reports of offences may contain some false allegations and therefore cannot be relied on as evidence that the offences happened, figures of convictions are much lower than the actual number of well-founded reports. An incidence rate based on criminal statistics would therefore be inaccurate whichever figures were used and would not establish either the number of offenders or of victims. The Howard League Working Party on Sexual Offences, pointing out the limitations of crime figures, stated that: 'Surveys based on self-reported sexual experiences, in spite of the difficulty of obtaining an unbiased sample and the danger of false answers, probably give a better indication of the incidence of sexual misconduct than do official statistics of crimes.'[9]

Other published information on sexual abuse refers to victims rather than offences. This material is subject to another source of ambiguity. The use of the 'case' as a unit for recording the sexual abuse of children can influence the final prevalence figures produced, which may be larger or smaller according to the different meanings the word can have. A 'case' can refer to an individual or a family. In Gorry's study of 'cases' of incest each 'case' was a victim; the number of cases over the five years studied was 171, some of the 140 reports concerning more than one victim, and an unspecified number referring to more than one abuser. The NSPCC in principle registers each child referred to them separately, so that if there were three children in a family, all of whom had been abused by their father, they should be registered as three cases. This would be likely to inflate their figures considerably and it certainly makes it difficult to compare the figures of the NSPCC with those of the social services, where 'cases' tend to refer to families, as they did in the child sexual abuse unit in the hospital where I worked. In practice, however, the NSPCC largely refers reported cases to other appropriate agencies. Since it takes time to reveal the abuse of other children in the household, their disclosures of abuse are made to other workers not the NSPCC. Of 59 children whose sexual abuse was reported to the NSPCC in 1984, there were only ten sets of brothers and sisters (23 children) registered separately as victims.[10] In general, unless one knows whether 'a case' refers to a child or to a family one cannot compare the figures produced by different agencies, for they may mean different things. The public was horrified by the figure of 160 children taken into care by the social services in Cleveland; but they came from a very much smaller number of families, about 44.[11] Thus the figures of sexual abuse quoted will decrease or increase according to whether cases mean families or children. Responsible reporting will make it clear which is referred to but much of the argument about the prevalence of sexual abuse uses figures with no thought of what is being counted.

Agencies whose aim is to protect and help children or families in trouble present several disadvantages where collecting evidence for estimating the extent of the problem of children's sexual abuse is concerned. The first they share with the police: it is that their records show only the cases that have been revealed. This fact may seem so obvious as not to need stating but it seems that it is often forgotten that prevalence or incidence rates should refer to all the examples of the behaviour that occur. Figures collected by the social services in a particular area or by the NSPCC are quoted from time to time as though they represented all cases, rather than cases that had been reported to those particular organizations. Thus the NSPCC published reports of their work which indicated that in 1984 10.8 per cent of children on their registers had been sexually abused.[12] This figure cannot legitimately be used to claim either that 10.8 per cent of all children may be sexually abused, since it refers only to children reported to the NSPCC, or that the incidence of sexual abuse is 10 per cent of children a year, because not all cases of sexual abuse are reported to the NSPCC and its branches do not cover the whole country evenly. The author does not make this claim, but it is not uncommon for such figures to be quoted by others who draw quite unjustified conclusions from them.

The Issue of Representativeness

A serious limitation on the use of figures collected by agencies which care for victims, as well as those produced by legal institutions, is that they are not typical of cases in Britain as a whole. This is most obvious when psychotherapists write of one case or a small number of cases they have seen, which is not uncommon. Any generalizations made from such very small numbers to the whole range of such incidents in the nation as a whole is obviously illegitimate. However, the quality of unrepresentativeness is not merely a matter of small numbers; it also affects the much larger numbers collected by the national agencies to which the sexual abuse of children is reported in the first instance. Although a larger number of cases is much more likely to provide an accurate picture of the range of variation, they have not been collected for this purpose. The figures are the product of a whole range of events which may determine which sort of case is reported, or placed on record with which agency, and which is not. Where the agency concerned does not rely on cases reported directly to it but on referrals from other agencies, as was the case in the hospital where I worked, and is the case to some extent with the social services, then the problem is compounded. The hospital cases provide a useful example of the process.

Origin of the Hospital Cases

The hospital cases came from a number of agencies. Most were referred by social service departments, either for diagnosis, where it was not clear if there had been sexual abuse, or for assessment as to treatment, or for therapy. Some cases were referred when a convicted abuser was due to be released from jail and an opinion was sought as to whether it would be safe for the victims for him to return home. Others were cases referred by the courts for an opinion at various stages in the legal process. A very few were referred by doctors, or as a result of a direct appeal by an individual concerned with the family. They were therefore a very mixed bag and the information contained in the files was very uneven.

The cases referred over the four years on which my research focused were not evenly distributed either in time or by the origin of the referral. There was a very rapid increase in the number of cases: from 14 in 1981 to 108 in 1984 (see total in table 2). These figures should not be interpreted as denoting a rapid increase in the number of cases that actually occurred; rather it reflected a growing awareness among various agencies of the possibility of children being sexually abused. Part of their new consciousness of the problem came from publicity given to the work of this particular hospital and the facilities it offered. The knowledge that the unit was able to diagnose and treat such cases resulted in a rise in referrals.

The growth in numbers of cases put great pressure on the unit's resources, which were not increased at all over the period concerned; one result of this was that it was forced to limit its intake by referring certain kinds of cases elsewhere. As a consequence of this, the cases referred in the early years are rather different from those referred later. More cases in which there was some legal obligation on the perpetrator to stay in treatment were taken and fewer purely diagnostic or assessment cases. In addition, with the rise in public awareness, more alternative facilities became available to which children could be referred, so that referrals also changed during the period.

The origins of all the cases in the study, where this information is known, are shown in table 2. As the table makes clear, the CSA Unit drew more cases from London than anywhere else, but within London it received referrals mainly from north and south London and within these areas mostly from those boroughs nearest to it. It is the local hospital for part of north London but the large number of referrals from south London is somewhat surprising; a new unit for cases of this sort was set up at Guys Hospital in 1984 and referrals from south London will probably decrease. Central and west London contribute fewest cases. This may be due to the existence of alternative sources of diagnosis and therapy which are easier to reach from the west.

As might be expected of a referral and teaching hospital, the unit has a wider catchment area than London itself; cases come from the home counties and beyond in southern England. But the cases are not evenly distributed over the whole region and they are certainly not the only cases to come to light in any of the areas concerned.

TABLE 2   Origin of cases referred to the child sexual abuse unit of a London hospital

Origin	to end 1981	1982	1983	1984	Total
London					
Central	0	0	1	8	9
North	2	3	9	25	39
South	5	4	9	10	28
East	0	2	3	9	14
West	2	0	2	4	8
Total London	9	9	24	56	98
Home Counties					
Kent	0	3	2	6	11
Middlesex	0	0	7	1	8
Surrey	0	4	5	9	18
Essex	2	3	3	7	15
Herts	3	2	6	11	22
Total Home Counties	5	12	23	34	74
Southern Britain excluding					
London and Home Counties	0	3	5	18	26
Midlands				2	2
Unclassified					4
Total	14	24	52	110	204

Source: Author's research.

The cases are not in any sense representative of cases which have come to light in the region over those four years.

This is easier to see if we consider one source of referrals in detail. Essex, a county adjacent to London, had started referrals early in the period under study. The absolute numbers of referrals to the CSA Unit from Essex increased but not in proportion to the increase in total referrals. Essex's share in the proportion of referrals declined sharply. In 1981 Essex provided nearly one in seven of all referrals but by 1984 it accounted for only about one in 16, although the number of cases referred from Essex had more than tripled. Essex does not refer a large proportion of its cases to this specialist unit, having other resources to call on. A check on whether they were a particular type of case which might indicate that distortions from outside London would bias the unit's cases in a particular way revealed some interesting differences between those Essex referred to the unit and the rest of their cases.[13]

There were 47 cases of the sexual abuse of children disclosed to the social services in Essex during 1984–5. These cases referred to 'families'; they involved 79 children, 65 girls and 14 boys. Sixteen, less than half of the total, were referred to the CSA Unit in London, mostly for therapy (nine); in seven cases the reason for referral was either for an assessment of whether the children had been abused (five cases) or for consultation as to how to manage the case (two); in one case diagnosis was followed by therapy. Nine of the cases which were not referred to the CSA Unit were referred to other similar agencies, such as a child guidance clinic, a child psychiatrist or another specialist organization. Altogether a little over half (25 out of 47) of the cases would have appeared as cases in therapeutic institutions; the rest would not.

The major characteristic distinguishing those not referred for specialist treatment seems to have been that it was unlikely that there would be a recurrence: either the parental couple had separated and the abuser lived elsewhere, or the victim had been only temporarily vulnerable (to a visitor or babysitter).[14] In two cases the perpetrator was subject to a probation order, which probably seemed sufficient guarantee of his future behaviour. In the four cases where there was only a suspicion that there had been sexual abuse, the person accused had left the household. It is of course the main duty of the social services to see that protection is provided for children at risk; it is not surprising therefore if it seems that in cases where there appeared to be no future risk the families were not referred for treatment or themselves did not consider it necessary. There is, sadly, a common misconception that if the child is removed from the person responsible for the abuse then the whole incident is closed. As we shall see in chapter 3, the damage and risk of recurrence do not disappear with the end of the abuse.

The other type of case referred was one in which there was uncertainty – over whether abuse had occurred or about continuing danger of repetition – or one where there had been serious emotional damage to the child for which there was no suitable alternative treatment. It was not possible to judge whether the cases referred were also those which were considered the most serious, for this would have meant a much more thorough study of the cases than was possible, but it seems likely. The cases Essex referred to the CSA Unit did include a slightly higher proportion of cases in which several brothers and sisters had been abused (seven out of 16, or 44 per cent) than the remaining 31 cases, of which 11 concerned multiple victims (34 per cent). None of the 31 had been referred to other agencies and five of them concerned cases with multiple victims. Altogether two-thirds of Essex cases where there was more than one victim were referred somewhere else for psychotherapy. It seems likely, then, that in Essex cases with multiple victims are more likely to be seen to require referral; if this were so in other social service areas then one might expect a large proportion of the hospital cases to be cases of multiple victims, since the hospital was a unit for this sort of referral.

In fact this seems not to be the case: only 29 per cent of the hospital cases involved several children. This may have been because in the early years a high proportion of single children were sent for diagnosis only or for consultation as to treatment; in addition it is likely that not all social service departments followed the same course as Essex. The difference between Essex cases and all the CSA Unit cases is not large enough to be of great significance, however, particularly as the overall number of Essex cases with multiple victims (18) is so very small and the total (47 in two years) not very large either.

The overall picture offered by these hospital cases and this discussion of Essex referrals suggests an unrecognized process of selection which takes place between agencies where cases are first referred and those further up the chain of organizations which may be involved after a case is disclosed. The hospital unit receives few direct referrals and its cases are therefore subject to this process before they are referred. There may be a qualitative difference between those which are not taken any further and those which are. Comparing figures from different institutions which represent different points in this process is to compare different selections. None of them represent the whole range of cases which come to light and still less the national picture of all sexual abuse. All information that is a byproduct of other work is unrepresentative to a greater or lesser extent. This does not mean that it is not useful, simply that generalizations based on it must be treated with caution. To generalize from these cases may result in a distorted view of what happens.

One such bias common to both criminal statistics and figures produced by the child protection agencies is that they appear to show that the problem is distributed differently among occupational classes of the population. A comparison with more representative material makes it clear that this is not really the case. Table 3 compares the occupational class (where this could be ascertained) of the households in the cases in the hospital CSA Unit with figures from the BBC survey. Where the percentage of abused is higher than the percentage of that class in the general population, then occupational class is likely to be associated with sexual abuse; the greater the discrepancy the greater the likelihood that there is some relationship.

TABLE 3   Occupational classes of victims: two types of data compared (percentages)

Class	Total population	Cases in BBC survey (weighted base)	Cases in hospital CSA Unit
AB	16	17	8
C1	22	29	13
C2	28	28	33
DE	35	26	45
Total	101	100	99

The class of victims in the hospital cases was counted as that of the main breadwinner, if any, in the original household. Of the hospital cases 6% concerned single unemployed mothers and 42% of the total could not be classified as the relevant information was lacking.

The figures for total population were taken from the BBC Special Projects research report, December 1987, p. 2. They refer to 1986.

In considering table 3 it should be borne in mind that the two sets of data differ in two respects. First, the hospital cases refer to children but the survey concerns adults reporting childhood experiences, so that they do not refer to the same period of time. Secondly, the hospital cases are all reported cases while the survey includes several that have never been revealed.

The hospital cases show a noticeable bias towards the lower

occupational classes when they are compared with the general population of the BBC sample. The more representative BBC survey shows a more even class distribution. The first national survey, undertaken in 1983 for Channel Four Television, using a wider definition of sexual abuse than that of the BBC survey, also showed an even class distribution.[15] The class bias in the hospital cases is not difficult to explain. The social services are more frequently concerned with children in poorer households, with single-parent families and the families of the unemployed; their prior involvement for other reasons may result in the discovery of cases of sexual abuse. Several of the hospital cases were of this kind and the majority of them were referred by the social services. There is no class analysis of criminal statistics for sexual offences but Gorry reports that incest may be revealed by police investigations of crime[16] which would also bias their records in the same direction as that of the social services.

The total numbers of people surveyed by both the BBC and Channel Four Television were rather small for a national sample; consequently the numbers of those who admitted being abused are too few for an analysis of the class factor to be completely conclusive. However, there is a considerable body of other evidence to suggest that they are not far wrong. Anecdotal material supplied to me by psychiatrists and psychotherapists and by professional lawyers suggest that the sexual abuse of children in the higher classes is less often reported to the authorities. Case material collected for Gorry and for me by one of the founders of the Incest Crisis Line, an organization that offers telephone help and counselling to victims and abusers, shows a preponderance of cases involving the highest social classes.[17] Over 30 per cent of the new cases recorded over three months and given to me were of members of occupational class A, that is they involved the families of professional people, business executives and higher civil servants. It seems likely then that while *reported* cases in Britain seem to confirm popular notions that the sexual abuse of children, like incest, is more prevalent among the poorer, less educated classes, they do so either because these children are more likely to appeal for help or because the adults are more subject to the scrutiny of either the police or the social services, or both. The actual prevalence is much more evenly spread.

Of course the popular stereotype contributes to the lack of

reports against members of the more affluent and influential members of the community, since it is hard for others to believe that they do such things. There is no statutory obligation on any British professional other than a member of the social services to report a case of sexual abuse, so that those who can afford to consult private doctors, analysts, psychiatrists or solicitors when they are involved in a case of incest or sexual abuse may be able to prevent it reaching public notice. In the United States, however, such professionals are generally required to report cases coming to them; in some states, even members of the public have a statutory duty to do so. It is therefore not surprising that cases reported in the United States are more representative of all cases. The only American national study of reported cases of sexual abuse concluded that there was no variation by class, although a later report based on it concluded that families where father/daughter incest occurred were predominantly middle-class.[18]

There is thus good reason to accept the two British national surveys, despite their small number of cases. The fact that the hospital cases show a class bias is the result of the way in which they came to be referred there. Were we to generalize from them as though they were nationally representative, we might be led to conclude that sexual abuse of children is commoner among the less privileged; the use of more accurate material shows that this is not so and that, on the contrary, the extent of sexual abuse among the children of the privileged is being effectively concealed.

Research

Studies undertaken specifically to obtain information on the sexual abuse of children are of many different kinds. Some of these, like articles commenting on the proposal to reform the provisions of the law on incest, are studies of particular types of case, but in general they are surveys that make use of questionnaires and are designed to provide statistics. Magazines such as *Cosmopolitan*, *Woman* and *19* have conducted surveys of their readers and the results have formed the basis for articles and, in one case, two books.[19] Television companies have done the same for programmes on the abuse of children. Such surveys employ professional pollsters or market researchers who are statistically trained. Surveys are generally based on a questionnaire but the design of the questionnaire and the methods of selecting the people who are asked to answer it may be an important source of bias. So too may be the decision as to whether to send the questionnaire by post for people to fill in themselves, or whether the interviewer should fill it in during an interview, but the effects of the mode of administering the questionnaire are less easy to detect.

To start with, the definition of sexual abuse may affect the final result of any survey. The national survey undertaken for Channel Four Television produced a prevalence rate of 10 per cent.[20] By contrast, the BBC national survey showed a much lower rate: 3 per cent. The first used a very wide definition of abuse, including exhibitionism and sexual remarks, while the second asked its correspondents to consider only a much more restricted range of behaviour. The difference in the two definitions also affected the survey's information on the perpetrator of the abuse (the next chapter discusses this aspect of the definitional problem). However, if we exclude the abuse which did not involve contact in order to make the two surveys comparable, the Channel Four survey still produced a prevalence rate of 8 per cent, nearly three times that of the BBC.

Not all the differences between surveys can be attributed to the differences in definitions of abuse. The method of selecting a sample of people to answer the questionnaire may have an important effect on results. There are a number of ways of doing this. The first is to publicize the subject on which information is required and ask the public to volunteer to fill in questionnaires; this is referred to as a self-selected sample because the respondents themselves choose to participate. The researchers have no control over who may fill in the questionnaires; even though a careful design of the questionnaire can show up those who are inventing information or filling in false answers for a joke, it cannot be shown that the respondents are representative of the population as a whole. If the response is sufficient, the questionnaires may be sampled to provide a more representative set of people but this procedure does not eliminate the probable bias in the results, which is that the subject being investigated has resulted in a higher number of answers from people specially concerned with it. This type of survey is a useful preliminary to further research since it gives a general idea of the features of the problem being studied. It can be more accurate than the figures produced by government departments or child protection agencies because it includes cases which have not been reported elsewhere.

The second type of survey can be made representative of a set of people or even of a nation. In a representative survey the respondents are selected as a sample which mirrors in various key ways the characteristics of the whole population. Where the sexual abuse of children is concerned features of class, age, gender and region of the country can be represented. Such a survey has the disadvantage that the people asked to fill in the questionnaire have not volunteered to do so and may be reluctant to answer with frankness or at all. This is a particular problem where sensitive subjects like the respondent's experience of sexual abuse in childhood is concerned; the reasons will be discussed in the next chapter. The BBC national survey mentioned above produced a prevalence rate for sexual abuse in childhood of 3 per cent, which is very low and is almost certainly the result of unwillingness to answer. This can be seen from the rather high figure of respondents (71) whom the interviewers felt were concealing their experiences, ten more than those who reported sexual abuse. Over three times as many respondents had known a child who was sexually abused than reported their own abuse. Very few men, only 12, revealed sexual abuse and there were six respondents who refused to complete the whole form after stating that they had been sexually abused in childhood. In the other, Channel Four (MORI), survey 13 per cent of the sample refused to answer, again more than those who reported abuse.

A well-conducted survey, with carefully trained, sympathetic interviewers can overcome much of the reluctance or inability to speak. A higher percentage of respondents revealing their abuse may thus be the result of more sympathetic interviewing. Diana Russell has argued that this is so. In discussing the methods of her own meticulously careful survey in San Francisco of women's experience of sexual assaults, she describes the long training she gave the interviewers. They were first carefully selected for their sympathetic view of victims of sexual assault and then taught to understand the subject they were investigating so that they were able to relax and not disturb the respondent with their tension or other emotional reactions. Interviewers were carefully matched to the respondents, who were all women but of different cultural origins; the interviewers were of similar background to the women they interviewed to ensure maximum sympathy between them. An important factor was that the interviewers were paid by the time they spent, not by the interview so that they were motivated to go slowly through the questionnaire and spend as much time as was necessary to obtain all the answers. She attributes the large proportion of respondents, 19 per cent, claiming to have suffered sexual abuse at the hands of relatives to the use of these methods.[21]

The highest prevalence rate for sexual abuse in childhood produced by British studies was the result of a study of women by Nash and West.[22] They chose a Cambridge medical practice whose doctors approved of their research and could act as an implicit guarantee to the patients of the researchers' good faith, for they assumed, probably rightly, that people would not be happy about answering a questionnaire unless they knew something about the research and the people doing it. They provided a measure of comparison by also surveying some female college students. In all, 223 postal questionnaires were completed. In addition Nash interviewed a proportion of the respondents. The prevalence rate for sexual abuse that they reported was startlingly high, 48 per cent (the average for their two samples). However, the definition of sexual abuse that they used was a very wide one and in 19 per cent of their cases there was only a single incident. Unfortunately it is not possible to tell how many of those did not involve contact. In addition the patients may have been typical residents of a small East Anglian town, although the presence of Cambridge University might be said to make it unusual. The social characteristics of people in the countryside or in large cities obviously differ from this segment of the population; these women could not be said to be a representative sample of British women. The university students, being largely from educated and wealthier homes, were even less representative of girls their age. (This survey did not attempt to address the question of the sexual abuse of boys.) Nevertheless the study was the most careful attempt of its time to provide information on undisclosed cases of sexual abuse and it made it very clear that far more cases are kept hidden than are revealed.

Two national surveys have attempted to overcome the problem of unrepresentativeness by using a sample that was specifically designed to be representative of the whole population of the country, male and female. Both were undertaken for television programmes, the first for Channel Four TV and the second for Esther Rantzen's programme, ChildWatch: the BBC national survey. The different results have already been used as a good example of how different definitions of abuse affect the estimate of rates of abuse. The definition used in the Channel Four survey which produced the higher (10 per cent) figure was similar to that used by Nash and West but there is still clearly a very great difference between the two results. The Cambridge study seems to show a prevalence rate nearly five times that of the Channel Four survey. How can we explain the discrepancy?

The higher proportion of reports of abuse in the study by Nash and West may be the result of their research techniques. To begin with, they were vouched for by the respondents' doctors as serious researchers who would maintain confidentiality. Then, as well as the postal questionnaire, a proportion of the respondents, some who had said they were not abused and others who had said they were, were interviewed. All the interviews were done by a single research assistant and not merely an interviewer with limited involvement in the project. The interviewer was a woman. Significantly, a surprisingly large number of those interviewed who had not reported their sexual abuse on the postal questionnaire did reveal it in the interview. Had Nash been able to interview all those who did not report sexual abuse in the questionnaire, the final figures might have been much greater. By contrast both the television surveys were done by professional interviewers. In the case of the BBC they were paid a set fee, calculated on the amount of time it was considered they would need to obtain a fixed number of completed questionnaires. They had thus every incentive to go through them quickly. It is also unlikely that the larger national surveys took care to have all respondents interviewed by someone of their own sex and class or cultural background. While one cannot be sure how much of the difference in the prevalence rates of different surveys is the result of all these factors, there is sufficient experience in research in the United States to show that they make a great deal of difference to the final figures. Russell's study of San Francisco women, which has been praised for its meticulous methods, produced the highest prevalence rate for American woman of any study in the United States. It seems unlikely that the Nash and West study inflates the prevalence rate unreasonably, bearing in mind that it uses a wide definition of sexual abuse.

A final, serious source of inaccuracy in surveys, which is probably unavoidable, lies in the assumptions about the sexual abuse of children which are taken for granted. These affect the methods used in a survey. The first assumption is that sexual abuse is randomly distributed among the population or, to put it another way, it is assumed that each individual has the same chance as anyone else of being abused. A random sample of individuals would thus reflect the prevalence rate in the population as a whole. However, as the qualitative study of cases shows, the brothers and sisters of a victim are likely to have been abused as well. Their chances of being sexually abused are much higher than those of children in households where no other child has been abused. Other factors, such as having a parent who was abused as a child, may also raise a child's chances of sexual abuse. Twenty of the 47 cases (43 per cent) dealt with by the Essex social services in 1984 and 1985 concerned more than one child and these 20 cases involved 52 children, more than all the rest of the cases. In 29 per cent of the hospital cases, nearly a third, there was more than one victim; in a few cases these were children outside the immediate household. One can hypothesize with some certainty that about a third of the victims who would be discovered in a survey would have been members of a household in which there was more than one victim of the sexual abuse. Sexual abuse is not randomly distributed but shows a clustering in affected households.

The second assumption follows from the first: if sexual abuse affects individuals, then a random survey will interview only a few individuals in each locality as though incidents of sexual abuse were evenly distributed geographically, over each neighbourhood, borough, town or county. Recent (1988) reports in the press have shown that quite large local networks of children may be involved in child pornography and prostitution. From time to time, there is a scandal involving many children abused in residential institutions such as children's homes or schools, sometimes over many years. Recording only a few individuals in any area makes it inevitable that such clusters of abused individuals in one locality are missed. In one of the cases dealt with in Cleveland it was thought necessary to trace all the children fostered by a couple where the husband had been suspected of sexually abusing a child; this immediately added 11 more children to the number of suspected victims.[23]

It might be argued that multiple victims are over-represented in reported cases, which are those available for study. This is plausible, since where there are more victims there are more chances that one of them may speak out. However, it is rare that all the victims of one abuser are recorded even in case histories; the confessions of some convicted men imply that there may be very many more than even reported cases suggest. Since many men are never found out or convicted, it is equally likely that as many of the undiscovered cases involve multiple abuse as those which are reported. Although it is impossible to say with any precision what proportion of all cases involve more than one child, it is clear that surveys, by assuming that sexual abuse is an event affecting single individuals, unconnected with others, rule out of account the incidence of multiple victims and hence seriously underestimate the prevalence rate.

To devise a strategy for ensuring that such cases were recorded in a survey would be very difficult. It would not be sufficient to ask the person being interviewed whether there were other children who had been abused as well as themselves, although the BBC volunteer survey did that. Nearly half their respondents (49 per cent) thought that other children had also suffered from their abuser, mostly brothers or sisters, but nearly a third (29 per cent) said they did not know if other children had been victims. Case histories show that sometimes the children do not know whether their brothers and sisters, let alone unrelated children, are also involved, although in some cases a child finds out when talking to a sister that she too has suffered abuse. In order to ensure that all the potential victims were identified, all brothers and sisters would also have to be interviewed.

Surveys interview adults, for reasons already discussed, so that the events of sexual abuse which are recorded refer to the household in which each informant grew up as a child; in the normal course of time, its members disperse to live elsewhere. If all the people who were children together in one household are to be traced and interviewed when a case of sexual abuse of children is identified, a survey would not be impossible but it would be an immensely difficult, expensive operation. Some brothers and sisters lose touch with one another; some members might agree to an interview and others refuse. It would take time and much effort to ensure that all the adults concerned were interviewed. To trace unrelated children, neighbours or former residents of a school or home would be prohibitively expensive and probably not feasible in practical terms. If there were a better idea of the incidence of multiple victimization then statistical techniques might be devised to take account of this in calculating prevalence rates from surveys of individual adults. A successful survey of the prevalence of abusers in the population and the number of their victims might provide this information, but so far it has not been tried. Surveys of victims will continue to underestimate the prevalence rate however well-designed they are otherwise, until they are based on more accurate initial assumptions.

It is in the nature of this particular problem that we are unlikely to be able to find a final and definitive figure for the prevalence rate. Most methods of collecting information on the sexual abuse of children underestimate the prevalence of sexual abuse rather than the opposite. Even the most reliable current estimates may prove to be too low. Using a rate midway between the two national surveys, about 6 per cent might give a reasonable basis to start with; the Essex and hospital cases indicate that excluding multiple victims underestimates the number affected by between two-fifths and about a third, so that the rate must be raised. If we then bear in mind the large numbers of children involved in prostitution rings and institutions, a minimum prevalence rate might be about 10 per cent. However, it must be remembered that not all the cases are of the same severity and duration; they do not leave the same scars, although it is impossible to believe that any child is untouched by this experience of betrayed trust. It is likely, too, that any minimum figure will be revised upwards by a national survey if it can be undertaken without the financial and other restraints hampering television companies.

If children are assured of a sympathetic hearing, it may be that we will be able in the future to assess with more accuracy how many children a year are abused, although it is likely that some secrets will always be kept. We will almost certainly never know whether there was more sexual abuse in the past than there is now, although the little evidence that we have suggests that it was merely more successfully ignored not less prevalent. The numbers of elderly people responding to a survey on their treatment in childhood are

subject to a number of additional sources of inaccuracy, all of
which work in the same direction: to produce a lower rate. The
smaller number of individuals surviving (particularly after two
world wars), the greater shame of revealing it and the likelihood of
memories being affected over such a long period make it risky to
extrapolate change from surveys carried out today. Diana Russell
has taken that risk, using her exceptionally reliable figures in San
Francisco; her conclusion is that not much has changed over the
lifespan of her informants.[24] There are indications that children
were sexually abused in the past and it seems likely, given the
insistence on respectability and not mentioning sexual subjects, that
it was at least as successfully hidden as it is now, and probably
more so. It depends on the measures we adopt now whether there
will be less of it in the future.

Research in this country on the sexual abuse of children has barely
begun and will undoubtedly improve as lessons are learned from
the mistakes of the past. Even in the United States where studies of
various aspects of the sexual abuse of children have been carried
out on a larger scale and for a much longer period of time than is
the case in this country, much is still unknown.[25] To understand the
sexual abuse of children, the research by people of many disciplines
using a variety of methods must be combined. Qualitative data
produced by detailed research into a small number of cases may be
useful for certain purposes. It can provide evidence on precise
circumstances, sequences of events and outcomes, making it
possible to detect common patterns. Statistics, or quantified
material, will be needed to provide reliable generalizations about
larger populations and test the conclusions arrived at by other
studies. Each method produces a certain type of information which
has its own strengths and weaknesses; the results of research can be
used more effectively if this is understood. But no single method can
be expected to find out everything or reveal 'the whole truth'.

There has been enough research to show that the sexual abuse of
children is not a negligible issue or a question of public hysteria but
a serious social problem. Even the lowest estimate of its prevalence
indicates that a large number of children are involved. The next
chapter considers who they are and how they are affected.

Notes

1 A. Baker and S. Duncan, 'Child sexual abuse: a study of prevalence in Great Britain', *Journal of Child Abuse and Neglect*, 9 (4) (1985).
2 C. L. Nash and C. D. West, 'Victimisation of young girls', in D. West (ed.), *Sexual Victimisation* (Gower, Aldershot, 1985).
3 R. Walmsley and K. White, *Supplementary Information on Sexual Offences and Sentencing*, Research Unit Paper 2, Home Office, 1980. This is an analysis of 1973 Home Office statistics cited in Howard League, *Unlawful Sex*, pp. 15–16.
4 N. H. Wells, 'Sexual offences as seen by a woman police surgeon', *British Medical Journal*, 2 (1958), cited in Howard League, *Unlawful Sex*, p. 16.
5 Ray Wyre, Director Gracewell Clinic, personal communication.
6 Gorry, 'Incest', particularly tables 4.16 (p. 38) and 4.19 (p. 40).
7 Ibid., p. 218.
8 Ibid., p. 26.
9 Howard League, *Unlawful Sex*, p. 12.
10 I am grateful to the NSPCC for letting me see some of their reports. Four of the 59 reports concerned only children.
11 *Observer*, 26 June 1988.
12 S. Creighton, *Trends in Child Abuse*, NSPCC, 1984.
13 The figures were collected by the social service teams in Essex. Each case was identified only by a number. The department felt this was necessary to protect the people concerned, so it has not been possible to identify them among the CSA Unit cases. Basic information such as the numbers, ages and sexes of the abused children and their siblings, the relationship the alleged perpetrator had with the victim(s) and what agencies were involved were recorded. I also asked for a brief account of why the referral had been made. I am most grateful to George Lane and the members of the various teams for undertaking this for me, putting as it did an extra call on their time. These figures are not the same as the figures in table 2 showing the origins of referral. The CSA Unit's file is opened when the case is received and refers to Essex cases recorded before 1984. The two years 1984 and 1985 were chosen for the convenience of Essex staff since it was already 1986 and older cases might have been closed.
14 Ideally, of course, those children where there was little danger of a repetition of the abuse should also have had some counselling to help them get over their experiences.
15 Baker and Duncan, 'Child sexual abuse'. This survey was undertaken for Channel Four Television and the fieldwork was done by MORI.

The consultants were Baker and Duncan, who were also consultants to the ChildWatch team. This survey, however, used a wider definition of sexual abuse than the BBC survey. See also J. S. La Fontaine, 'Preliminary remarks on a study of incest in London', in N. Scheper-Hughes (ed.), *Child Survival* (Reidel, Holland, 1987).

16 Gorry, 'Incest'.

17 Ibid.; La Fontaine, 'Preliminary remarks'.

18 American Humane Association National Reporting Study 1978 (Denver, Colorado) and L. Browne and W. Holder, 'The nature and extent of child abuse in contemporary American society', in *Sexual Abuse of Children* (American Humane Association, Denver, 1980).

19 D. Sanders, *The Woman Book of Love and Sex* and *The Woman Book on Men* (Sphere, London, 1985).

20 Baker and Duncan, 'Child sexual abuse'. See G. E. Wyatt and S. D. Peters, 'Issues in the definition of child sexual abuse in prevalence research', *Child Abuse and Neglect*, 10 (1986), pp. 231–40, for a discussion of the effect of definitions of sexual abuse on American prevalence rates.

21 Russell, *The Secret Trauma*.

22 Nash and West, 'Victimisation', see note 2 above.

23 Cleveland Report, p. 16, paragraph 20. Ray Wyre, Director of the Gracewell Clinic, told me that most of his patients recalled a large number of victims, far more than those for which they were prosecuted (see note 5 above).

24 Russell, *The Secret Trauma*.

25 See Finkelhor, *Child Sexual Abuse*, pp. 227–31.

3 The Victims

I don't want you to think I was in any way responsible. I tried everything to avoid it.
Girl aged 17, Bucks

I don't think a 13-year-old is able physically to resist a man of 17 stones.
Married woman aged 35, Yorks

The girl who wrote the first of these comments on her questionnaire left home at 16 because she could no longer bear being abused by her father. It was no more than a year earlier, so the memory was fresh in her mind. Her plea is a defence against one of the common and quite erroneous opinions that add to the pain inflicted on victims of sexual abuse. Children who are sexually abused are often believed to have provoked it in some way, by being seductive, either because they are sexually precocious or even just 'naturally wicked'. Alternatively, when children do ask for help to stop sexual abuse, they may not be believed; their accounts of abuse may be dismissed as fantasies or even as lies made up out of malice against the person they accuse.

The myth that a child is responsible for what happens to him or her is an easy excuse for those who abuse children. Refusing to accept responsibility for what happened is a common characteristic of perpetrators of sexual abuse; interpreting the child's behaviour to exonerate the adult from blame is one of the commonest forms that this denial of accountability takes. Children who are too embarrassed or frightened to say 'No' to an adult are said to have consented to the sexual behaviour. One man in a therapy group who had abused his daughter answered a question about what his daughter had felt by saying that she had said nothing; her failure to complain was put forward as evidence of consent. He totally ignored the fact that he was a violent father of whom his children were clearly frightened. In some cases, the physical pleasure with which a child's body may react mechanically is taken as justification. Even a child's mother may express her pain by asking 'Why didn't you stop it?', when an outsider might consider that the more appropriate question, addressed to the abuser, would be 'Why did you start it?' The conviction that children may not be innocent victims can make any discussion of the problem of sexual abuse very difficult so it is necessary to begin by discussing it.

There is a general reason for the blaming of children. The Christian doctrine of original sin, the inherent wickedness of human beings who have not been purified by religion is, in that form, no longer widely held. However, the general notion that there are traits and characteristics which are part of an individual's own identity, like the colour of their hair, is by no means discredited. One of its most potent forms, relevant to this discussion, is the idea that some children, particularly girls, are 'naturally' sexually precocious and promiscuous. Child pornography makes lavish use of this idea.[1] Children who are photographed in sexual activities are shown smiling, to indicate their enjoyment. The myth has even been the basis of an internationally famous novel, *Lolita*, in which the fictional narrator of the story asserts his amazement at being seduced by his 13-year-old step-daughter.

The idea that some children are sexually seductive rests on the misinterpretation of several facts taken out of their context. Overt sexualized behaviour is not uncommon among children who have been abused. The children who display their bodies, assault other children or touch adults' genitals have learnt to behave like this because it has earned them adult approval or prevented trouble for them. Their behaviour is the result of their experiences and is not seen in children who have not been abused; it is taken by experts as a sign that there has been sexual abuse. To interpret it as the cause of the earlier events is like saying that because a child cries when it trips and bruises a knee, the tears are the cause of the fall! Similarly, while early and promiscuous sexual behaviour among teenagers is not an inevitable sign of earlier sexual abuse, it is not an uncommon consequence of it; yet it may be taken as a 'proof' that the adolescent concerned is immoral by nature. One man who had admitted abusing his step-daughter lost no opportunity in the therapy groups to refer to the fact that she was living with her boyfriend, although she was only 16. By implication, her seduction by him at a much earlier age was her fault.

It is important to recognize that all these ideas depend on

adult interpretations of children's behaviours in terms of adult feelings, adult desires and adult knowledge. While children may demonstrate their sensual enjoyment of cuddling, the physical contact with those they love, it is only an adult interpretation which makes this pleasure sexual. The flirtatiousness of very small girls may amuse adults; it cannot be held to be evidence that the child is aware of the meaning it has for those who encourage it by their approval.

It is rarely recognized how much children's behaviour is interpreted by adults without reference to the child's own motives or understanding of what they are doing. This reinterpretation of a child's behaviour can be seen clearly in what abusers say about their victims and it can be taken to extraordinary lengths. One anecdote told me by a child psychiatrist concerned an elderly male patient who asserted that his 18-month granddaughter was being sexually provocative because, when she lay on her back on the bed to have her nappy changed, she lay with her legs apart. In such an extreme case it is easy to see that the adult's interpretation of the child's behaviour is unacceptable and a matter of special pleading. However where a child is older, the reality may not be easily recognized.

Can Children Consent?

Most sexual abuse of children is not violent. Although some children may be subjected to rape or sadistic sexual assault, these are not the commonest forms of sexual abuse. When sexual abuse starts, as it often does, with relatively mild touching by a familiar adult, the child may not be distressed. 'When I was about three and a half years old, Dad kneeled down by my bed and put his hand inside my pyjama trousers and started to rub what I thought was my tummy and said "this is our secret, you mustn't tell mummy".' Her father 'had a great deal more time to spend with me than my mother' and she reported that her best memories were also to do with things she did with her father. It would be hard to say a child was particularly upset at such behaviour, particularly if it is not violent or forced. This fact has sometimes been taken to mean that the child is a willing partner in the sexual activity. The conclusion then raises the question of whether it is possible for children to suffer no harm from a sexual relationship with an adult.

The argument that children can consent or have consented to sexual activity is advanced by adults, not children. Apologists for paedophilia argue that if sexual activity takes place in a loving and gentle relationship a child may give its consent and is entitled to do so; they even argue that such activity is beneficial. Most experts in the field of child sexual abuse dispute this.[2] Their arguments rest on the fact that consent depends on the individual's being in possession of enough knowledge to know what they are consenting to, and being free to refuse consent. In the case of children neither of these conditions are fulfilled. Children's knowledge of what sexual activity is depends on their age, but even teenagers can be remarkably ignorant of what it entails. Small children entirely lack the information and understanding of what they are being asked to engage in. This is particularly so when the initial actions are merely the preliminaries to other and rather different activities. The woman whose words have just been quoted went on to tell how she was then asked to touch her father and then masturbate him; she began to get frightened. She was unable to refuse then, because her father told her she had liked it earlier. This case also makes it clear that, even where violence is not used, consent is not a free choice. There are many means of non-violent coercion and where the abuser is in a parental relationship with a child, the relationship itself is one that implies obedience. Once the implications of what consent involves are made clear, it is obvious that children are unable to give it.

Do Children Lie?

It is also believed by many people that children may say they have been sexually abused when they have not been, either to get the person they accuse into trouble or because they have been made to believe this or told to say it by another adult. During the Cleveland affair, it was said of several children that they had been made to believe in their own sexual abuse by the questioning they had been through. The *Sunday Times* made a feature article of the story of one mother who reported that her son said to her: 'I must have been abused because that is what Dr Higgs told me, but I didn't know it had happened.'[3] In another case a mother whose child's disclosure of abuse she believed reported that she had been told by Stuart Bell, the local MP, 'the bairn's been told to say she was abused.'[4] These instances were products of a crisis, but there is also a much more general conviction that children are liars. Just over half (53 per cent) of the respondents to the BBC national survey agreed that 'children tell lies about being abused', and although this statement applied to all forms of abuse, it does indicate how general is the disinclination to believe children.

Children do not expect to be believed, rightly in many cases, as we have just seen. Just under a quarter of the BBC national survey respondents who claimed to have been abused said they had not told anyone because they did not think they would be believed. Where it is a question of an adult's word against a child's, public opinion and the law are both on the side of the adult. Even men who are prosecuted for sexual abuse may successfully deny the accusation. One of the teenagers who appeared on the ChildWatch programme spoke bitterly about how the police had believed her and prosecuted her father for abusing her and her sisters; but he had denied it and had walked out of court past them, laughing. Why then would children tell lies about being sexually abused, when they are so often not believed?

These considerations make it seem unlikely that children would falsely accuse someone of sexually abusing them. But there have been arguments that the figures recording cases of sexual abuse which are not substantiated are instances of false accusations. One of the expert witnesses brought by Parents Against Injustice to the Cleveland inquiry is reported to have suggested that 65 per cent of all reports were unfounded.[5] There is no record of supporting evidence for his statement and the Cleveland Report's use of the term 'suggested' indicates that there may not have been any. Fortunately there is also a careful study of such reports that shows that unfounded reports are not the same as false accusations. It is worth considering it in some detail.

Jones and McCraw studied all the reports made to Denver Department of Social Services during one year, 1983.[6] There were 576 in all, but in 24 per cent there was insufficient information for the cases to be assessed. Of the remaining 439, 70 per cent were considered to be reliably founded; of the 30 per cent considered unfounded, most (22 per cent of the total) were unsubstantiated suspicions reported by an adult about a child, which reflected the fact that Colorado law requires individuals to report suspicions of sexual abuse of children. Thus the proportion of unfounded accusations where the report of sexual abuse was not true was only 8 per cent, a figure which is similar to that produced by other studies. However, these 8 per cent consisted of three times as many fictitious reports by an adult (6 per cent) as by a child (2 per cent). The incidence of false reports by a child in that study was very small indeed.

Phase two of this study assessed 21 fictitious cases seen at the Kempe National Centre in Denver between 1983 and 1985. Nine of the reports were made by adults, five by children and in seven it was not clear who first made the allegation. Four of the five children who had made fictitious reports had been sexually abused in the past and the other was the subject of a custody dispute. The latter situation is not uncommon and will require more detailed consideration later (in chapter 7). Careful investigation of the other four made it clear that there were reasons why the children had made their accusations. Two of the four had been abused by their stepfather, were in care and made new (fictitious) allegations referring to an access visit, because they were afraid they were going to be sent back to live with him. One five-year-old child gave an account of abuse which had happened two years earlier; she *had* been sexually abused then but not by the person she was now accusing. A significant feature of the cases where adults had made fictitious reports was that in a large number of them no one had interviewed the child! The authors conclude that 'fictitious allegations are unusual',[7] and they also show that they are even more rarely made by children.

While children do not often make false accusations of sexual abuse, they do retract the accusations they have made. The same pressures that ensure that only a fraction of the sexual abuse that happens is every reported may operate to make children change their stories. The Denver study described above noted that in 4 per cent of the total number of cases children retracted their statements 'under duress'. Once the allegations have been made, victims are often reluctant to repeat them or to talk about what happened.

The Enforcement of Silence

Only a fraction of the sexual abuse of children that happens is ever reported. The difficulties of discovering the dimensions of this social problem come largely from the fact that the victims are silent. Or rather they are silenced. For a variety of reasons the victims of sexual abuse as children either do not tell anyone or, if they tell, the information goes no further. Adults who have been victims may record what they remember of their feelings at the time. There are those who still consider these to be fantasies, the disordered imaginings of neurotic individuals, in order to deny the reality of children's sexual abuse, but the weight of the evidence is against them. What little is gleaned from child victims, either when they are in treatment or when they talk to a sympathetic social worker or foster parent, shows clear parallels with the retrospective accounts by adults of their childhood experiences. The coincidence is too great for the biographical accounts of adults to be dismissed as fantasy. This chapter makes use of what was written by adult respondents of the BBC self-selected survey. Seven per cent of them were under 18 and so, legally, they were still children; some were clearly quite young. Their experiences were recent, and in a few cases the abuse was still continuing. What is made clear by many of these accounts is that sexual abuse can endure through long years of painful childhood.

The reasons for the silence are produced by the unequal relationship between adults and children. The power of adults is greatest when children are young and weak but much of it continues long after that stage. Power refers to the ability to enforce one's wishes, by physical means, non-violent coercion or persuasion, rather than through the recognition of rights which are an issue of public morality and/or law, although parents have rights as well as power. Parental authority is a matter of rights which are much more often talked about than parental power.

Children lack power for many reasons, some of which are publicly recognized but others are so taken for granted that they are not often considered. The first lies in the condition of being immature in body with little physical strength. Babies and small children are picked up, carried around and taken from place to place. From a very early age children in any society learn that they are weak relative to adults. This lesson, that a child's ability to resist an adult is limited, is well learnt before any awareness or understanding of the fact that some adults, parents and others, have not merely the power to command a child's obedience but the right to do so. The teaching may be gentle or it may be instilled with threats or violence which emphasize the force behind adult commands. Writing of the abuse that she suffered for several years, a middle-aged woman recorded that if she cried when she was being sexually assaulted, she was beaten till she stopped, 'and you learn quickly as a child'. Part of what adolescence may bring is a growing realization that the balance of physical power is changing; it does not seem coincidental that it is then that many victims gain the ability to tell of their abuse or to break away from home.

A large number of adults recalling their experiences refer to the threats that were used to induce compliance with the abuse, and silence thereafter. Similar threats are referred to in the cases of children referred to the hospital unit. These range from the authoritative, 'All fathers do this with their little girls but no one talks about it, so you must not talk about it either', to threats of beatings and worse. A very common threat is to tell the child what will happen if the sexual abuse is disclosed, making it seem that the consequences are the results of telling rather than of the abuse. Thus the child may be told that (s)he will be taken away and the family broken up, while the perpetrator will go to jail. Even if the child is longing to have the abuser removed, the threat of separation from mother, siblings and all that is familiar is a very potent deterrent.

Often there are threats to another member of the family. A woman in her late twenties to early thirties wrote:

> I remember getting up one morning and my mother had two black eyes and bruises round her neck. She just said not to worry, she'd rather he hit her than hit us. He very rarely smacked us and then it was only one smack so he didn't mistreat us in that way . . . The worst memory is when I told him I was going to tell Mum what he was doing and he said if I did he would kill her and chop her into little bits. As a child I believed he would do this and by not telling anyone I felt as if I was protecting her in some way.

Not a few victims believe that by sacrificing themselves they are protecting a mother or sisters from violence or abuse.

The financial dependence of a mother and her children may also prevent a woman from revealing the abuse. One girl reported that she had told her mother that her father, described as a very senior policeman, was abusing her. Her mother was angry with her, declaring that her father was within a few years of retirement and she was not going to be allowed to jeopardize his pension. Yet another woman who had suffered abuse from a professional father for ten years gave as the reason for her silence, 'My mother would have had nothing had she reported him. She would have lost her home and her only means of support.'

Some abusers are loved as parents or friends. 'Samantha', a girl who told her story to the Cleveland inquiry, said of her father who had abused her since she was four and had had full intercourse with her since she was ten: 'I loved my father so much. I respected him as a father. But I was confused, didn't understand. I wanted it to stop. I hated that part of it so much.'[8] A young woman slightly older than Samantha wrote of the neighbour who abused her: 'We'd been friends for about one to two years before the abuse started. We'd done things together and he'd made things for me my Dad never had time to do.' She didn't want to get him into trouble or lose a friend. The desire to please is a powerful incentive behind the acquiescence and silence with which victims may seem to condone what is done to them. Children need love and acceptance as much as they fear punishment and violence. When a parent or a relative whom they love demands sexual services as the price of such love a child is faced with a terrible dilemma. A 13-year-old girl in a therapy group at the hospital produced a poignant description of her desperate wish to be liked. She wrote in the book which, like other members of the group, she had been given to help her express her feelings: 'people will like me very much for what I have give them. If the boys do not like me I can go around kissing them and go in there [sic] bedrooms at night and let them see my tit and all the other things.' (Her father served a seven-year sentence for what he had done to her to teach her how to please him.)

Children's ignorance is a major source of their weakness. They very quickly believe that they are at fault for something that happens. Thus it is easy to convince children that if they tell of their sexual abuse, it is they who will be despised or punished for it.

Some adults insist that the child likes the sexual acts, pointing out to them that the physical sensations are pleasurable. This adds to the confusion they feel and convinces them of their guilt. The combination of physical sensations, that are pleasant though unwanted, with guilt may be recounted as the most painful part of the whole experience.

Children may make pathetic efforts to protect themselves from abuse. One woman reported that she used to put on several pairs of pants and thick woolly tights when she went to bed, hoping this would prevent her father touching her. It was to no avail. Another spent a great deal of energy ensuring that she was not alone, either in the house or on the farm. A third recounted how she and her sister banded together, hoping that if they went everywhere together they would be safe. Others stay late at school, hoping their mothers will be home before them. Their efforts are rarely successful but the strain adds to a miserable life. A grandmother writing her story for me described it like this:

> Daddy was an ever-present threat. If I was safe from him, when Mum was going to be home first, life was rosy. I could run the race and win it, lose myself with my friends and not worry too much about the humiliation of reading aloud in class. When, as usual, he was to be home first, the day was filtered through this dread.

Some children seem better able than others to protect themselves against abuse by reacting strongly at the first approach. Deidre Sanders records one or two such incidents reported by respondents to the *Woman* survey. In one, a man named as Alex confessed:

> My daughter is now 19 and I masturbated her from the age of nine to 15 about 25 times . . . I once touched my other daughter who politely said: 'Don't do that' and that's as far as it went. Because my youngest never asked me to stop I carried on. I try to please the three women in my life constantly and I thought I was pleasing her.[9]

As Sanders rightly comments, 'Alex almost seems to hold his daughter responsible. Because, when as young as nine or ten, she did not tell him to stop, he convinced himself that she wanted him to continue . . .' A similar incident occurred among the hospital cases, but the girl concerned there had to threaten to tell her mother and run out of the room to protect herself.

It is sometimes suggested that children do not understand that such behaviour is forbidden. It is then argued that it is only when they learn at a later age that such sexual behaviour is wrong that they are disturbed. A few retrospective accounts by victims lend some support to this idea. But the abuser's own behaviour more often gives a child the idea that something is wrong. As one young woman from Hereford reported 'Even at seven I knew it wasn't right – he was so furtive always hiding his actions.' There are other confusions too. One young woman recalled: 'I was once told off by my mother for touching myself – I couldn't understand – Daddy could do it so why couldn't I? I felt very isolated and confused but still wasn't really aware that anything was wrong.' Even if adult behaviour did not indicate that it was wrong, the insistence on not telling which is an almost universal accompaniment to the sexual abuse of children raises questions in a child's mind. However, it is quite clear that what is more important to the child's emotional health is not whether s/he knows it is forbidden or not but whether s/he can stop it when s/he does not wish it to go on. The great majority of these children are not allowed to say 'No'.

Different Kinds of Abuse?

The label 'sexual abuse of children' covers a range of behaviour and, as we have seen, there are even differences of opinion as to what should be included. Exhibitionism or verbal abuse has been excluded from the definition used in this book, but other authors include it. Within the general category of sexual abuse, however it is defined, distinctions may be made according to the severity of the abuse. The most important of these is that made between those victims who have suffered sexual intercourse, whether anal or vaginal or oral, and those whose abuse involved other forms of sexual activity such as masturbation and digital penetration or 'merely' genital fondling. The distinctions owe a certain amount to the laws prohibiting sexual activities with minors, where the presence or absence of full intercourse is critical for the definition of the offence. Children may, however, be severely damaged emotionally by rather minor sexual acts and the degree of harm they may suffer seems to depend on a range of other factors rather than what is actually done to them.[10] The danger of making these distinctions is that they come to seem different subtypes of abuse, some being less 'serious' than others. Since more incidents of the 'less severe' type of abuse are recorded, because they may also happen in serious cases, the greater proportion of these 'milder' forms may be taken, quite wrongly, to mean that most sexual abuse is rather mild.

These different 'kinds' of abuse are not mutually exclusive. A child may suffer any or all of the different forms of sexual abuse from the same person, either in different incidents within a short period or as a gradual escalation of sexual activity. In relationships within the household it is very common for the sexual abuse to start young with relatively mild touching. In most cases the abusive behaviour does not stop at touching the child. One young woman reported: 'When I was very young, my father used to touch me in my private parts when there were no other people in the house. At times, when I tried to refuse him, he used to get mad with me, but kept on doing it. At first I thought it was a natural thing in families.' This girl was so innocent that when she finally became pregnant by her father at just 14 she did not realize what had happened; it was he who told her she was pregnant and then forced her to have an abortion. She did not like what he was doing and made it clear from the beginning. But 'he kept on doing it'. A child's relative lack of freedom to refuse a powerful and loved father makes children completely vulnerable to exploitation.

It appears to be easier for a child to accept being touched than being asked to touch an adult's penis. The child in the story above was later asked to touch her father and then to masturbate him. She reported that she began to get frightened. One man, referred to as Rory, who responded to a survey carried out by a magazine, recorded 'My grandfather used to sit me on his knee and feel my genitals. He once tried to get me to feel his, but I wouldn't. After that I wouldn't let him near me.'[11] It is seldom pointed out that the sexual arousal of a grown man may be very frightening to a small child. A woman of 65 reported that from the age of about two she used to play with her father's penis and suck it. She went on, 'This was what led to disaster because there came a time when he got really aroused and went on to have an orgasm in my mouth. The whole change, from affectionate gentleness to that, was terrifying to me.' This account like many others shows that mild sexual touching rarely stops at that but progresses further, because the adult becomes more aroused or demands progressively more from the child. If the child resists then it may be forced into doing what the adult wants, so that fear, anger and humiliation are added to the emotions that already exist. The abuser's feelings may also add to the child's pain. 'The problem was, I often cried during the interference', wrote a young woman from Kent, 'he knew it upset me. What hurt was that he cried too, yet was unable to stop himself.'

The Consequences of Abuse

The consequences of sexual abuse in children obviously depend to some extent on the age of the child when it started and the nature of the abuse. Other factors which affect the outcome are whether the abuse was long-standing or short-lived, occasional or frequent and whether force or physical abuse accompanied it or not. It is only in rare cases that it can be said not to damage the child in some way; many of those recorded in the literature have only been superficially assessed. As Mrazek points out, it is naive to assume that being married and having a job indicates that there have been 'no harmful effects'.[12] Sexual abuse which seems less serious is not necessarily less damaging. In fact, the reasons for suspecting sexual abuse which are given in many textbooks are themselves indicators of damage. Some of them are physical: there may be genital or rectal damage, some of it so severe that it needs surgical repair, with bleeding, pain and infection. Children may show evidence of sexually transmitted diseases in the mouth, vagina or anus. They may be badly bruised. However in many cases of sexual abuse there are no physical signs or none that can easily be detected or exclusively related to sexual abuse.

The sexual abuse can also trigger psychosomatic responses. Asthma, eczema and anorexia nervosa are common syndromes, but there may also be abdominal pains, headaches and illness of various sorts. Commonly there are also emotional problems, often long-lasting, which are shown in various ways at different ages. Younger children may show open and even compulsive sexualized behaviour, or regress to an earlier stage with wetting and soiling. School-age children may manifest sexualized behaviour less often but may have problems in school, sleeping and eating disturbances, lack of self-esteem and nightmares. Adolescents may make suicide attempts, mutilate themselves and generally display hatred of themselves. They may be promiscuous and/or aggressive, or run away from home; girls may become pregnant.

All these symptoms show the effect of severe disturbance of the normal patterns of development, the trauma, pain and lowered self-esteem which characterize victims of sexual abuse. They do not go away with the passage of time after the abuse has ended, for a wide variety of later effects have been pointed out, including sexual difficulties, inability to form lasting relationships, a serious lack of self-confidence, marital problems and inability to be good parents. Sometimes these may remain under control until pregnancy, until children are born or until they reach the age the adult was when he or she was abused, when they cause a re-emergence of symptoms. Sexually abused boys may grow up to abuse their own or other people's children, while women who have been abused as children may be found among battering mothers.[13] Girls who survive sexual abuse as children may find themselves attracted, tragically, by men who are, or become child molesters, and be unable to offer their children any protection. As a consequence of her own earlier abuse, such a mother may be unable to tolerate the recognition of what is happening to her own children, or if she does understand it, she may feel powerless to do anything to stop it. Repetition in the next generation is not inevitable; not all abused children grow up to be abusing parents. Nevertheless, the identification and treatment of sexually abused children becomes even more vital when it is likely to help the next generation as well.

Who Are the Victims?

In our current stage of knowledge in Britain, it appears that girls are more vulnerable to sexual abuse than boys. The Channel Four survey showed 12 per cent of women were abused as girls but only 8 per cent of men reported their abuse as boys. The nearly four thousand people who wrote in to the BBC offering their experiences as material for the programme ChildWatch were very largely women; and almost 40 per cent of the men who wrote to ask for the questionnaire did not complete and return it. The representative national survey that the BBC conducted later revealed very few men who reported that they had been sexually abused as children: 12 men as opposed to 49 women. Another six men answered 'not sure/don't remember' to the question whether they had suffered sexual abuse.

In general there has also been less interest in the abuse of boys. Most research has concentrated on girls, perhaps because of the feminist influence on this whole subject. But the abuse of boys is also taken less seriously than that of girls: the possibility of damage to the reproductive organs is greater where girls are concerned and there is also the possibility of a girl becoming pregnant. Some people appear to feel that boys recover more easily from sexual abuse. Even in the United States, where there is much more information on the sexual abuse of children than in Britain, research on the sexual abuse of boys is thin.[14]

The fact that relatively few men reveal their childhood experiences of sexual abuse cannot be taken as it stands as an indication that boys are less at risk than their sisters. The sexual abuse of boys is under-reported to the authorities and under-represented in surveys. Men and boys are more strongly motivated to conceal that they have been sexually abused. Since most perpetrators of sexual abuse are men, boys who have been abused fear that they may be admitting to homosexual tendencies. Parents may share these anxieties and encourage silence, even when the abuser is not a close relative or member of the household, lest their son and they themselves acquire the stigma which still attaches to homosexuality.

The sexual abuse of boys may also be considered less serious and damaging emotionally than that of girls. Boys are expected to protect themselves and not complain; some sexual experience with older boys and men may even be considered a normal hazard to be overcome, which should then be forgotten about. It is a 'phase' which is grown out of. The accounts of school life by former public schoolboys make it clear that the sexual abuse of younger boys by their elders was, in some schools at some periods, almost a normal practice. One of my informants, an Old Etonian, made it clear that little boys would mostly find it impossible to resist the overtures of a prefect, or particularly the 'head of house'; it was even an advantage to have a protector who was of sufficient seniority to prevent other assaults. While such behaviour was officially forbidden, the former practice of giving the senior pupils the responsibility for keeping discipline in the houses where the boys lived in fact conferred powers on them which made the exploitation of the weak and least able to protect themselves much more likely. Even where there are no relationships which can be called abusive, the great interest that boys develop in the physical sensations of sexuality colours behaviour and creates a charged atmosphere which enhances the likelihood of sexualized relationships and sexual abuse in all-male institutions such as schools or children's homes for boys. We shall come back to the difference between boys and girls as far as their sexual development is concerned in later chapters, in connection with incest between brothers and sisters (chapter 6), and at the end of the book in discussing the problems involved in preventing the sexual abuse of children.

Some adults who are attracted to children may choose to work as teachers in boarding schools; since men are usually employed in such schools when the pupils are boys, boys may also be at risk from the occasional member of staff. It may be a long time before a boy is bold enough to reveal what has been going on there. Most never do. However, the view that boys go through a period of adolescent homosexuality which is not significant for their later development is not confined to those who went to public school and who send their sons there. The working-class parents of one boy who was referred to the hospital clinic seemed to share it. According to the social worker on the case, they felt that homosexuality was a normal stage in a boy's sexual development; they were not keen to discuss it or for him to have counselling; their attitude was 'The less said the better.' Many of the men in the parents' group gave instances of either sexual abuse or approaches they had suffered when young; they agreed that most boys would experience one or the other.

The shame of having been a sexual victim when males are expected to be the initiators of sexual activities may also be a factor in preventing boys or men disclosing their experiences. In the public school system it was the weak who were abused. In accounts of all-male institutions like prisons, mining camps and the army, it is similarly made clear that physical and sexual abuse of new recruits or inmates is a demonstration of their weakness and of the abusers' masculine power.[15] Admitting to having been abused is confessing to being weak and humiliated; disclosure by boys is thus made much less likely by the socially approved masculine image they must live up to. The American expert David Finkelhor has suggested that boys may have more to lose than girls from revealing that they have been abused.[16] As they are allowed more freedom and independence than girls, the fear of having their activities curtailed and being supervised 'like a girl' may make them reluctant to tell anyone that they have been sexually abused or assaulted. Certainly the higher proportion of boys abused by men outside the immediate family circle indicates that the relative freedom of boys, and the fact that this independence starts at an earlier age than girls are allowed out alone, affects the pattern of their abuse.

The unwillingness of boys to tell when they have been abused, for whatever reason, can be seen in the fact that among the hospital cases boys much more often appeared as victims in cases where more than one child had been abused. Boys figured in very small numbers among the single victims, 11 per cent of the children, but in cases where there were multiple victims, they formed twice as large a proportion, 22 per cent. In many cases a boy's abuse was only discovered when the abuse of his sister had already been revealed. Where there are several victims, one child may tell and disclose the abuse of the others, as in the case of five boys abused by a neighbour, revealed by the one child who told his mother.

Boys in Britain, like those in the United States, appear more vulnerable than girls to sexual abuse by outsiders, 'friends of the family', uncles and those like scoutmasters and youth workers who organize activities for boys. This generalization rests on figures from the Channel Four survey, which indicates that 44 per cent of boys but 30 per cent of girls had been abused by known outsiders. The BBC survey shows the opposite result (23 per cent of boys and 31 per cent of girls) but it recorded only 12 cases of men abused during boyhood, too few to make any comparison reliable. Most of the boys in the hospital cases had been abused by a member of their own household. A greater liability to abuse by non-household members is consistent with boys' greater independence and their involvement in activities organized for boys outside their homes which may offer opportunities to adults with paedophile tendencies. However, the category of known outsiders who may abuse boys is a very mixed one and includes friends of the parents or neighbours, so that there is no reason to blame boys' groups in particular. Only two of the boys among those referred to the hospital were abused in such a context. The man who had abused five boys including his own son was greatly respected in his community; his relationship with the mothers of his other victims, most of whom were single parents, was that of a kindly and helpful neighbour. A large proportion of the boys referred to the hospital were abused, like the girls, by senior relatives: fathers, stepfathers, uncles and older brothers.

Finkelhor has remarked that as the public became more aware of the possibility of abuse, more boys and men were prepared to disclose the fact that they had been abused. He reported: 'Whereas five years ago, many treatment programs saw only a few cases of abused boys, today some programs report that as many as a quarter or a third of their cases are of that sort.'[17] With the recognition that sexual abuse can have just as serious an effect on boys as on girls, more information is likely to become available in Britain as well. As yet the information on the sexual abuse of boys is patchy and unreliable so that it may be some time until there is research which will allow us to estimate the prevalence of this form of abuse and establish the relative vulnerability of boys and girls. At the moment it seems as though girls may be twice as vulnerable as boys but that is an estimate which may change when there is better information available.

While the information we have, scanty as it is, indicates a difference in the patterns of abuse suffered by girls and by boys, this does not appear to indicate two different phenomena. Girls, like boys, are involved by adults in mutual masturbation, and girls, like boys, may suffer anal and oral intercourse. There is some indication that abusers may show a preference for children of one or other sex (see below) but it would be quite unwarranted to conclude that abusers of girls are more 'normal' than abusers of boys or that homosexuality always involves a fondness for sexual relations with young boys.

The Age of Victims

There are a number of general misconceptions about the age of victims of sexual abuse. It is often assumed that children, particularly girls, are sexually abused as they begin to reach physical maturity. The attractiveness of young girls who are at this stage is widely accepted and in turn these children (for that is what they still are) are often thought to try out their newly-acquired sexual powers by acting seductively. Girls who are adolescent are in a sort of limbo, not quite children and not yet adults: their sexual status is uncertain.[18] The fact that in other parts of the world girls are married very young, while they are still what we consider children, adds to the impression that the sexual abuse of girls merely anticipates by a short while their adult status. The present minimum age of marriage is relatively recent. Until 1929 the legal age of marriage was 12 for a girl but 14 for a boy; since the enactment of the Age of Marriage Act in that year, 16 has been the minimum age for either party to a legal marriage.[19] Public opinion strongly supports the law in this case. An attempt by an Iranian student a few years ago to obtain a place in school for his 12-year-old wife caused such a public outcry that he was forced to send her back to Iran.

Gorry's study of 140 incest cases reported to the Metropolitan Police over a period of six years, ending in 1985, appears to lend some support to the view that newly matured girls present an irresistible temptation, in this case to their fathers. The majority of victims in these cases were between 13 and 15 when the first act of intercourse was alleged to have taken place. Of course, as we have seen, full sexual intercourse often follows a long period of other forms of sexual abuse. The requirements of police reporting for this particular crime make it seem as though the age at which incest occurred was the beginning of sexual abuse; even so, there was a substantial minority (26 per cent) where the victim was 12 years or less and nearly 12 per cent were ten or less when this happened.[20]

Much of the available evidence on the age of victims is confusing because social service departments and hospital clinics often record the age of their child patients not at the time at which the abuse started but at the time at which the abuse was revealed or the case referred (Finkelhor notes the same for a study in the United States[21]). A table of ages of victims in the report of the CSA team at Great Ormond Street hospital gives information on when the abuse started, but in nearly a third of the cases it was not known.[22] For therapeutic purposes it may not be particularly important to determine the precise age when the child was first abused. Some of the children are so young that they are unable to answer questions about when the abuse started, although there are ways of establishing this in some cases.

In many of the files of the CSA Unit cases, it was impossible to tell when the abuse started, so table 4 shows the age of children at referral. Even so, some cases had to be omitted, either because the child's date of birth was not available or the date of referral was missing. In many cases the abuse had started years before referral but this information was not available in enough cases to make it worthwhile to try and reconstruct putative ages at the time of the first incidents for all the cases. In addition, the abuse of some of those included in the table was only discovered when the abuse of a younger brother or sister was discovered; this information that others had been abused in the past largely accounted for the presence of eight girls and three boys over 17 who formed part of the study but have not been included in the table. Since the referral process itself may take as long as a year or a year and a half, the ages given in table 4 represent a considerable overestimation of the age of victimization. Even so, nearly half the victims are under 12 *at referral*.

TABLE 4   Age at referral of patients of the child sexual abuse unit of a London hospital

Age	Girls	Boys	Total
Under 6	24	3	27
6–11	61	20	81
12–16	121	18	139
Total	206	41	247

Source: Author's research.

Nearly half the children (108 out of 247, 44 per cent) were under the age of 12 by the time they reached the hospital unit. Nineteen girls and four boys were 12 at the age of referral and were certainly abused while they were 11. If one includes them in the pre-pubertal category then there are almost as many pre-pubertal girls (99) as there are those referred after puberty (102). At Great Ormond Street 'The age of onset was evenly distributed in the age-groups 3–5, 6–8, 9–11, 12–14 . . .'[23] The authors also note that in 6 per cent of cases the child was under three. The evidence from clinical cases suggests that in a large proportion of them the girls are well under the age of puberty; in a minority, the children are very young indeed.

The BBC national survey confirms the finding that the sexual abuse of children often starts when they are very young. It shows that a majority of the respondents claimed it started before puberty, as table 5 shows. Despite the apparent certainty with which these adults responded, it is not always easy to establish the age at which a child was first sexually abused. There are many reasons for this. One woman who wrote to me to volunteer the story of her father's abuse of herself and her sister over many years started her account: 'If my sister is born I am three and a half, if not I am younger.' Others deal with their painful childhood by suppressing the memory entirely; one young woman began to answer a question asking for her childhood memories with the words: 'I hear many people talking about times when they were a child going to school, etc. but find I cannot remember any of my school days or home life until about the age of nine to ten years old.' Still others carry the mental scars with them until late in their life: women of over 60 wrote vivid accounts of their experience of sexual abuse in childhood. Some victims have dealt with the pain of the experience by burying it deep in their memories and it takes time for the therapeutic process to reveal it. During therapy, children may reveal that the abuse started much earlier than was originally thought; the initial disclosure of abuse usually refers to the most recent incident and this may be recorded as the date of onset; it is only after the child's confidence gradually improves that the full

TABLE 5   Age when sexual abuse first started, by sex, of respondents to the BBC national survey

Age at onset	Males	Females
Under 6	1	8
6–11	6	27
12–16	1	10
Not stated	4	4
Total	12	49

duration of abusive behaviour comes to light. One respondent to the BBC survey, now in her late forties or early fifties, reported that she had had therapy for eight years, which brought the memory back. She wrote: 'There are a LOT like me. When I was in therapy, out of all the girls I went with [who] had an incest-bound problem (20–30) only ONE had recall of the events that had led her to seek help. The rest of us spent years looking for the truth' (her emphasis).

Events may trigger off the memories which have been suppressed. A senior social worker experienced in the field of caring for the mentally handicapped described to me her experience of being in charge of a hostel when the ChildWatch programme was shown on television. There was uproar among the residents, all of whom wanted to telephone the number given to tell of their experiences. The staff were taken by surprise for they had not known that any of their clients had been abused, despite their close association with them. In the hospital clinic it was common to find that the therapy in which mothers of abused children took part resulted in their revealing their own experience of abuse which they had 'forgotten' until their own child was abused.

Some therapists consider the silence of severely abused children as one symptom of a more general condition which may also affect the survivors of large-scale accidents or other disasters: post-traumatic stress disorder (PTSD). Loss of memory, depression and other psychological disturbances are other symptoms. The fact that some victims of sexual abuse cannot remember or cannot speak of their abuse, for whatever reason, makes sexual abuse a difficult subject to study and adds to the possibility of underestimating prevalence rates. In particular it makes one somewhat sceptical about the reliability of information on the age when victims were first abused. There seems good reason to suppose that any figures overestimate rather than underestimate the ages of victims. Finkelhor has argued, and Russell shares his opinion, that in the United States the abuse of girls actually declines when they reach puberty.[24] Certainly in a few of the hospital cases the abuse stopped when the girl started menstruating, possibly for fear of a possible pregnancy. It is not uncommon to find that a younger child was then approached. In one such case two sisters had been subjected to sexual intercourse, both anal and vaginal, since they were about ten or 11. One report in the file records that sexual abuse of the eldest

daughter had started when she was six. The question arose as to
how their younger sister, then aged 11, had escaped. The social
worker reported: 'Mr P's approach is to draw pictures on his
daughter's legs, which he has just started doing with Theresa [the
youngest daughter].' The combination of the fact that she was the
youngest of the three and that her sisters disclosed the abuse when
they did had protected her.

There is some difference between boys and girls as far as their
ages of victimization are concerned. More of the boys in the
hospital set of cases were 11 and under than 12 and over, a finding
that is supported by the survey evidence both in this country and
the United States, which shows that the majority of boys are abused
at a younger age than the majority of girls. All but one of the men
who answered this question on the BBC national survey were 11 or
under when the abuse started; half were eight or under. The very
small numbers of men in the survey who claimed to have been
sexually abused makes it unwise to base too many conclusions on
the survey alone. However it is consistent with much of the other
data which show that boys past puberty are much less often
sexually assaulted.

Is the Sexually Abused Child a 'Special' Child?

It is sometimes believed by adults that men may 'fall in love' with a
particular child (usually a girl), either because she resembles her
mother when young or for some other reason to do with individual
appearance or character. Individual instances to support this
conviction can be found; there are CSA Unit cases which seem to
confirm it. In one, the abuser had met his wife when she was very
young, 13 or 14; her parents were Travellers, who strongly
disapproved of her association with a non-Travelling youth.
Because of their opposition, at 15 she ran away from home and they
were married. Her eldest daughter, 14 at the time of her referral,
had been born when her mother was only just 16. She was said to
be the image of her mother. In the opinion of the therapist
responsible for the case, her father, who had abused her since she
was 12, was passionately in love with her. In a confused way he saw
himself as returning to his youth and could not really distinguish

between his daughter and his wife when young. What she thought was not clear.

The idea that the sexual abuse of children is a misguided love affair may seem to imply both mutuality and the child's consent. In a second case a youth worker had clearly fallen in love with the 13-year-old boy concerned; unlike the girl in the first case, this boy appeared to reciprocate these feelings. His parents said that the young man had been very good to their son. They were reluctant to end the association because, they said frankly, of the material benefits he had received. However, as is all too often the case, the boy's feelings were not recorded in the file and, while one may not doubt that he felt affection for a man who had taken notice of him, helped him and given him presents, this does not mean that he necessarily accepted the sexual relationship.

Not a few women report that they were told that they were abused because they were 'special' in some way. Abusers may argue that the abuse was a manifestation of love and an attempt to please. One father in the parents' therapy group I attended spent a long time in one session demanding that someone give him a clear definition of the difference between love and sexual desire, implying in his remarks that since he could not tell where one ended and the other began, his sexual involvement with his daughter was a matter of his love for her. The excuse that sexual abuse is 'love that goes too far' is common and too important to be dismissed lightly.

This question is also of vital practical significance because social workers and other child protection agents may act on the assumption that if one child in a family is abused, either sexually or in any other way, then others are also at risk. Such pre-emptive action was said to have accounted for the large numbers of children taken into care in Cleveland. If, in some cases, the abuser is attracted only by one particular child, then the wholesale removal of children from their parents may not always be necessary. The examples given above are unusual among the hospital cases, and there is much more evidence that the sexual abuse of children has little to do with love that goes too far.

However, systematic analysis of cases provides more reliable evidence than a few case histories selected to support a conclusion. It might still be true that there is a difference between those cases where only one child in a family has been abused and the smaller number of cases where there are many victims. In the first type of case there is the possibility that the child concerned may be 'special' to the abuser in some way, even if it is not clearly expressed. The case files do not provide enough information to give a direct answer to this question but it can be inferred indirectly. The single victims have a number of general characteristics which show up as a pattern when all the cases are considered. Where many children prove to be similar in a certain respect, then it is harder to believe that they have each been singled out as individuals.

Among my CSA Unit cases, there were 130 cases of one child's having been abused but in only 95 of them was there enough information to be reasonably certain that no other child had been abused. In another four the perpetrator was not a member of the household, so these were excluded to make a more homogeneous set of cases. There were thus 91 remaining cases; only seven of them involved boys, the rest of the victims were girls.

As far as the boys were concerned, the situation was clear. Either they were only children, so that the perpetrator had no other children in the household from which to make a choice, or the other children were all girls. In the latter situation it is probable that a sexual, rather than an individual preference was being exercised; there were other children but the man concerned was attracted only to boys. As far as the 84 girls were concerned, 16 were only children and another 36 had brothers but no sisters. If a similar sexual preference for girls was being shown, then over three-fifths of the girls (52 out of 84, or 62 per cent) were the only available victims. Altogether in nearly two-thirds of the cases, no obvious choice of a particular child was being made; the victim was the only available child.

As far as the remaining 32 girls were concerned, in 22 cases the victim appears to have been singled out not for her personal characteristics but from her position in the household. Twelve were the eldest girls and in such cases one cannot be certain that the other girls would not have been abused had the abuse not been revealed when it was. It is a common pattern in cases of the sexual abuse of children for the children to be abused one after the other. There were several such cases referred to the CSA Unit. Other studies have noted that an eldest daughter is particularly at risk, possibly because she often has a more distant relationship with her mother, who is preoccupied with the younger children. For a variety of reasons she may be forced into the role of substitute for

her mother in doing housework or as companion for her father.
The eldest daughter is probably therefore a more likely victim
because of her position in the household, not because of her
personal attractiveness to the man who abuses her.

Just under half the abused girls were step-daughters of the man
who abused them. In ten of the 18 cases where there were other
children in the household, the victims were the only step-daughters.
Step-daughters have also been shown to be particularly vulnerable
to sexual abuse.[25] The high proportion of only step-daughters
seems to suggest that they have been picked out as different from
the other children in the household but not because they were
particularly attractive as individuals. (In chapter 5 the reasons for
step-daughters' vulnerability will be discussed more fully.) Overall,
of the 84 girls, only 14 seem not to fall into any particular category.
The information is not good enough to say whether all of these
cases really did confirm the stereotype but a large majority did not.
All the rest of the cases, 83 per cent, concerned either the only
available child, or one who occupied a position in the household
that other studies have shown to be a particularly vulnerable one.
In over four-fifths of these cases, the term victimization is clearly
the most appropriate.

The common myths about children hinder our understanding
about how they can be sexually abused. The evidence set out in this
chapter shows how much younger, and hence more vulnerable,
they are than generally supposed. The victims are not mostly newly
matured girls, eager to use their sexual powers, or boys whose
latent homosexuality makes them attractive to others who share
this sexual orientation, but young children below the age of
puberty. Their common characteristic is a general vulnerability to
all adults by virtue of the differences, in size and strength, that are the
consequence of their immaturity. Children lack the social and
sexual knowledge which might protect them and they are brought
up to respect and obey adults, whose relationship with them is
based on the inequality of generational differences. Where children
are also completely dependent on adults, as they are on those they
live with, then their vulnerability is very great. Their silence can be
enforced by threats and by feelings of shame and guilt, so much so
that they find it difficult to speak about it even when the secret is
revealed. Their allegations may be retracted out of fear of the
consequences so that when children do tell of their sexual abuse, it

is only in very special circumstances that it is not the painful truth. Children cannot be thought to have any responsibility for the sexual abuse they suffer; it is rather those adults who are responsible who should be the objects of our scrutiny.

Notes

1 J. Ennew, *The Sexual Exploitation of Children* (Polity, Cambridge, 1986), p. 120ff.
2 A. Bentovim and E. Vizard, 'Sexual abuse, sexuality and childhood', in Bentovim et al. (eds), *Child Sexual Abuse*; Finkelhor, *Child Sexual Abuse*.
3 *Sunday Times* magazine, 29 May 1988, p. 31.
4 Cleveland Report, p. 46, paragraph 2.605.
5 Ibid., p. 205, paragraph 12.7.
6 D. Jones and E. M. McCraw, 'Reliable and fictitious accounts of sexual abuse to children', *Journal of Interpersonal Violence*, 2 (1) (1987), pp. 27–45; also D. Jones and A. Seig, 'Child sexual abuse allegations in custody or visitation disputes', in E. B. Nicholson (ed.), *Sexual Abuse Allegations in Custody and Visitation Cases* (American Bar Association, Washington DC, 1988).
7 Ibid.
8 Cleveland Report, p. 9, paragraph 34.
9 Sanders, *Woman Book of Love and Sex*, pp. 167–8.
10 Baker and Duncan, 'Child sexual abuse'.
11 Sanders, *Woman Book of Love and Sex*, pp. 167–8.
12 P. B. Mrazek and D. A. Mrazek, 'Definition and recognition of sexual child abuse: historical and cultural perspectives', in Mrazek and Kempe (eds), *Sexually Abused Children*.
13 Bentovim and Vizard, 'Sexual abuse'.
14 Finkelhor, *Child Sexual Abuse*, p. 153.
15 J. M. Coggeshall, 'Ladies behind bars: a liminal gender as cultural mirror', *Anthropology Today*, 4(4) (1988).
16 Finkelhor, *Child Sexual Abuse*, p. 157.
17 Ibid., p. 151.
18 I owe this point to Amanda Sackur but see also Ennew, *Sexual Exploitation*, p. 53.
19 See J. Levin (ed.), *Family Law by His Honour Judge Brian Grant*, 3rd edn (Sweet and Maxwell, London, 1977).
20 Gorry, 'Incest', p. 26.
21 Finkelhor, *Child Sexual Abuse*, p. 161.

22 A. Bentovim and P. Boston, 'Sexual abuse: basic issues – characteristics of children and families', in Bentovim et al. (eds), *Child Sexual Abuse*, p. 21.
23 Ibid., pp. 36–7.
24 D. Finkelhor, *Sexually Victimised Children* (Free Press, New York, 1979), p. 61; see also Russell, *The Secret Trauma*, and K. A. Kendall-Tackett and A. F. Simon, 'Molestation and the onset of puberty', *Child Abuse and Neglect*, 12(1) (1988).
25 See Finkelhor, *Child Sexual Abuse*, pp. 25–6, and discussion in chapter 5 of this book.

4   The Offenders

. . . I was his favourite and I loved him very much and would do anything to please him.   Woman aged about 40, Hertfordshire

I never felt completely free till my father died last year. Now I *am* safe.   Woman aged about 50, Bedfordshire

Since the sexual abuse of children cannot be dismissed as the fantasies or lies of disturbed or malicious children, nor the cause found in the nature of the children themselves, their emergent sexual powers, or the sensuality and precocity of individuals among them, the responsibility is clearly seen to lie with the adults who are the abusers. Explanations have been sought in the nature of the individuals who initiate sexual activities with children. The first such attempts sought them in the personalities of the offenders. They were thought to be a small group of individuals with psychological abnormalities, whose emotional disturbance resulted in an inappropriate sexual interest in children. The condition, labelled paedophilia,[1] was believed to be comparatively rare but opinions about its causes were divided. Various characteristics of offenders, such as low intelligence, unusually strong sexual drive or psychopathology were given prominence as 'causes' of the sexual offence. Later explanations moved away from focusing on individual pathology to a consideration of factors which might distort normal development. Some theories start from Freud's view that all individuals are initially attracted to children but are weaned away from these feelings by social conditioning and repression. The question then became: what are the factors that prevent normal development happening, because most adults do not engage in sexual activities with children. The answers have posited various reasons, either for some adults becoming 'fixed' at the early stage or for their regression to it when suffering traumatic events in their lives.[2] Other investigators used different theoretical approaches but they were asking similar questions about what differentiated sexual offenders against children from the majority of adults who do not engage in sexual activities with children. The answers were sought in the psychology of the offenders themselves.

More recently it has been argued that the motives behind the sexual abuse of children are largely non-sexual; these explanations stress the expression of negative feelings and issues of domination and control which lie behind it. Feminists have pointed out the extent to which sexual domination is an expression of men's power over women; this argument can be extended even more to children who are weaker even than adult women.[3] It has also been suggested that sexual abusers of children are characterized by a lack of self-esteem and a fear of adult women; as a result they can only find beings much smaller and weaker than themselves attractive, or that they compensate for their feelings of powerlessness in this way. Several of the women who participated in the BBC self-selected survey remarked that the men concerned appeared to be motivated more by hate than love, or by a desire to inspire fear, or to punish either the child or her mother. While there can be arguments about the mix of sexual and non-sexual motives which impel individuals to abuse children sexually, none of these arguments challenge the dominant assumption that the main reasons for the sexual abuse of children are to be found in the nature of individual offenders.

The use of alcoholism as a factor in explanations can be taken as a good example of this kind of thinking. The part attributed to it has varied: from being a prime cause of sexual abuse it has been relegated to a precipitating factor. Since alcohol is known to lower inhibitions, it seems plausible that men who drink too much may give way to sexual impulses that they would otherwise control. In popular thinking 'being drunk' may explain disapproved behaviour by implying that the culprit 'did not know what he was doing'; abusers themselves may claim this. One of the earliest studies, by Maisch, of offenders convicted under the West German incest laws, examines the role of alcohol carefully. Just under a quarter (24 per cent) of his sample were chronic alcoholics but he concludes that, although alcohol may have significance in some of the individual cases, 'It would be a mistake to deduce from suitable cases a direct specific, causal connection between alcohol and incest.'[4] His view of all individual characteristics that have been associated with incest is that although they appear in a proportion of the offenders, they are not characteristic of the majority.

A more recent description of abusers figuring in cases referred to the sexual abuse unit in Great Ormond Street Hospital showed that alcohol was referred to in 19 per cent of cases; in 15 per cent the report mentioned a long-standing problem with alcohol and, one might infer, chronic alcoholism. As they note, the diagnosis was impressionistic and therefore probably unreliable, particularly since alcohol is expected to be associated with sexual crimes. The percentage is slightly lower than Maisch's figures but the authors refer to it as 'high'.[5] Yet the prevalence of alcoholism among the general population is unknown so that one cannot compare this rate against one which might occur by chance to demonstrate a statistical significance. There is a far higher incidence of alcoholism among perpetrators of violent crimes or even those involved in road accidents. In 5 per cent of Great Ormond Street cases alcohol was specifically ruled out as a factor. However, it is the absence of any information at all about alcohol abuse in the vast majority of cases (76 per cent) that makes this study inconclusive.

Recent research in the United States seems to indicate more caution in accepting alcohol as a cause of the sexual abuse of children. Parker cites a 1984 analysis by the American Humane Association of all cases of child abuse and neglect which reported that sexual abusers were lower than other kinds of abuser in their use of alcohol.[6] Herman argues that incestuous fathers were frequent users of alcohol but not significantly more so than a comparison group.[7] It seems likely that the persistence of this explanation and others like it owes more to popular stereotypes of the anti-social individual than to solid evidence on the question. As Maisch argued 15 years ago, the attempt to find explanations for incest and the sexual abuse of children in the ' "abnormal" and socially undesirable personality traits' of individual offenders is the result of the 'manifest incomprehensibility of the incestuous act to the average mind', for generalizations from some of them do not apply to the majority.[8]

Explanations in terms of the psychological abnormalities of the offenders are related to the fact that most studies of sexual offenders with children are based, for obvious reasons, on convicted offenders. They are, as Finkelhor remarks, likely to be more extreme and obvious in their behaviour.[9] Until comparatively recently it was reasonable to suppose that they were a tiny minority of deviant people. Now, however, there is evidence to show that only a small fraction of offenders are caught, let alone convicted of their offences. Moreover, as we have seen, the abusers in child-care cases are not representative of all abusers. The convicted form a minority, not only of the population as a whole, but of a larger category of offenders about most of whom little or nothing is known, except that they are a heterogeneous category, with a variety of motivations for sexual involvement with children. Only a minority appear to have a permanent and exclusive sexual interest in children; in others the interest in children is combined with other sexual interests and the activities can be aimed at personal gratifications other than the purely sexual.

The prevalence of sexual interest in children is hard to assess. There is evidence that enough people find children sexually attractive to provide a market for child pornography and clients for child prostitutes of both sexes, both in this country and abroad. Although both these activities are criminal offences in Britain, the revelations in the press from time to time about prosecutions indicate they have not been eliminated by being proscribed; in some other countries the law is either not so strict or more easily evaded. In Britain an association of paedophiles, the Paedophile Information Exchange, was formed to attempt to change the general disapproval of such activities to one of acceptance; at one time it claimed to have 2,000 members. The organization was eventually banned, but we cannot assume that its former members have changed their views or that the ideas and feelings it expressed have disappeared. It may be, too, that many more people who do not sexually abuse children and do not consider themselves paedophiles feel sexually attracted to them. Judith Ennew, in her book on *The Sexual Exploitation of Children* points out the suggestive use of children in advertising; its effectiveness may draw on such latent ideas and feelings.[10]

Sexual offenders against children are not obviously different from other people. The most striking characteristic of the parents of abused children who came to the therapy groups at the hospital was that they were so ordinary. While waiting for the sessions to start they chatted about the difficulties of transport, of cars and the weather or helped each other to the coffee and biscuits that were provided. It might have been any committee meeting of a neighbourhood organization. On closer acquaintance it became clear that the women, who were all wives of sexual offenders, were mostly rather quiet and retiring; they spoke little and were diffident about offering their opinions, or unwilling to express their emotions. Some of them, however, were containing their anger and pain in this way; they were by no means as indifferent and lacking in emotion as they appeared. The men revealed themselves as lacking confidence, but very self-centred, unable to put themselves in the place of someone else and, most of all, reluctant to take responsibility for their actions. One or two were very aggressive and the group was liable at any point to turn into a chorus of accusations against social workers and probation officers, whom they blamed for their difficulties. All these men had abused at least one child; most of them their own daughter or step-daughter; few would have stood out in a crowd.

Social Factors

The recognition that the sexual abuse of children is much more common than was realized hitherto has encouraged greater attention to social and cultural factors which might facilitate or encourage sexual activities with children. Early popular theories posited a connection between sexual crimes against children and some or any of the following: overcrowded living conditions, ignorance or lack of education, criminal behaviour, unemployment. These reflect the general acceptance common at that time that incest was found only among the 'lower classes' in society. Some figures do appear to give credence to this view. The closer examination carried out in chapter 2 showed that this impression is misleading. It is largely the result of the methods by which the figures were collected.

Stereotypes of incest suggest that remote communities or certain subcultures or ethnic groups are more prone to incest. Gorry[11] shows that the figures in police reports of incest show larger numbers of reports in the metropolitan areas of England and Wales; the differences are not great, however, and he attributes them to the greater density of urban populations. It may also be that he is thinking of the fact that, as he remarks elsewhere in his thesis, incest may be discovered by the police in the course of investigation of another crime. Urban areas have a very much higher crime rate and a correspondingly greater police intervention rate, which might lead to a greater number of cases of sexual abuse of children being discovered. In the United States, there is one study which appears to show the opposite pattern to that of Britain: Finkelhor's study of Boston students shows an association between a rural upbringing and sexual abuse,[12] but the study is not based on a national representative sample. The BBC survey which is nationally representative shows the abuse of children, including sexual abuse, evenly distributed by region. The popular stereotype of remote, rural areas appears to be inaccurate. No research has yet been undertaken in Britain to determine the relative prevalence of incest or sexual abuse in its different cultural or ethnic subgroups. Lukianowicz's study of some Irish psychiatric patients, which draws the conclusion that incest is a subcultural, working-class pattern there, has been shown to be so flawed methodologically that it cannot be accepted.[13] The only national survey undertaken in the United States (of reported cases) indicates that there is no statistically significant association between sexual abuse of children and ethnic origin. Abusing fathers are less likely to be black Americans. Abusing mothers are more likely than fathers to be black but blacks are still in the minority among abusing women.[14]

The popular British notion that incest is normal in 'other' cultures has no basis in facts established by research. When research on distribution by ethnic origin can be done it will almost certainly show that this idea is mistaken. There is evidence that baby-battering (the physical abuse of children) is more frequent towards the lower end of the social scale and relates to deprivation and stress. Some children who are sexually abused also suffer beatings and other physical violence. But on the whole, as we have seen in chapter 2, the available evidence strongly suggests that, unlike physical abuse, the sexual abuse of children occurs at all levels of society.

Social Change as a Factor

Some popular commentators have looked to social changes for an explanation, associating the sexual abuse of children with the decline of traditional family patterns, such as easier and more frequent divorce, the employment of women outside the house or greater sexual permissiveness. Child pornography, instead of being seen as revealing the extent of adult sexual attraction to children, may be held responsible for encouraging it. All these arguments assume that the sexual abuse of children did not occur before the social changes that are picked out as causes took place. As chapter 2 showed, it is not possible to say how prevalent the sexual abuse of children was even two generations ago, so that arguments which start by characterizing this social problem as a new one are on very weak ground.

Gender and Abuse

Differences of sexual orientation associated with gender roles, as distinct from general ideas about sexuality, became the focus of attention in the United States when it became clear that children were almost always sexually abused by men, not women, unlike the cases of physical abuse where perpetrators might be of either sex. Finkelhor considers that the sexual abuse of children is a problem directly related to the socialization of men; many other American experts take the same point of view.[15] All the available research in Britain indicates that here, too, the abusers are men (see tables 6 and 7 below). While women are as often accused as men of battering children, very few are suspected, let alone convicted, of the sexual abuse of a child. One man among those interviewed for the BBC national survey reported sexual abuse by a woman, his mother, but he also accused his father. There were three children referred to the hospital CSA Unit for sexual abuse by a woman, two of them by their mother (the case is described below). All three children were very young boys. Some additional information can be obtained from the study of police reports of incest already referred to.[16] Just over 2 per cent of cases, four out of 171, involved a mother and her child, but one of these was the case of a young man who brutally raped his mother. The proportion of women probably responsible for incest was thus even smaller: 1.8 per cent. It is higher than the incidence among the cases in the hospital unit where just under 1 per cent of the cases involved women, but it is still very low.

The relative absence of women from the ranks of sexual abusers cannot be attributed to any universal or instinctive feminine protectiveness, for women have been convicted of terrible physical damage to their young children. It is much more likely to be the result of social and cultural factors, for it has been suggested that mother/son incest is a subject of much public concern in Japan where it seems to be the predominant form of sexual abuse.[17] There is some controversy over the opportunities for women to perpetrate sexual abuse. First, it is sometimes alleged that women are permitted such a degree of physical familiarity with children that it is difficult to know when it becomes abuse. This view, which has even taken the form of asserting that there is a double standard in these matters which favours women,[18] would indicate that the abuse by women never comes to light. There may be differences between individuals and perhaps even between sectors of the same society about what physical contact between a mother and child is appropriate.

The anthropologist Jill Korbin has pointed out how what is considered normal may also vary in different societies.[19] One hospital case showed a conflict of opinion, clearly based on cultural differences. A young woman, brought up in another country, was astonished to be told by the British health visitor that her practice of kissing her little boys' genitals when she was putting a clean nappy on them was abusive. She considered that she was merely expressing maternal affection; they were then aged two and a half and one and a half. As they showed no signs of resenting this attention, the hospital staff did not consider this really constituted sexual abuse. However, they agreed that the practice might lead to abuse and the mother was persuaded that, at least as far as the elder child was concerned, it was time for it to stop.

However, against this view that sexual abuse by women may be going unreported, Finkelhor argues 'that women learn earlier and more completely to distinguish between sexual and nonsexual forms of attraction'.[20] In addition, one might add that women are less motivated by cultural attitudes to find children sexually attractive, and more socialized to be sensitive to the child's wishes. A second CSA Unit case indicates that this latter quality is probably critical; its absence indicates, too, that it is the effect on the child that makes clear what is sexual abuse. The boy in this case was abused by his grandmother, with whom he and his mother lived for some years. His mother went out to work leaving him in the care of the older woman. The child had complained to his mother but she did not understand his allegations until much later, when he was about ten years old and they had stopped living there. In that particular case the boy was clearly abused, he had not liked it at the time and tried to get help to stop it. Although the identity of the perpetrator of the abuse was most unusual, his failure to get his mother to understand him is extremely common, even typical. It did not occur to his mother that there might be a sexual element to the relationship between her son and his grandmother; moreover she was living in the other woman's house and, as a single parent, it would have been difficult for her to manage without this and the help in looking after him. Later they moved to their own flat; it was only later still when her son required treatment for his emotional difficulties that his earlier attempts to tell her of his abuse could be recognized for what they were.

In some other hospital cases, accusations were made against the mothers of the children, either by other adults or the children themselves. They were mostly unsubstantiated, although in two cases a mother was said to have taken part in sexual activities involving her children and other adults. Even where mothers have no direct involvement, however, in many cases the victims of the abuse may feel as much betrayed and abused by the failure of mothers to prevent or stop sexual assaults. It is possible that the male respondent in the BBC survey was accusing his mother of complicity in this way.

There are some indications that sexual abuse by women may be under-reported, but the evidence so far is rather weak. A careful examination by Finkelhor and Russell of the American evidence adduced in support of this view, concludes that it does not carry enough weight to change their original conclusion that the socialization of women makes them much less likely to be abusers.[21] Much of the evidence, when examined closely, can be seen to refer to the practice in some states of recording mothers as guilty of sexual abuse when they failed to prevent it happening. In Britain a free confidential telephone service for children, called ChildLine, was established as a charity in October 1986. It has made available information on the calls children made to it in the first year of its existence. During three months in 1987 nearly two-fifths of the boys who reported sexual abuse accused women; nearly half of them accused their own mothers and a slightly smaller proportion other female relatives.[22] However, no details of their allegations are given so that the information is intriguing rather than clearly demanding a radical revision of views held so far. The insistence that there is much sexual abuse perpetrated by women which is never revealed may be the product of discomfort with the idea that this sexual problem is solely a masculine one. The effort to find indications of female abuse of children may, like the denial that the problem exists, be a reaction to the overwhelming evidence that sexual abuse is perpetrated by men, who are the figures of authority in Western, as in most, societies. Nevertheless the possibility that more women will be revealed as abusers in the future cannot be dismissed.

Identifying Abusers

The social characteristics of perpetrators of sexual abuse have not been properly established. Those who are convicted are not representative of all offenders and figures based on studies of them are as likely to be as biased as the figures for abuse revealed to the authorities. In Britain there are few studies even of convicted offenders.[23] Most generalizations about perpetrators are derived from information provided by surveys of victims. They assume that the social characteristics of offenders are similar to those of their victims. This is obviously justifiable where sexual abuse takes place within the household, but equally clearly unreliable where strangers, neighbours or even family friends are concerned. As we have seen, children of all classes are abused; nor are the victims particularly located among ethnic minorities or distributed regionally, in urban or rural areas, or in marginal or backward communities. Deviant characteristics of an individual sort do not seem to identify the sexual abusers of children; the assumptions that there is an association with alcohol addiction or criminal behaviour have already been shown to depend on rather unreliable information. The best information on offenders concerns their relationships to their victims which shows that the general stereotypes of such offenders are not well-founded.

The Myth of the Abusing Stranger

If people do think of the possibility of sexual assaults on children they see them as a risk from casual encounters in the street. The belief in the natural relationship between parent and child is the basis for the firm conviction that if danger threatens any child, it can only come from 'outside' the family. When the damage inflicted is sexual, the offending person must be an unknown, a shadowy and frightening stranger, not anyone with whom one has daily contact, let alone someone who is part of the familiar circle of family and friends. This belief has persisted for at least a generation during which parents have warned their children not to talk to strangers, accept lifts in their cars or presents of sweets from them. Newspapers report the rarer and more dramatic cases of children who disappear and in doing so reinforce the general idea that strangers carry a risk to children involving acts of the greatest perversion, serious damage and even death.

Finkelhor argues that the persistence of this belief that strangers are to blame for sexual abuse is not one of misinformation. His own research has demonstrated how very resistant even well-informed parents are to the idea that children may be at risk from people they know.[24] The reason is not therefore a matter of ignorance but the fact that this truth is a very difficult one to accept. Even doctors may ignore symptoms which indicate sexual abuse by someone close. The Kempes, in their book on child abuse,[25] tell how a clinic treated four members of the same household, girls aged 18, 16 and 14 and a boy of nine; they all had gonorrhoea, a sexually-transmitted disease. The particular (and unusual) strain of infection they had was the same as that shown by the stepfather of the three eldest, the father of the youngest; yet they were all treated without comment. Further investigation would have presented too much of a challenge to fundamental beliefs. As Finkelhor remarks, 'It is unpleasant for people to harbor suspicions about friends, neighbors, relatives, members of their own family. So people continue to hold the image of the sexual abuser as a stranger, because the other image is so disconcerting.'[26] Where there is an accusation against someone of the child's own family, many people find it impossible to believe.

Today it is less likely that silence would be kept in such a case.

The myth that children are mostly at risk from the occasional compulsive pervert outside their homes is being widely challenged. There is evidence that the idea is not only inaccurate but positively harmful, for it diverts attention from the real danger to them. Case material published by those who deal with sexually abused children and the work of organizations of adult survivors suggests very strongly that when a child has been sexually abused, the perpetrator of the abused must have been the child's father or stepfather. Such an idea is an outrage to the common assumption that parents love their children and would do nothing to harm them. It has, not surprisingly, aroused strong reactions, of the sort that are to be expected when fundamental beliefs are challenged. In England, the organization called Parents against Injustice, which was involved in the Cleveland crisis, seems to see the accusations made against parents as part of an attempt by state bureaucracy to infringe the rights of parents and destroy the family's traditional freedom from interference from outside. In their enthusiasm to defend 'the family' in this way some go even further and deny that the sexual abuse has happened at all. Against this and in defence of themselves, those who are concerned with the protection of children may appear to be saying that all sexual abuse is perpetrated by parental figures. This argument about whether children are, or are not, at risk in their own homes was an important element in the Cleveland affair. It clouds the whole issue of how, where and why children are vulnerable to sexual abuse by advancing competing bogeymen: the stranger or the father. It is therefore even more important to consider carefully what has been found out about the offenders in cases of the sexual abuse of children.

Abusive Relationships

The main characteristic which these abusers have in common is that they have had the opportunity to be alone with a child or children. This obvious point is rarely mentioned but it needs to be stated. It refers as much to relationships in an institution where children live or spend much of their time as it does to those in their homes. The next chapter shows that where a child may go and with whom depends on the organization of social worlds that include children but give them no recognized position except as dependants of parents. The social relationships between adults and children which offer opportunities for abuse are largely ignored. Since there are relatively few occasions when children are alone with strangers it is not unreasonable to suppose that children were less often abused by strangers than by men with whom they had some sort of socially recognized relationship. Yet the results of British research appear, at first sight, to contradict this. The survey undertaken for Channel Four Television by Baker and Duncan in 1984[27] produced a result which supports the general conviction that children are most at risk from strangers. Their figures showed that over a half of those who reported that they had been abused (51 per cent) had been abused by people they did not know. Girls seem to have been slightly more at risk from strangers than boys (56 per cent of their abusive experiences were with strangers as against 43 per cent of the boys') but boys were more likely than girls to have been abused by someone unrelated but known to them: a neighbour, family friend or by an adult in a position of authority such as a teacher or leader of a youth group. If we consider the result of this survey alone it does appear that girls, if not boys, are most often sexually abused by strangers.

However, if we consider the kind of experiences that they had, rather than how many girls were affected, the danger appears much less. Two-thirds of them involved a single incident and nearly as many were experiences involving no contact with the abuser (exhibitionism or being talked to in an erotic way), which in this survey were included in the definition of sexual abuse. There was a statistically significant correlation between abuse by a stranger and these milder experiences, showing a firm association between them. Baker and Duncan comment that 'Exhibitionism probably accounted for a large proportion of such experiences.'[28] The Nash and West study of Cambridge women[29] confirms the conclusions of the Baker and Duncan survey. It shows both a high proportion of strangers claimed to have been abusive and that the kind of abuse inflicted by strangers was relatively mild. The wide definition of abuse used in these two rather different pieces of research is clearly responsible for the numbers of strangers described by respondents as responsible for their sexual abuse in childhood. These two research results also show that where more serious sexual abuse is concerned, the perpetrator is far more likely to be someone known.

So the danger to children from strangers, according to these studies, is the danger of 'flashing', of sexy remarks, and only in a very small proportion of cases is it the danger of the sort of action which most people would consider more serious sexual abuse. Even with that wide definition of sexual abuse, boys were less likely to have been abused by strangers than by people they knew. This research does show how common it is for children, particularly young girls, to be perceived as sexual objects, even if they usually come to no serious harm from it.

The cases from my hospital study, which involve sexual abuse in the narrower definition used in this book, show that an overwhelming majority of these children were abused by a man they knew. Table 6 sets out the abusers in 192 cases of children referred to the hospital child sexual abuse unit, grouped to show the broad risks. (In 12 of the total of 204 cases it was not clear who the abuser was so they have been omitted.) In some cases there were several children so that the numbers of children are greater than the number of cases. The table makes it clear that strangers are not the main risk. There were only three cases where the abuser was referred to as a stranger. Four-fifths of all the children were abused by people they lived with, members of their own household; nearly a fifth, however, had been abused by someone outside it whom they

TABLE 6   Abusers of children referred to the child sexual abuse unit of a London hospital, by number and sex of children abused

Abusers	Girls No. (%)	Boys No. (%)	Total No. (%)
Male			
Strangers	2 (1)	1 (3)	3 (1)
Known			
Unrelated	18 (9)	12 (30)	30 (12)
Related	10 (5)	4 (10)	14 (6)
Members of child's household	179 (85)	20 (50)	199 (80)
Female			
Members of child's household	0 (0)	3 (8)	3 (1)
Total	209 (100)	40 (101)	249 (100)

Source: Author's study.

knew. The table also shows a clear difference between boys and girls: two-fifths of the boys had been abused by someone outside the household and nearly a third by a man who was known but unrelated, while the proportion of girls who had suffered abuse from known people outside the household, whether related or unrelated, was less than half that figure. There were rather small numbers of boys involved in the hospital cases so that conclusions as far as they are concerned must be tentative, but as far as girls are concerned it is clear that the picture presented by these cases is that sexual abuse is in the vast majority of cases likely to take place at home.

As has already been demonstrated, the cases in the CSA Unit were referred to the hospital in a number of different ways; they do not provide us with a representative set of cases. For a national picture we have to use the BBC national survey which shows a rather different distribution of abusers between the various categories. Unfortunately, this survey has two flaws: first, a proportion of respondents refused to identify the perpetrators by role, merely indicating that they had been abused; secondly, in a much higher proportion of cases all that was coded for the identity of the abuser was 'someone else'. It has proved impossible to retrieve the original forms to check whether the respondents did fulfil the request to specify who that someone else was, except in nine cases where an earlier sorting of the replies by hand had revealed these to be 'strangers'. Despite these imperfections, the survey clearly indicates a much higher proportion who claim to have been abused by people other than household members.

Table 7 sets out a comparison of abusers identified by respondents to the BBC national survey and in the hospital CSA Unit. There are some areas of agreement between the two sources of information. The survey, like the hospital cases, shows that most abusers are known to their victims; strangers form a larger proportion of the abusers in the survey than they do of the hospital cases, but they still represent only 15 per cent. In other respects the survey data show a rather different pattern of abuse: about a third of the abusers (34 per cent) are shown as people who are known but are outside the household. The highest single category is that of household members, but known outsiders, who form 21 per cent of the total, come close to that proportion; moreover the numbers are so small that the difference between these two figures is certainly not statistically significant. Male relatives other than household

The Offenders

TABLE 7 Identity of abuser by numbers and percentages: two sources of data compared

Abuser	BBC Survey No. (%)	Hospital CSA Unit No. (%)
Household member[a]		
Male	18 (28)	199 (80)
Female	1 (2)	3 (1)
Male outside household		
Unrelated	13 (20)	30 (12)
Relative[b]	9 (14)	14 (6)
Stranger	9 (14)	3 (1)
Other ('someone else')	8 (13)	0 (0)
Not stated/not known	6 (9)	10 (4)
Total	64 (100)	259 (104)

[a] One man accused both his father and his mother, two other women indicated abuse by two men.

[b] One respondent lived with an aunt but was abused by a more distant relative of hers who did not live with them.

members (15 per cent) constitute about half the proportion of household members (30 per cent). In the hospital unit's files, where the initial information was amended by later interviews, it is clear that one or two girls referred to their mother's boyfriend as a 'friend of the family'. It is possible that the latter category in the national survey contains some men who are *de facto* stepfathers. The study of individual cases also makes it clear that the closer the relationship, the greater the unwillingness of a former victim to reveal it. It is highly likely that the refusals in this survey resulted in the omission of more known and related people than strangers.

Individuals and Relationships

To classify abusers in this generally accepted manner, as we have been doing, is slightly misleading; it implies that each abuser can be clearly identified by a relationship with a single victim. But the retrospective accounts of survivors of sexual abuse in childhood and the case histories of child protection agencies and therapists all indicate that a single relationship between an adult and one child is not a feature of all cases: there may be both multiple victims and multiple abusers. Where one child is abused by more than one person, which is by no means rare, each abuser has a different relationship with the victim. A girl may be the victim of her father in one case and a stepfather in the other; there are two different relationships used to identify the men involved. But where a man abuses his own child and one or more of the child's friends, the different relationships concern the same man. In one of the hospital files it was noted that the abuser of the child referred had been arrested in connection with the sexual abuse of 'several boys in the neighbourhood'. How are the men with a variety of victims to be classified: as abusive fathers, stepfathers, grandfathers or neighbours? They may have abused a child in each of these capacities. It may be almost a matter of chance that a man becomes labelled as an abusing stepfather, when similar offences as a father or neighbour might have been used to identify him. Clearly, we must distinguish between the relationships in which abuse can occur and the men concerned. The latter may have many relationships with children and commit an abuse in only one, or in many, or all of them.

A different limitation affects the information derived from the survey and makes the comparison with that based on the hospital cases less conclusive. Surveys of victims cannot pick up instances where a man has abused several children. In about a third of the hospital cases, more than one child is known to have been abused, mostly brothers and sisters of the original patient. In order to show the numbers of children abused by the different categories of perpetrator in table 9 below, each relationship concerned in cases of multiple abuse was counted as a separate instance. For example, a man who abused both his daughters represents two instances of paternal sexual abuse. The hospital cases might show a disproportionate number of children who were abused by household members simply because they include cases of multiple abuse.

We know that it is not only children in the same house who may be involved in the sexual activities of adults. In the last three or four years the police have uncovered networks of several children, boys and girls, involved in both sexual abuse and child prostitution. The adults concerned may not have included the children's parents, although they were not unknown to them. These cases of multiple abuse would increase the number of children recorded as abused by individuals outside the household. However, the evidence does not support either case unequivocally.

The commonest kind of multiple abuse is where one individual abuses several children. In nearly a quarter (46) of the 204 CSA Unit cases, there were several children abused by one man. These cases involved at least 107 children, 84 girls and 23 boys. It is not possible to be more exact about the number of children involved because in six of the cases, although it was known that children other than the hospital unit's patient had been abused, there was no record (it may not have been known) of how many other children were concerned. In almost all these cases of multiple abuse, the children were brothers and sisters or half-brothers and sisters, living in the same house or staying there as visitors. These were also the children whose abuse was most likely to be uncovered by the hospital unit when one child was referred to them. In some cases, a man abused his step-daughter or son and during the investigations it was discovered that he had earlier abused his own children, from whom he had been separated by divorce. In five out of the six cases where it is not clear how many children had been abused, the other children were neighbours' children, mostly friends of the abuser's own child or step-child; one case concerned a child abused in the children's home where he lived. In every case the perpetrators of the sexual abuse could be placed in the victim's social world: as neighbour, friend of the parents, or relative, whether distant or, more often, intimate. Most of them were members of the victim's own household.

Alternatively, multiple abuse can involve one child being abused by more than one person. It seems that once a child is known to have been abused, other people may take advantage of him or her; in some cases a child appeals for help against one abuser only to be abused again. One of the women who filled in a postal questionnaire for the ChildWatch programme reported that she had consulted an older sister and her husband about what her father was doing to her, only to have her brother-in-law try and abuse her. And another wrote (of her brother, nine years older than herself): 'He must of said something to the two younger boys because before long they were doing the same thing, that was when I was about ten.' Sometimes even an abusing father or stepfather encourages further abuse by others; there was a clear indication of this in two of the hospital cases.

As the last chapter made clear, abused children may display sexualized behaviour as the result of their experiences and this makes them even more vulnerable. Among the CSA Unit cases there were five girls and a single boy who had been abused by more than one person, but with such very small numbers the preponderance of girls is almost certain to be by chance. Four of the five girls were known to have been abused by two people, the other by three. In each case one of the abusers, usually the first, had been a father or other father figure. The only boy had suffered anal intercourse often and over many years but it was never established how many men had been responsible, or whether his father had been one of them.

In a few cases there are complex tangles of relationships in which several children are abused by several adults. Some of these cases resemble what is generally imagined to be the incestuous household, and some of the children in them are abusers as well as victims. Such cases pose difficult problems of presentation. To concentrate on the relationship between victim and perpetrator obscures the characteristics of these complex cases, which do present features that distinguish them from the majority. As they form only a small proportion of the cases, about 10 per cent of the total, they will not be considered here but will be dealt with separately in chapter 6. After these complex cases had been excluded there were 176 files. Just under half (130) were of cases involving single victims, as far as could be discovered. The rest of the cases concerned 84 girls and 23 boys, 46 people being responsible for their abuse. Since it was not possible to discover all the victims in some of the cases, the figure of 107 children is a minimum one.

A comparison (Table 8) of the figures for the abuse of single children and those where several victims were involved shows that the cases of multiple abuse do not differ very greatly from the other CSA Unit cases. The cases of multiple abuse do show a larger proportion of abusers who are closely related to their victims: a higher proportion of both boys and girls in cases of multiple abuse are abused within the household. This is particularly true of boys, where the proportion rises from 5 per cent of single victims to 15 per cent of victims abused with other children. The numbers are too

The Offenders

TABLE 8   Single and multiple abuse compared

| Abuser | Single abuser, single victim | | Single abuser, multiple victims | |
	Girls No. (%)	Boys No. (%)	Girls No. (%)	Boys No. (%)
Stranger	2 (2)	1 (7)	0 (0)	0 (0)
Outsiders				
Unrelated	8 (7)	5 (36)	8 (10)	5 (22)
Related	7 (6)	2 (14)	2 (2)	1 (4)
Household member				
Male	99 (85)	5 (36)	74 (88)	15 (65)
Female	0 (0)	1 (7)	0 (0)	2 (9)
Total	116 (100)	14 (100)	84 (100)	23 (100)

Source: Author's study of cases in a London hospital unit for child sexual abuse

small to be reliable but support the general impression that boys' abuse is more likely to be found out when there are several children involved. Girls involved in multiple abuse are usually sisters and many of the boys were found to be abused together with their sisters. The proportion of unrelated outsiders (neighbours and friends of the family) is lower where there are multiple victims, boys or girls, but here it is likely that lack of information is the reason for the difference. No strangers are seen to be involved in multiple abuse, for obvious reasons: unless more than one of an abuser's victims are referred to the same agency, the victims will remain unconnected, even if the identity of the stranger is discovered.

A consideration of how multiple abuse is discovered is very revealing. The question of whether the victim's brothers and sisters had been abused was always raised in the CSA Unit; given the family focus of the unit, these children were included in the therapeutic process. As a result, few brothers or sisters of a child referred to the unit did not reveal their abuse, even though in some cases it was not possible to confirm the finding beyond all doubt. But the unit was dependent for information on the referring agency and their reports did not usually enable the unit staff to find out how many children outside the household had been victims of any particular abuser, nor what their relationships to him were. In one particularly well-reported case of the multiple abuse of boys it was the man's son who was the hospital's patient. The other boys were referred to another clinic in order to protect them and their parents from having to meet the abuser when they visited there for therapy. In the case already mentioned where there was a note in the file that the man responsible had been arrested 'for several offences concerning boys of the neighbourhood', the number of children involved was not recorded. On occasion the referral history or the process of therapy would refer to other children but they could not be taken account of systematically. It is significant that five of the six cases of multiple abuse where it was not possible to find out how many children had been involved were all cases where children outside the household had been abused as well as children within it. It may have been that in other cases, too, children other than the hospital's patient but outside the household had been abused and it was not noted in the file of the case.

The Channel Four survey reported that girls are somewhat more at risk than boys of being abused by more than one person but the difference was small, 5 per cent.[30] The number of people who reported multiple abuse in the BBC survey was very small: one man and two women. No conclusions can be drawn from these figures. The national extent of multiple abuse is thus impossible to calculate until further research has been done. The available information does suggest, however, that a child who has been abused needs protection against further abuse. Removing the abuser does not wipe out further danger.

Abuse Inside and Outside the Home

There is one important difference between the survey data and that drawn from the study of the hospital child sexual abuse unit and this must now be explained. The hospital data show that by far the largest number of children are sexually abused by members of the same household, whether multiple victims are included or not. Even the cases of single victims show a significantly different distribution of offenders from that of the survey. The more representative survey does not support the conclusion that one would draw from the hospital cases: that the great majority of children were abused in their own homes. While over one in five of the respondents

(22 per cent) did not identify their abuser, those who said they had been abused by someone other than a household member outnumbered those abused at home in the ratio three to two. The hospital cases involving multiple victims are not so many or so different from those involving a single child as to have biased the whole pattern; they cannot therefore be considered the reason why the hospital cases and the survey support different conclusions about who the abusers are.

The main reason for the differences in the 'facts' gathered by surveys of adults reporting on their childhood experiences, and similar 'facts' derived either from clinics who treat the victims of sexual abuse or from the agencies concerned with the protection of children, is the result of another and inevitable kind of bias. To begin with, the child protection agencies deal with cases that have been disclosed while the survey attempts to record a more representative set of facts. But there is a more significant reason for the difference. This is the result of the context in which the information is collected. In most circumstances, parents have complete responsibility for their children. Where a child has been hurt or sexually abused by someone else it is left to the parents to decide what to do. They are very likely to do nothing unless the case is serious and many of these incidents may not seem very serious. In fact many parents are reluctant to bring their child for therapy, feeling that children will forget all about such incidents and that talking only keeps the memory alive. It may only be later, when the child gets into trouble at school or is otherwise obviously emotionally disturbed (and this is not uncommon), that a child may come to the attention of a child guidance clinic or a sexual abuse unit. In many more cases the abuse is never revealed. However, when the sexual abuse has been perpetrated by someone who is normally responsible for the child, then child protection agencies have a statutory duty to intervene. Their role is precisely to protect children where the parents do not do so. Hence information based on cases of children which come to agencies concerned with the protection of children is likely to over-represent the responsibility of the male members of the household for a child's sexual abuse.

Table 9 shows the range of people who were reported to have been perpetrators by the adults interviewed for the BBC survey and in the CSA Unit cases. The difference between the two sources of information is marked. In the hospital cases the great majority of

TABLE 9   Comparison of distribution of relationships between abuser and victim in two sets of cases (percentages)

Abuser	BBC Survey		CSA Unit	
	Women (N = 51[a])	Men (N = 13[b])	Girls (N = 220)	Boys (N = 39)
Male				
Stranger	10	31	1	3
Neighbour	12	8	5	5
Friend of family	12	8	2	13
Male relative (not close)[c]	14	8	2	8
Grandfather	2	0	3	0
Father[d]	16	8	50	28
Stepfather	6	0	25	18
Brother/half-brother	10	8	3	3
Foster father/brother	n.a.	n.a.	4	3
Others (male)[e]	14	0	1	13
Female				
Grandmother	0	0	0	3
Mother	0	8	0	5
Stepmother	0	0	0	0
Sister	0	0	0	0
Not stated/not known	6	23	5	0

[a] Two women identified two abusers.
[b] One man accused his mother and father. This set of cases is included for comparison but is so very small that 8% represents one case. No firm conclusions at all can be drawn from it.
[c] Both the BBC survey and the hospital cases include one case where victims were living with the relative concerned.
[d] The hospital cases include three adoptive fathers.
[e] Include, in BBC survey, a teacher, and in hospital unit cases, childminder's son, scoutmaster, father's girlfriend, worker in children's home.

perpetrators are the children's older relatives: fathers, stepfathers and grandfathers. These three categories account for 160 of the girls (73 per cent), though only 18 of the boys (46 per cent). By contrast the BBC survey shows that these male relatives together constitute just under a quarter of abusers of girls (24 per cent). The same proportion of abusers are either neighbours or friends of the family. Fathers still form the largest single category of abuser of girls (16 per cent) but are closely followed by other male relatives (14 per cent). In the survey, men most often identified strangers as their childhood abusers but more of them, proportionately, would not record the abuser's identity.

Table 9 demonstrates that the more representative BBC survey shows a much higher proportion of individuals who claimed to have been abused by men outside the household. Probably in many cases the parents do not get told, since children sense when sexual matters are not considered mentionable, or they may be afraid of getting into trouble. These incidents of sexual abuse may get reported to interviewers doing a survey of sexual abuse. The respondents are then adult and the assault safely in the past, and there are not usually the same inhibitions about talking about a stranger's behaviour, however upsetting it had been at the time. Moreover these adults have been asked if they had ever had such an experience; children are hardly ever asked such questions, even by their parents, and most people are not knowledgeable enough about the symptoms a child may show to judge when such questioning is important. It is all too easy for a child not to tell. This is probably one of the reasons that a larger proportion of sexual abuse by strangers is reported in surveys using adult respondents than in cases derived from clinics or child protection agencies concerned with children. But as many as one in five of the children referred even to the family-oriented hospital unit were not abused by members of their own households.

Any conclusion drawn from the national survey must take into account the known weaknesses of all surveys: they cannot deal easily with cases of multiple victims. This means that many individuals, particularly brothers and sisters of those interviewed, will be missed. In addition the single interview by a stranger does not offer the safest situation for an adult to recall painful incidents from the past, unless the interviewer is much more specifically and carefully trained than most are at the moment. The numbers of people who refused to identify their abuser are a clear indication of this lack of trust. Yet surveys, however flawed, cannot be dismissed out of hand. They do pick up some of the cases that have been hidden, secrets which no one has talked about, and so give a more balanced picture of the whole range of behaviour which is labelled sexual abuse. Children are social beings and their sexual abuse may place many adults under suspicion of having abused their relationship. It is not likely that the perpetrator will be a stranger and it is certainly someone whom the child may have had cause to trust and to obey; however, although the men of the household are indeed responsible in the majority of cases, the investigation must always range more widely as well.

More information is collected from child protection agencies than from national surveys, since the agencies are continuing to deal with and record cases, while surveys are only undertaken on rare occasions and are expensive. We need a more accurate national survey, carried out without the constraints that are felt by television companies. Those that have been undertaken to date indicate that the old myth of the pervert who hangs about school playgrounds is just that, a myth. But it is not surprising that the child protection agencies seem to be developing a new picture of the sexual abuse of children which is not entirely accurate either. The conviction that when a child is sexually abused it can *only* be a member of the child's own household, a father or stepfather, who is the guilty party, is based on knowledge obtained from cases coming to the attention of the social services and child protection agencies. In a high proportion of these, children have been abused at home. Social workers cannot be blamed therefore for acting on the information they have. However, the pattern of abuse they are reacting to is produced by the way these agencies have been set up to intervene when children are in danger from those who look after them. In addition, the understandable unwillingness of victims to tell of their abuse and the right of parents to conceal the sexual abuse perpetrated by their neighbours, relatives or friends when they *are* told of it, contributes to a picture which appears to place so much of the blame for sexual abuse on members of the family. There is a significant number of cases where children have been sexually abused by relatives or people they know but who do not live with them. If parents were prepared to accept that this may happen, to listen to children and then take action to report the offender and seek help for the child to get over the experience, then the regular sources of information about the sexual abuse of children might represent the problem more accurately. At present many parents keep their child's abuse a secret even if they know of it; in this way they are unwittingly contributing to the general conclusion that children are sexually abused at home.

Despite the differences between the information provided by surveys and that from other sources, there are certain consistencies. Both indicate that children are more at risk from men they know than from strangers. This implies that any explanation of the problem must consider more than merely the characteristics of the offender. It must look, as well, at the relationships men have with children.

Notes

1 Strictly speaking, paedophilia refers to sexual attraction to pre-pubertal children. I shall use it in the wider, but common, sense of sexual attraction to children in general.
2 See Finkelhor, *Child Sexual Abuse*, pp. 33–69.
3 See ibid., p. 35, Herman, *Father–Daughter Incest*, and Russell, *The Secret Trauma*.
4 Maisch, *Incest*, p. 130.
5 Bentovim and Boston, in Bentovim et al., *Child Sexual Abuse*, pp. 35–6. The factors listed in tables 2.12 and 2.13 probably reflect the fact of a large number of referrals through the social services.
6 H. Parker and S. Parker, 'Father–daughter sexual abuse: an emerging perspective', *American Journal of Orthopsychiatry*, 56(4) (1986), p. 533.
7 Herman, *Father–Daughter Incest*.
8 Maisch, *Incest*, p. 134.
9 Finkelhor, *Child Sexual Abuse*.
10 Ennew, *Sexual Exploitation*, pp. 125, 132–5. She records that convicted offenders against children may send for Mothercare catalogues as stimulants.
11 Gorry, 'Incest'.
12 Finkelhor, *Child Sexual Abuse*.
13 Lukianowicz's article on 'Incest' in the *British Journal of Psychiatry* is criticized by Mrazek in 'Child sexual abuse: methodological considerations', in Mrazek and Kempe, *Sexually Abused Children*.
14 American Humane Association National Reporting Study 1978.
15 D. Finkelhor and D. Russell, 'Women as perpetrators', in Finkelhor, *Child Sexual Abuse*. See also K. C. Meiselman, *Incest: A Psychological Study of Causes and Effects with Treatment Recommendations* (Jossey-Bass, San Francisco, 1984), S. Nelson, *Incest: Fact and Myth* (Stramullion Co-operative, Edinburgh, 1988), and Russell, *The Secret Trauma*, among others.

16 Gorry, 'Incest', p. 30.
17 Personal communication from M. Lock, an anthropologist working in Japan.
18 See R. S. Kempe and C. H. Kempe, *Child Abuse* (Fontana, Glasgow, 1978), p. 65.
19 J. Korbin (ed.), *Child Abuse and Neglect: Cross-Cultural Perspectives* (University of California Press, Berkeley, 1981), and see also Karl G. Heider, 'Dani sexuality: a low energy system', *Man*, 11(2) (1976).
20 Finkelhor, *Child Sexual Abuse*, p. 12.
21 Finkelhor and Russell, 'Women as perpetrators', in Finkelhor, ibid., pp. 171–87, especially pp. 182–3; and compare Russell, *The Secret Trauma*, pp. 296–312.
22 *ChildLine: The First Year*, report for 1987 issued by ChildLine, London, unpublished.
23 But see T. C. N. Gibbens, K. L. Soothill and C. K. Way, 'Sex offences against young girls: a long-term record study', *Psychological Medicine*, 2 (1981), pp. 351–7.
24 Finkelhor, *Child Sexual Abuse*, p. 99.
25 Kempe and Kempe, *Child Abuse*, pp. 68–9.
26 Finkelhor, *Child Sexual Abuse*, p. 99.
27 Baker and Duncan, 'Child sexual abuse', p. 27.
28 Ibid., p. 25.
29 Nash and West, 'Victimisation'.
30 Baker and Duncan, 'Child sexual abuse', p. 25.

5   Natural and Unnatural Fathers

The complicated psychological chemistry between blood relations cannot be substituted with something new and unfamiliar. As a step-parent, there is little you can do about this . . .

James Runcie, 'Tips from a wicked stepfather', *Observer*, 3 April 1988

His [Runcie's] assertion that blood ties will always outweigh the reinforcement of a consistent and caring presence (including the occasional punishment) is an insult to every parent of an adopted, foster or, in my case, step-child.

What I have learned from my own three step-children and three 'blood' children is that their love for me and mine for them is indistinguishable, with no regard to genetic origins . . .

Dr L. O. Hughes, letter, *Observer*, 10 April 1988

The generally accepted view of society implies that it is composed of adults. Children are largely regarded as dependants of their parents or as pupils in school, since these two institutions are accepted as concerned with the bearing and rearing of children. The social life of children if it is considered at all is seen as consisting of relationships with other children: brothers and sisters, friends at school or in the neighbourhood. But very few children are abused by other children.[1] Children are not expected to have independent relationships with adults other than parents or teachers; even their relations with relatives are believed to derive from the parents' own relations with them or from the teaching of their parents about what such relationships should be. Preferences for a particular relative are explained either by greater familiarity with him or her or by the adult relationship. Thus the greater affection many children show for their mother's sisters rather than those of their father is explained by the closeness of (the adult) sisters. On the other hand, children who express a dislike of a particular person who has a good relationship with a parent may be scolded.

People are reluctant to believe that their neighbours, friends or relations might abuse a child; if they are told they may not believe it. As one woman said of her mother: 'how could I expect her to believe that of her brother?' Where an adult is being helpful by caring for someone else's child temporarily there is normally no suspicion of their motives for doing so. A working mother often depends on such help; even doing the family shopping or visiting an elderly relative may depend on the child's being left with another adult. The fact that children are abused by neighbours, friends of the family and relatives outside the immediate family circle indicates that the relationships between adults are not a reliable guide to the nature of the relationship between the child and these adults.

The range of children's contacts and relationships with adults depends on the stage of their development. As they grow older they are brought more and more into contact with adults outside the circle of close kin. Until they are of school age children do not usually leave the house without a parent. Parents may leave them with a relative or babysitter in their own home, or in the homes of grandparents or other kin, for them to be looked after while the parents go out on their own, but the opportunity for children under five to meet a complete stranger comes rarely. Their circle of adults is restricted to their parents, their close friends, a neighbour or two and grandparents or other relatives who come to the house or whose houses they visit with parents. Even at this stage, however, the child's relationship with any of these adults may make him or her vulnerable to abuse. At a later stage, children go to school and meet teachers and the parents of their friends to whose houses they may go. They are also allowed to run errands in the immediate neighbourhood. Children who go out without a parent may meet adults on their way to and from school or doing errands, but most are shy of those they do not know. Moreover children are expected to be accompanied by other children on these occasions; they normally conform to adult expectations that they do not go out alone. However, children may visit relatives on their own and the practice of getting a babysitter when parents go out brings adults, related or not, into the child's home or places a child in another household temporarily.

These stages by which children come to participate in social relationships with adults are reflected in the patterns of children's sexual abuse. Over a third (35 per cent) of the people who filled in a postal questionnaire for the BBC survey claimed that they were seven or under when the abuse started; none of them was abused by a stranger. About two-thirds of the respondents of the representative survey were 11 and under when they were abused; five out of six of them suffered this at the hands of someone they knew. Some of them were abused by an uncle or grandfather, usually in their own home where the relative was a guest or babysitter, or in the relative's home. The comparative freedom of boys to go out of the house on their own is reflected in the larger proportion of men and boys who claim to have been abused by strangers or by people other than relatives, neighbours or friends of the family.

The general restriction of children to their own homes and those of close relatives focuses attention on these people. Despite the larger proportion of individuals in the BBC survey who claimed to have been abused by someone other than a relative, about half the women (24 out of 49) and a third of the men (four out of 12) had been abused by relatives. While relatives other than the closest were named as often as fathers, brothers or stepfathers, one must remember that there are many more of them so that proportionately there is a greater likelihood that there will be someone among them who might abuse a child. The research that would be needed to show the likelihood of a child's being abused by a close or a more distant relative requires much more detailed studies of the victims' whole range of kin and how frequently they see them, but the data available now suggest a disproportionate amount of sexual abuse occurs just where children are assumed to be safe: in their own homes. Those responsible are father figures or brothers, which raises the question of how much of the sexual abuse of children is incest. This chapter and the next will therefore be concerned with this.

Father Figures

Nearly half the victims in the cases from the hospital child sexual abuse unit – over half the girls and nearly a third of the boys – were abused by their fathers. Stepfathers accounted for another quarter of the abusers, slightly over (26 per cent) in the case of girls and under (18 per cent) where boys were concerned. Altogether nearly three-quarters of the children in this set of cases were abused by fathers or stepfathers. If one adds the foster fathers and adoptive fathers identified as having abused their charges, the total percentage of father figures rises to 76 per cent. This fact is shocking because the majority of men are fathers and their authority is an essential element of the constitution of the family. The revelation that even some of them are untrustworthy appears unthinkable. It can be accepted that men who are teachers or neighbours may prove to have molested a child but the guilt of father figures has much more disturbing connotations.

In popular opinion it is vital to distinguish between 'real' fathers and 'substitute' fathers, which is believed to affect the likelihood of their abusing children in their care. However, not everyone holds that the significance of fatherhood lies in the biological relationship; many people consider that fatherhood is a matter of behaviour and feeling, of living together. The difference between these points of view is well displayed in the argument about stepfatherhood in a Sunday newspaper, quoted at the head of this chapter. James Runcie asserts what many people believe, that there is a quality in 'blood relationships' which makes them unlike any other. Dr Hughes alleges, quite as categorically, that there is *no* difference in the nature of the emotional relationship between father and child and stepfather and step-child, when they are living happily together (the 'consistent and caring presence'). Dr Hughes's view is not an unusual or eccentric one; similar ideas are to be found among a whole range of people, particularly those who have been influenced by psychological theories which emphasize the importance of care of the child.[2] In such a view the position of father is occupied by any man who lives with and takes responsibility for a child. This particular discussion in the newspaper concerned normal relationships between adults and children but the same conflicting assumptions appear when the question at issue is sexual abuse. It raises the question of how much sexual abuse is attributable to 'true' fathers, how much to father substitutes.

A familiar (the term includes fathers and stepfathers) relationship makes sexual abuse seem worse to most people than a more distant one. A man in one of the parents' groups I observed, who had abused several young children placed in his care by their parents, alluded on more than one occasion to the difference between himself and the others who had abused 'children in the family'; the implication was that his offences were less blameworthy than theirs. Many people believe there is a special relationship between a man and the child he has begotten that makes incest far worse than the sexual abuse of an unrelated child. Another man in the parents' group justified himself by saying: 'Well, I told myself she wasn't my own daughter and that didn't seem so bad.' A third, who had also abused his step-daughter, seemed genuinely shocked at the idea that there were men in the therapy group who had abused their own daughters. Although these men were keen to show that there were others whose actions were even more culpable than their own, and so were probably guilty of special pleading in their own defence, their remarks reflect a very common belief that the genetic connection between father and child makes incest or incestuous abuse both more unlikely and more culpable.

The idea of fatherhood as combining a physical connection with a recognized social position is a powerful notion with a wide influence in social life. This emphasis on a biological connection between father and child is not universal in human societies; it seems to have been less important in Britain in the past as well. Although all known societies accord social significance to having two parents, the biological element in paternity may be of little importance. However, in most societies the fact of being a father is a vital component of a man's standing in his community; in many societies it is an essential prerequisite to his assuming any other authority. Those who are not fathers are somehow incomplete. In early modern Britain, a close parallel was drawn between God's authority and that of fathers; the latter was believed to derive directly from the former.[3]

The conviction that the 'real' father is the individual with a genetic connection to the child (and hence that no other person can be more than a substitute, however effectively they may act the part) is fundamental to the modern culture of Western societies. The idea of family is based on the belief that children should and do live with the adults whose biological offspring they are. In the absence of any information to the contrary, children are assumed to have a genetic relationship with the man they live with and whom they call 'father'. It is not uncommon for a couple to conceal the fact that the husband is not the physical father of 'their' child in order to give his position the appearance of conforming to social expectations. The generally negative attitudes to stepfathers as deviations from the ideal of fatherhood have been noted in a study of step-parenting[4] and are implied in the title of James Runcie's article, 'Tips from a wicked stepfather'. Probably the majority of Westerners see fathers and stepfathers as distinguished by the presence or absence of a genetic link with the child and by its correlate, the incest taboo. All sexual abuse by father figures may be attributed to stepfathers rather than 'real' fathers; this protects the ideal of fatherhood by deflecting all guilt on to their substitutes who clearly are not good enough.

To some people it is because there are more couples getting divorced and more likelihood of children's living with a stepfather that sexual abuse is occurring. They see the sexual abuse of children as an indication of the 'breakdown' of the institution of marriage and as likely to increase. This argument ignores the fact that in past times marriages were broken by the death of one or other partner nearly as frequently as they now are by divorce. The role of stepfather (or stepmother) is as much a part of 'tradition' as natural parenthood, although only the latter is seen as such.[5] Neither incest nor the sexual abuse of children are recent phenomena as far as we can tell. However, the question whether there is a protective instinct in 'real' fatherhood that makes a man unable to abuse his 'own' child is not answered by referring to the traditional role of stepfathers; it must be addressed directly.

Incest and Incestuous Abuse

Incest, in the sense of vaginal sexual intercourse between specified relatives, is a small proportion of the sexual abuse of children. Just under a quarter, 24 per cent, of the men involved in the hospital CSA Unit cases had committed incest. The BBC national survey showed a much lower figure: only 8 per cent of men reported by respondents to have abused them were accused of incest, although another 6 per cent were said to have attempted it, leaving one father who had sexually abused his daughter but had not attempted full intercourse with her. In both sets of data, moreover, incest was almost entirely committed by fathers. All the incestuous men in the

BBC survey were fathers and all but one of those reported in the hospital cases.

In another 28 per cent of the hospital cases it was not clear whether the sexual abuse had included intercourse; it was certainly incestuous abuse. In eight of these cases of incestuous abuse the girls were under ten; since, as we have seen, there is a progression in the course of sexual abuse, incest might have occurred in these cases too, had the incestuous abuse not been discovered. Altogether only 20 per cent of the fathers had certainly not been involved in incest.

The legal definition of incest as vaginal sexual intercourse is responsible for the low rate of incest as distinct from other forms of incestuous abuse. However, the numbers of fathers involved in incestuous abuse (including those where it was not clear if there had been incest or not) was almost equal to those who committed incest. Both categories together accounted for nearly half of all abusers (46 per cent) in the hospital study. Incestuous abuse is not necessarily less serious than incest: it can involve oral and anal intercourse and be accompanied by physical violence and humiliation for the child.

Incestuous abuse also involved people other than fathers: brothers and grandfathers. Half of all those men who had sexually abused girls were one of these three kinds of male relative. The few abusers of boys who were reported in the BBC survey showed as many brothers accused as fathers; but the only man who reported having suffered anal intercourse accused his father. We shall return to the subject of incest between brother and sister in the next chapter, but it is worth noting here that the brothers and grandfathers in these two sources of information are virtually all accused of incestuous abuse rather than incest, whereas there is other evidence that full intercourse is quite likely.

Fathers and Stepfathers

Most sources of information agree that by far the commonest form of incest in Western societies is that between father and daughter. However, as we have seen, paternal incest does not form a large part of reported sexual abuse. This evidence might be interpreted to mean that children are less often sexually abused by their fathers than by other men, were it not for the clear indication that fathers may be guilty of other forms of sexual activities with daughters or sons, or both. Fathers were the most often accused of perpetrating the sexual abuse recorded in the files of the CSA Unit; stepfathers were the next most frequent offenders. This was true whether the victims were boys or girls. If one lumps together all kinds of sexual abuse by a father, whether incest, incestuous abuse or sexual abuse of a son, it is twice as common in these cases as sexual abuse by a stepfather. In the more representative BBC national survey, fathers are three times more often accused of all forms of sexual abuse than stepfathers.

These figures, particularly those from the survey, seem open at first sight to the interpretation that fathers are *more* likely to abuse their children than stepfathers, since so many more are accused. However, this conclusion would only be justified if there were a statistically equal chance for stepfathers and fathers to be accused of sexual abuse. This is not really the case: far more children live with fathers than with stepfathers, but it is impossible to discover what the proportions actually are. The General Household Survey in 1982 recorded that 82 per cent of children under 16 were living with both natural parents but only 6 per cent with a mother and stepfather.[6] The proportion varies according to age: 90 per cent of children aged 0–4 are with both parents, but only 77 per cent of those aged 10–15. Only 2 per cent of the youngest but 10 per cent of the oldest age-group were living with a mother and stepfather. However, since there are often several children in a family, the number of children living with a father or a stepfather does not tell us how many men have children or step-children living with them. Then of course some, probably many, households are mixed in this respect. Dr Hughes, part of whose letter formed an epigraph to this chapter, had three of each in his home. Until research on this subject is done, one cannot tell what percentage of households consist of a couple living with the children of both of them and what proportion contain fostered, adopted or step-children, although one might hazard a guess that the percentage of the former kind is lower than generally recognized. However, a conservative estimate would be that fathers are five times as common as stepfathers. If fathers were as likely as stepfathers to abuse children in their care they would appear in the figures in similar proportions.

Table 10 compares the figures for all sexual abuse of girls by

TABLE 10   Sexual abuse of girls by fathers and stepfathers: two sources of data compared (percentage of all abusers identified)

	BBC Survey	CSA Unit
Fathers		
Incest	8	24
Incestuous abuse	8	22
Total	16	46
Stepfathers		
Full intercourse	0	14
Sexual abuse	6	13
Total	6	27

fathers or stepfathers, distinguished by whether it involved full intercourse or not. Since the aim is to compare the frequency of paternal incest and incestuous abuse with forms of sexual abuse by stepfathers this table refers only to cases where girls were victimized. The figures for the representative BBC survey show only three times as many fathers as stepfathers; fewer fathers than one would expect. The hospital CSA Unit figures show fathers outnumbering stepfathers by only two to one. On the evidence of both these sets of figures, stepfathers *are* more dangerous to children than their own fathers.

Abusers who are fathers or stepfathers appear in the BBC survey in much lower proportions than in the CSA Unit cases. There are two likely reasons for this. To begin with, as I argued in chapter 2, the survey probably under-reported the extent of abuse, particularly where the abuser was a close relative. More strangers, neighbours and friends of the parents were reported in the survey so obviously the proportion of the total who were fathers and stepfathers is lower. In addition, most (80 per cent) of the hospital cases concerned sexual abuse 'in the family'; one would therefore expect most of the abusers to be fathers or stepfathers, as indeed they are. The discrepancy between the evidence of the survey and the hospital cases is the result of the less representative nature of the latter. The number and proportion of abusers in the CSA Unit cases who are stepfathers may also have been artificially inflated by the biased class composition of the clinical cases. Since the divorce rate varies according to class, class I having a divorce rate which is a fifth of that of the unskilled in class V,[7] any bias towards the lower end of the class spectrum would result in a higher proportion of stepfamilies than is characteristic of the population as a whole. This partly explains the differences between the large percentage of stepfathers among abusers in the CSA Unit cases and the lower one in the national survey. However, the under-reporting of sexual abuse in the survey will also have affected the distribution of cases of fathers and stepfathers in ways impossible to assess.

However, in both sets of data, fathers account for much more sexual abuse than stepfathers. The BBC survey shows three times as many fathers as stepfathers recorded as abusers by women. There were five reports of paternal incest (full intercourse) but no reports of intercourse with stepfathers, although one woman reported an attempt by her stepfather. In both sets of cases, fathers formed the largest single category of abusers, but the survey showed only 6 per cent of respondents who accused stepfathers, far fewer than reported strangers (15 per cent), other relatives (11 per cent) or male neighbours (10 per cent). By contrast, among the abusers in the CSA Unit cases, fathers and stepfathers were the two largest categories of offenders. While there is no information on the number of men who are stepfathers it seems unlikely that they are half or even a third as numerous as fathers. Stepfathers are represented in a rather higher proportion than one might expect from the proportions of stepfathers among the married population, but the difference is not so great as to justify attributing sexual abuse mainly to father figures who lack the qualities of 'real' fathers, whatever these are said to be.

Although sexual relations between father and son are not incestuous in law, a comparison with the figures of boys sexually abused by fathers and father figures is interesting. The evidence regarding them is contradictory. Boys referred to the hospital CSA Unit show a greater tendency to suffer abuse, including anal intercourse, by stepfathers than the girls do; stepfathers are only slightly less often the abusers of boys than fathers. The figures for the childhood abuse of men in the BBC survey suggest the opposite conclusion: that more fathers are guilty of sexual abuse of boys, particularly when it involves intercourse, than stepfathers. But there were so few men and boys reporting sexual abuse in the survey that the difference between fathers and stepfathers is affected by even one case: one man reported a father as having had full intercourse (12.5 per cent of all cases) and none reported a stepfather for this. But to say that fathers are twelve and a half times more likely to have anal intercourse with their sons than stepfathers with their stepsons would not be legitimate on such a tiny sample of cases. Clearly, more male victims and survivors will have to report their abusive experiences before there will be enough cases to decide whether boys as well as girls are more at risk from stepfathers and reach a conclusion on whether stepfathers are more of a risk to stepsons than to stepdaughters.

The question now is: how do we explain the difference in risk between fathers and stepfathers? Is it the case that the genetic link between fathers and their children is such that only a small minority of fathers will engage in sexual activities with them? Or is it the social relationship between them which is the more important? The categorization of sexual offences as more or less heinous is based on the basic distinction between a 'real' father and other father figures, so it is likely that the sexual self-restraints learned by an individual are equally differentiated. It is plausible then that in Western societies it would take a stronger compulsion to motivate a man to incest than to the sexual abuse of an unrelated, and particularly an unknown, child. From this point of view, however, it is the social significance of being a 'real father' or a stepfather that has the effect on behaviour, not the presence or absence of a genetic link.

Two Americans, a counsellor and an anthropologist, have addressed some of these issues in a study aimed at testing whether the biological relationship between father and child protected the latter from sexual abuse. Hilda and Seymour Parker follow Westermarck in their hypothesis that it is the early association of the two in the same household which is the more significant factor.[8] Like those who explain the infrequency of incest by paternal instinct, the Parkers assume that incest or sexual abuse is motivated simply by sexual attraction. But while those who argue that there is a protective instinct in biological fatherhood assume that it precludes a child's being sexually attractive to its father, the Parkers assume that a child *is* sexually stimulating unless a father is conditioned not to respond. They argue that familiarity reduces sexual arousal through repetition of the stimulus and point out that while this conditioning does not produce an aversion to incest, by raising the threshold of arousal it makes it less likely. They also draw on a theory of mother–child bonding, associated with the name of the developmental psychologist, J. Bowlby. This claims that the establishment of a strong, protective relationship between mother, or mother-substitute, and child develops from closeness in the earliest period of the child's life. The Parkers argue that a similar bonding could be expected between a man and the child he cared for in the same circumstances. They adapt the Bowlby theory rather freely in other ways as well, since they take a much longer period to be critical than he did, the first three years as opposed to the first few months and for a rather small proportion of that time.

Their research compared two samples from the same sources (penal and social-psychiatric institutions). The first sample consisted of 56 men known to have abused their daughters or step-daughters, the second of 54 men with no such known background. In choosing the men, no distinction was made between genetic fathers or other 'father surrogates', either within a sample or between samples.[9] The results of the study show that the 'biological relationship' is not the most significant factor. What distinguishes statistically between abusers and (putative) non-abusers is the degree of closeness leading to bonding with the child. Two measures were used to assess this. The first was time spent in the house during the first three years of the child's life. Some men were not living there at all at the time; many more of these were abusers (36 per cent of the sample) than non-abusers (6 per cent). The reason for this is not difficult to discover: there was a very much higher proportion of stepfathers in the abusing group (46 per cent) than in the control group (17 per cent). Stepfathers are, by definition, less likely to have a close relationship with their step-children in the latter's early years (as has already been noted, only 2 per cent of British children under four were living with a stepfather). This might seem to indicate that stepfathers pose a much higher risk just because they cannot develop a bond with the children who later become their victims. However, the Parkers go on to consider the men who *had* been living in the same household with the children, 36 who had abused them and 51 who had not. They report the result as follows: 'It appears that it is not biological status (i.e. step-parent or natural parent) as such that is important in explaining the relationship between stepfathering and abuse. Rather, it is the absent stepfather during this early period who is at risk [sic]. Stepfathers are more likely abusers than fathers, they argue, because they are absent in the victim's early years, not because they are unrelated.

This research demonstrates that the presence of a genetic connection between a father figure and child is not a significant factor in preventing abuse. Dr Hughes's view that there is no difference in relationships gains some support from this study. If that is so, then there is no qualitative distinction between incest or incestuous abuse and sexual abuse by an unrelated father figure. The fact that there are proportionately more stepfathers than fathers who abuse children under their care is the result of the fact that stepfathers are rarely around when a child is very young.

However, the idea that it is conditioning against arousal and paternal bonding which act as mechanisms to explain the differences between abusers and non-abusers is less convincing. A study in preparation by the anthropologist Arthur Wolf uses very large numbers of Chinese cases where women were brought up from childhood with their future husbands and shows that males do not appear to develop a sexual aversion to girls they have known from the latter's early years.[10] In addition the activities that are used by the Parkers as evidence of behaviour likely to condition fathers seem rather to reflect progressive ideas of what a 'good father' in Western society *should* do,[11] than to demonstrate any theoretical argument or empirical evidence that there is such a conditioning process or that these particular activities actually do promote bonding or condition responses. The involvement in child care might be evidence that these men are already devoted fathers, rather than that the child care was responsible for their commitment. The men in both groups were asked whether they regularly undertook any of five types of activity that were used to define 'child-care and nurturant activities' and which might create a bond between father and child. Men who had not abused a child were likely to have undertaken more of these activities than the abusers, whether they were 'biological' fathers or not.[12]

The theory requires an assumption about why men do or do not undertake child care which has not been proved. Recent studies in England indicate that these kinds of measurement are not satisfactory indices of paternal involvement and much more sensitive measures of both attitude and behaviour are necessary before one can say how committed a man may be to fatherhood.[13] The degree to which men care for or play with their young children is highly variable, across societies and even across classes within Western society. The man who baths a baby in some societies would be considered suspiciously abnormal; in societies where 'child-care and nurturant activities' are not undertaken by fathers, a man can be a good father in local terms but without, according to the Parkers' theory, ever achieving any bonding with the child. There is no evidence that in such societies there is more sexual abuse of children than in Western societies; many people would argue that it occurs less often. It is difficult, therefore, to link child-care activities with commitment to the paternal role or their absence to subsequent abuse. What is established by the Parkers is the importance in Western societies of the way a man behaves to the child, not their biological connection. This means that the different proportions of fathers and father figures among abusers must be understood in relation to the social relationships that they have with the children.

The relationships men may have with children in their care are complex and the sexual element may coexist with a range of emotion and behaviour. It is too simple to characterize them merely in terms of the presence or absence of bonding. As the discussion of offenders in chapter 4 noted, it is not uncommon to find relationships of great ambivalence in which affection is clearly present, on either or both sides. It may be the close bond with their daughters, sometimes amounting almost to an obsession on the father's part, that provides an occasion and the motivation for sexual abuse. A few brief case-histories will show the range of variation.

One of the cases in the CSA Unit, that of the Beards (not their real name), might almost have been chosen to demonstrate bonding between father and daughter:

Frances Beard was her parents' first child and her mother felt she could do nothing right for the baby. From babyhood, her mother declared, Frances had preferred her father. Her husband could stop the baby crying and took over most of the child care; she clearly felt rejected by the baby and resented it. The relationship between mother and daughter was poor but Sheila Beard felt compensated by her good relationship with their second child, a boy. Leslie Beard's abuse of his daughter did not include intercourse or the use of force but Frances was very sexualized in her behaviour and clearly at risk of further abuse. She and her father continued to appear deeply devoted to one another. He declared on more than one occasion that his sexual abuse of her had been the result of his inability to distinguish between sexual activity and an appropriate physical expression of paternal love.

In a second case, concerning a family I shall call Haws, the relationship between father and daughter was much more ambivalent; it showed the resentment and hostility that is also not uncommon and which may be displayed in violence as well.

Linette Haws, aged seven, was referred by her GP. She had been involved sexually with her father for the last year or more before referral but the occasion which precipitated it was her rape by her father which caused serious injuries. She was reported to have asked her father how babies were made. He'd taken her into the bedroom and demonstrated, threatening her with a beating when she struggled.

Linette's mother, a pretty woman, looked more like her sister than her mother. She reiterated that she had known about the incestuous abuse, had disapproved of it but had been unable to stop it. She and all her sisters had suffered incest or incestuous abuse by their father and she reported that she had earlier acceded to her husband's demands to dress as a child when they had sex, 'in case he got interested in Linette'. Geoffrey Haws was the son of a violent father, who had been convicted of three serious rapes and habitually beat his wife and children; he himself was occasionally violent. According to his wife, he was very jealous, even of Linette: 'he holds me back from showing affection' to the child.

One thus cannot assume that all relations between fathers and daughters are similar. To do so is to mistake the ideal of such relations for their actuality. Similarly, to characterize the difference between fatherhood and stepfatherhood in terms of bonding is also to oversimplify. Few relationships between stepfather and daughter approach the intensity of the Beards', even where a stepfather has known the child from babyhood; many of them resemble the second case, where motives for the abuse appear very mixed. However, there are social factors which distinguish between the two relationships which mean that they cannot be considered equivalent, whatever the personal relations of the adults and children concerned. These involve legal and financial differences which are much more important than generally assumed.

The Social Context of Fatherhood and Stepfatherhood

It is common to hear people speak of the rights of parents as though mother and father have the same rights over their child(ren), exercised jointly. They are spoken of as though they are intrinsic and 'natural' rights, which derive from the fact that the child owes its physical existence to them both. In fact, these rights have been established by legislation, that is by the state; they are not simply a public recognition of the physical relationship. Over the last two hundred years, paternal rights have undergone considerable reduction, to begin with because mothers acquired rights that they did not have before, and later because the principle of the child's own interests became a significant factor in deciding between the rights bestowed on either parent.[14] The justification for the award of legal rights to a mother was based on the recognition of her biological link with the child, her bearing, nursing and caring for it and also on the principle that 'children need their mothers', that is on the child's interests.

Paternal rights, on the other hand, are not acquired as a consequence of a genetic relationship to the child, for a man who begets a child does not automatically acquire paternal rights over it; these depend on marriage to the child's mother. Formerly a man's 'natural' children were those for whom he assumed no responsibility and over whom he had no rights. This was the case even before a mother had acquired any rights of her own over her child. Paternity is thus not simply a relationship between a man and a child but one which is defined by a relationship to the child's mother.

A stepfather's relation with his wife's children is also based on his relationship to their mother; it is this which makes him their stepfather. But the marriage which makes her his wife does not give him a legally based relation with them. A stepfather has no legal rights over his step-children, even if he supports them.[15] Some stepfathers declare that they hate the term stepfather. It underlines the ambiguities of their position; acting as a father but forever prevented from being recognized as 'the real thing'.[16] It is possible for stepfathers to adopt their step-children which gives them full paternal rights and some do so for that reason. More commonly, the absence of the legal rights and responsibilities of fatherhood undermines the authority of stepfathers. If children are born of the second marriage, their existence may emphasize this and alter both the relation between stepfather and step-children, and the position of the latter in the household as a whole. The existence of children who are 'theirs' makes a 'family' of the married pair and leaves the step-children representing a former broken marriage and a 'family' that no longer exists. Conflict between half-siblings is a common feature of societies where there are plural marriages, whether they follow one another (serial polygamy) or are contemporaneous.

The association of rights over children with property rights is also common in human societies. It has been noted of some fathers accused of incest that they apparently feel they have the right to do what they want with 'their own' children.[17] This possessive attitude is by no means confined to abusing fathers; to a greater or lesser degree it is very general to find resistance among parents to any limitation of their rights over their children. In some writings published during the Cleveland crisis, the idea that children 'belong' to their parents was particularly strong.

This belief has a variety of different consequences for the child. Children's relationships with the parent they are living with after a divorce are often adversely affected by conflicts over custody.[18] The children may be angry with their mother (it is usually she who keeps them with her), or one or all of the children can come to represent the former partner and suffer dislike or neglect for that reason. Daughters, particularly eldest daughters, seem particularly likely to be alienated from their mothers after a divorce; they also seem more likely to be sexually abused. If they live with their mother and her husband, their attitudes to their stepfather may vary from warm acceptance of him to active dislike or outright rebellion. His reaction to them may be equally varied. The insecurity, anger and grief caused by the conflict and separation of parents may make the initial relationship between a step-parent and child very difficult for both of them.

Since children are so strongly identified with their parents, the motive for the abuse of a child, whether physical or sexual, may be primarily an indirect attack on one or other of its parents. Men may 'get their own back' on their wives or their wives' former husbands by damaging their child. One or two of the women who replied to the BBC request for information indicated that they felt their abuse was the result of anger or hatred directed against their mothers. An important element in a stepfather's attitudes seems to be whether he regards the children as 'their mother's' or 'another man's'. The abuse of a child on an access visit to an estranged or divorced father may be the result of his feelings about the separation and his (ex-)wife, or a demonstration that this is still 'his child', as much as sexual attraction to the child. A case reported in Beatrix Campbell's book about the Cleveland affair, *Unofficial Secrets*, gives an example of this. She interviewed the mother of three girls who had been diagnosed as sexually abused; the woman told her that she had first been worried when her daughters began to show reluctance to visit their father for their weekly access visits.[19]

Fatherhood is indissolubly linked with the idea of authority and discipline. While both parents have the right to control and discipline their children it is commonly a father who assumes the role. Paternal authority is backed by the legitimate use of punishment, including corporal punishment, although public opinion no longer approves of the beating of children, and excessive use of force is now considered physical abuse.[20] The issue of a stepfather's right to punish his step-children is often a matter of great sensitivity; he may meet resistance from the child's mother or the child itself. On the other hand, some mothers may be so relieved to have the help of a man again in controlling a child that they virtually abdicate responsibility for discipline to their new husband.

The exercise of paternal authority requires little display of force, especially when the child is very young. Physical strength and a child's habit of obeying adults may be enough to ensure compliance. Even when they are older, children may obey adults with little coercion. But it is frequently noted that men who sexually abuse children are domestic tyrants.[21] Even those men who present a mild, ineffectual image to outsiders may be violent. It is not merely stepfathers who resort to force, lacking the authority of a father. The respondents to the BBC national survey who reported that they had been sexually abused, by fathers and stepfathers, all reported that they had been physically abused as well. The sexual abuse itself may be used as a punishment: one man made his daughter submit to it when he caught her smoking and again when he saw her with a girl he had told her not to be friendly with. A man in the parents' therapy group admitted he would make his daughter submit to him sexually if she had been 'cheeky'. But there is also a typical development of violence in a long-standing sexual relationship with a daughter or step-daughter which is not characterized by force to begin with. During adolescence she begins to resist him more strongly, which may result in much more violent behaviour from him, until she finds the courage to tell someone. Often it is the support of a boyfriend which enables a girl to break free of her abusive father, or a rebellion against restrictions placed on her ability to join in the activities of her friends which precipitates a violent confrontation. It may be that such men do feel unsure of their authority and so exert their masculine power instead.

Paternity is not merely a matter of rights but of responsibilities. A father has the legal obligation to maintain his children,[22] although it is not easily enforced. The question of maintenance of the children is an important element of the paternal role and may be bitterly fought over by divorcing parents. A man's financial responsibilities for the children he lives with is an important influence on his attitude and behaviour to them and theirs to him. The financial obligations of paternity and its rights often appear to be linked so that a man who maintains a child feels that he should have some rights over it. In a study of step-parents Burgoyne and Clark point out that the men seemed eager to take on the financial responsibility for their step-children, particularly if this meant a reduction in contact with their father.[23] The concern of these stepfathers to support the children seems to be motivated (at least in part) by a desire to establish some rights over them, even informal ones. The fact that they do so in this way exemplifies the informal equation of control over children with degree of financial responsibility; it may also reflect the widespread association between children and property.

Children are made aware of their dependence by the words and actions of their parents; they are expected to accept paternal rights and their dependence on the parents for shelter, food and clothing. Men who marry a woman with children may be involved in additional expenditure for them as well as supporting their mother; the cost of step-children may be assumed willingly or unwillingly but may come to seem a burden, particularly if the 'real' father cannot be made to support them himself. A stepfather who provides support may expect perpetual gratitude for it. The maintenance of the relationship betwen a woman and her husband may come to seem vital to her children's financial support, in their eyes as well as hers; consequently they feel forced to submit to all his demands. One woman among the cases in the hospital CSA Unit was very angry with her daughter for disclosing her stepfather's abuse of her; she said her husband had been very good to the girl and never denied her anything. The implication was that she was either lying out of malice or, if she was not lying, she was being ungrateful in not complying with his demands in silence.

Financial obligations for 'genetic' children and legal rights over them which continue after divorce may also be the source of much tension and conflict. If a divorced father marries again, he may then reduce maintenance payments to his former wife.[24] This reduction of his support of his children will have a direct effect on the income of their stepfather, who must now assume more financial responsibility for 'another man's children'. A stepfather's resentment of his situation may be directed against them. Anger at the man who placed the liability for his children on someone else is seen very clearly in one of the hospital cases, although the man concerned was the victims' uncle by marriage and foster father, not their stepfather.

The mother of Daniel and Teresa Maddock had died when they were about eight and six respectively. Their father did not want to take care of them and moved a new girlfriend in with him, handing his children over to the care of his sister and her husband. This proved an unworkable arrangement as his sister had her own small children to look after, so George Maddock made over his house to his dead wife's sister and her husband, the Goldens, in exchange for their taking over the children. From the beginning, the two Maddock children were treated worse than their three younger cousins and soon both of them were being sexually abused by John Golden. At the initial interview with them, he told the hospital therapists that he had been angry with George Maddock for 'dumping the children on him' and was bored because he was unemployed.

It was evident that Bill Golden felt that the two children, unlike his own, should not have been his responsibility, that he had earned the right to use them as he wished and also that, by maltreating them, he was revenging himself on their father. The sexual element in his behaviour was probably the least important part of it.

The Antecedents of Sexual Abuse

The idea that divorce may be the significant factor underlying the finding that proportionately more stepfathers than fathers sexually abuse their children is not new. But hitherto it has merely been implicit in various hypotheses: that sexual abuse does not happen in a 'traditional family', that it is stepfathers rather than fathers who abuse children sexually, or that divorce puts children at risk. Finkelhor's work provides an explicit account of the effect of divorce in cases of sexual abuse in the United States. On the basis of his own research he lists 'living with a stepfather' as a major factor putting a girl at risk of sexual abuse. This conclusion is much quoted but usually out of context. Finkelhor goes on to show that the important factor is what is implied by having a stepfather at all: that the child has been separated from its own father. Girls separated from their fathers by divorce are not merely at risk from their stepfathers, but from other men as well.[25] The effect of separation from her father would seem to make a girl more vulnerable to men generally. Girls who are or have been separated from their mothers are shown to be even more vulnerable, so it is probably the insecurity which results from the loss of a parent that is the reason for their vulnerability rather than the need for a father figure. Divorce or disruption of a child's relationship with either parent may deprive it of continued affection and care, and of possible protection.

A child's added vulnerability in a relationship with a stepfather is not the only effect of the changes which have resulted from divorce and remarriage. It is well known that stepfamilies have difficulties peculiar to themselves:[26] the legacies of death or divorce which have preceded a man's assumption of stepfatherhood are not wiped out and forgotten, although in the public view this family is now 'reconstituted'. According to studies of step-parents, questions of discipline and support of the children, relations with the absent parent and disagreements about where the children 'belong' may introduce conflicts and tensions additional to those of a normal household. As Chesser pointed out thirty years ago, 'Divorce may solve the parents' problems but not that of the child.'[27] The presence of a stepfather is, in almost all cases, a reminder of a past separation as well as a possible source of problems in the present.

Men who are stepfathers vary in their antecedents and these have their effect on the way the family learns to live together.[28] Some men become stepfathers without experience of fatherhood, either because they have not been married before or because their first marriage did not result in children. Others, like Dr Hughes, are fathers as well as stepfathers; their children may be living with them and their step-children, or separately with their mother. A man's step-children may or may not have a continuing relationship with their genetic father, just as he may or may not have continuing relations with children by a former wife. These ties to people elsewhere at best make distinctions among the members of a step-family, but at worst may be the source of conflict among them.

Even if attention is paid to the variety concealed under the term step-family, to view children's sexual abuse solely as a product of their present family situation ignores the effect of the earlier relationships in other families of both abuser and victim. In particular it fails to consider that the daughters of broken marriages may be more vulnerable because they have been sexually abused before. Alternatively a man may abuse both his children and, later, his step-children. The following case history from the CSA Unit is a demonstration of how it may be misleading to characterize a man by the role he happens to be filling at the time his abusive activities are exposed.

> Jenny Palmer aged 13 went to the police and reported her stepfather, Dan Grimshaw, of sexually abusing her and her younger sister Louise. Both of them had suffered a similar pattern of abuse: exhibition of his penis, mutual masturbation and finally sexual intercourse. Jenny had tried to object but he bullied and threatened her till she gave in, telling her when she complained, 'You'll get used to it.'

This case of abuse seems to fit a common stereotype of abuse by a stepfather of a newly pubertal girl. Their relationship was not good: Jenny's attitude to her stepfather was hostile and he alternated between threats to hit her and gifts of money. Louise was said to be more passively accepting of him. Their little half-sister, Dan's child by their mother, had not been abused by her father. At first sight the case demonstrates the expected distinction between behaviour as father and as stepfather. However the full history of the household reveals something rather different.

> The Palmers and the Grimshaws had been neighbours and friends. The eldest Grimshaw girl, Tina, was the same age as Jenny. The affair between Iris Palmer and Dan Grimshaw broke up both marriages. Dan married Iris and they moved to London with her children. The Grimshaw children stayed with their mother.
>
> Mrs Grimshaw had found her husband in bed with Louise two years earlier (when she had been eight or nine); he had admitted having intercourse with her and his wife had threatened him with the police if he didn't stop. This apparently had no effect on him. It was a visit from Tina Grimshaw to her father that led to Jenny's going to the police. Tina asked Jenny if her father had involved her in sexual activities, saying that she had been made to participate since she had been about six (she dated it by her return from having been hospitalized as a result of physical abuse). Dan Grimshaw was later convicted of incest with Tina and unlawful sexual intercourse with Jenny. Louise was not considered suitable as a witness in court so he was not charged with her abuse.

Dan Grimshaw was convicted of two separate offences but the case was recorded in the hospital files as one of sexual abuse of a step-child, since Jenny was the patient.

A number of men in the cases in the hospital CSA Unit had married again and abused a second set of their own children; other victims had been abused by both a father and a stepfather. In the latter type of case, the children have been taught sexualized behaviour which may draw a man to join the household because he finds the children an attraction. The children's subsequent abuse is the result not simply of his role as stepfather but of the circumstances which preceded his becoming a stepfather at all. It is as likely that men become stepfathers because they are attracted to the children as it is that they abuse children under their care because they are not fathers. It is not usual to think of a man's choice of partner as motivated by the fact that she is already a mother, but the idea receives some support from the CSA Unit cases.

The term 'stepfather', like 'father figure', brings together a wide variety of different relationships under a single term. There are some men whose marriage to a woman with children can be seen as the establishment of a permanent relationship with them as well, but others whose position, either as recognized lovers or as resident members of the households, is much more tenuous, lacking in responsibility and short-lived.[29] In the latter case, it is often unclear how appropriate it is to refer to these men as stepfathers at all. Sometimes they may be referred to by the children as boyfriends of their mothers but all too often the nature of their position in the household is not examined but merely assumed to be that of a substitute father. A man's sexual relationship with the child's mother or the fact that they are living together is translated in terms of the 'ideal' pattern of the family into a 'marriage'. It becomes a form of fatherhood, a relationship with the children, whereas in reality it may not be considered as such either by the child(ren) or by their mother.

Among the cases in the CSA Unit, nearly half (48 per cent) of the men referred to as stepfathers were not married to the mothers of the children they abused. Many had not been members of the household for long, although in some other cases there was clearly a common-law marriage and the use of the term stepfather was appropriate. If the doubtful cases are taken out of the stepfather category, the proportion of stepfathers relative to all abusers is reduced to 12 per cent, a figure much closer to that which might be expected to result by chance.

The relationships between men and any unrelated children they may live with is obscured by the common use of stepfather as a generic term for a common-law husband, resident lover of the children's mother and so on. The terminology is the result of the assumption that a man and a woman living together with children form a family. While the ideal form of this group is that the couple should be married and the children the offspring of them both, variations in the pattern are fitted into the form by the use of the term stepfather. Since a woman with children is referred to as a mother, these men are assimilated to a pattern of the family by referring to them as stepfathers. The important difference is felt to be the distinction between 'real' (genetic) fathers and all others; as substitutes for the father, they are all stepfathers.

Common Factors

The contrast between stepfathers and fathers is less important than it appeared at first sight. Cases where a man is both an abusing father and an abusing stepfather underline the artificiality of the distinction between incest and the sexual abuse of step-children. What all these men have in common is not that they are types of 'father figure', more or less 'real', but that they are living with the children they abuse. If the distinction made by classing incest as a separate offence is ignored, then the largest single group of abusers of children are those who live in the same house, members of the same household.

Households and families are not the same. Although this is seldom remembered, it is easily demonstrated. Families may be concieved of as undergoing a life cycle in which a couple starts a new family, which grows with the birth of children, matures as the children leave home and start new families, and finally dissolves with the deaths of the founders.[30] When the children are young, the family is contained in a single household; when they are adult the same relationships, of parent and child or siblings, links several households. The importance of this distinction between family and household is that although the idea of the family includes the notion that its members live together, it is removed from the full implications of household organization. The idea of the family refers to idealized feelings and behaviour associated with the genetic relatedness between parents and children; households are practically oriented organizations which concern property, financial management and household chores. Their members must cope with daily strains and difficulties but the privacy and freedom from interference which being a 'family' ensures, allows the ideal of the family to survive unaffected by public acknowledgement of any negative effects of living together.

The strength and persistence of the idea that children live in families makes it appropriate to describe it as a social dogma. The common features of household patterns show how idealized the family ideal is: marriages may not last, children of both sexes may not be born, or they may not be the biological offspring of both those who occupy the position of parents. The majority of households in Britain are not families in the sense of containing a couple and their children of both sexes. Even those households which are classified in official figures as 'family households' are merely those with children in them, whether they are adopted, fostered or step-children. Deviations are fitted into the ideal pattern by referring to them in terms which imply normality. Today, households formed by a second marriage of one or other partner may be referred to as 'reconstituted families'. The term is obviously a misnomer because the new unit differs from the old; it is not the old one reforming. Nevertheless, the label serves to give the household an acceptable status as a kind of family. The relations between their members are seen as deriving from their life together. Stepfathers and men associated with a child's mother may be referred to as father figures, father surrogates or even fathers. These usages make it easy to continue to refer to households as families and hence to ignore what actually shapes relationships within them.

The nature and operation of the actual organization of households depends on legal, economic and political features of the wider society; the antecedents of its members may also affect their relations with each other as we have seen. The financial resources of the household are usually distributed unequally between adults and children and between men and women, which make their relationships unequal; there are differences in strength between men, women and children, in the kind of work that they do and the amount of time it takes. The relationships within a household are a composite of many elements, of which the family relationships they form occupy only one strand.

Children are most often abused in houses where they live, by the people with whom they live. These are the significant facts. Domestic life throws adults and children together in conditions of intimacy which make opportuities for abuse much more frequent and much easier to conceal even from other members of the household. Abusing a child in other circumstances carries a much greater risk of discovery, despite the privileged position occupied by many men who have children in their charge. There is much less privacy, and intimacy between the adults and children concerned is not expected. Children may complain to their parents if other adults abuse them but they are much less likely to complain about parents to other people, since to do so is to be tainted by the shame.

What the majority of abusers have in common is not that they are types of father figure, more or less 'real', but that they are living with the children they abuse. In only two of the hospital cases was a child abused by a father she was not living with; in one of them it was clear that the abuse had started before the parents separated. All the accused stepfathers were living with their victims. Incest, like the sexual abuse of children, takes place within a household. Those in which the children are not the offspring of the male householder are merely a particular form of household. There are special strains in it that make the children particularly vulnerable but similar factors may also be found in 'normal families'. Some of the people who abuse children are defined by society as fathers, brothers, grandfathers; others are seen as 'unrelated'; the context of the abuse is not that they fail to conform to the ideal family but that their intimate social relationships are many-stranded and are played out in privacy, without outside interference.

The identification of those involved in sexually abusing a child in terms of family relationships ignores the personal characteristics of the people who live together and the way that their lives are actually organized. The relationships within the family are seen as of a different quality to any others because they are believed to be given, the result of natural requirements for rearing the young.[31] Unlike other relationships they cannot be chosen or broken off; one may not see or speak to one's father but he remains one's father nevertheless. The expected behaviour and appropriate feelings are seen to be natural, that is outside the control of individuals but inherent in human nature. Those who do not conform to these ideals are seen as 'bad' or even as 'unnatural'. Family relatedness implies sharing and altruism but in fact the notion legitimizes certain rights over people and over property as well as setting out ideals of appropriate behaviour and feeling. Contrary to what many people believe, these notions have long affected domestic life, regulating inheritance and establishing the rights of mother and father over their children and the relations of spouses to one another and to their joint property. Whereas the idea of the family contains much about 'natural' affection, and some conceptions of how authority should be exercised, it is silent on the question of the different interests of its members or their relative power to pursue those interests at the expense of other members. Where brothers and sisters are concerned, this element in their relationship is crucial, as the next chapter will show.

Notes

1 Some girls and one boy among the hospital patients were victims of young abusers but the latter were a good deal older, and hence stronger, than their victims in almost all cases. They were mostly boys in late adolescence and hardly to be referred to as children.
2 Herman, *Father–Daughter Incest*, p. 70.
3 R. A. Houlbrook, *The English Family 1450–1700* (Longmans, Harlow, 1984), pp. 144–5.
4 J. Burgoyne and D. Clark, 'From father to stepfather', in L. McKee and M. O'Brien (eds), *The Father Figure* (Tavistock, London, 1982), p. 197.
5 Houlbrook, *The English Family*, pp. 215–19.
6 General Household Survey 1982 (HMSO, London).
7 I. Reid, *Social Class Differences in Britain*, 2nd edn (Grant McIntyre, London, 1981), pp. 163–5. See also J. Haskey, 'Social class and socio-economic differentials in divorce in England and Wales', *Population Studies*, 38 (1984), quoted in J. Burgoyne, R. Ormrod and M. Richards (eds), *Divorce Matters* (Penguin, Harmondsworth, 1987), p. 34.
8 Parker and Parker, 'Father–daughter sexual abuse'.
9 Ibid., p. 542.
10 A. Wolf, unpublished manuscript. This research considers Chinese couples where, in a traditional form of marriage known as Sim pua, the wife was brought up by her future in-laws from a small child or even a baby to be a future daughter-in-law. See also A. Wolf, 'Childhood association, sexual attraction, and the incest taboo: a Chinese case', *American Anthropologist*, 68 (1966).
11 Parker and Parker, 'Father–daughter sexual abuse'. They are clearly chosen as activities normally undertaken by mothers and shared by progressive fathers. The Parkers found a rather low participation in these activities in both samples; they refer to the 'low paternal involvement of American fathers' (p. 547). One of their conclusions is that their study demonstrates the need for joint parenting.
12 Ibid., p. 542.
13 L. McKee, 'Fathers' participation in infant care: a critique', in McKee and O'Brien (eds), *Father Figure*, pp. 26–30.
14 N. V. Lowe, 'The legal status of fathers: past and present', in McKee and O'Brien (eds), *Father Figure*, pp. 26–30. Houlbrook, *The English*

Family (p. 215), describes the early modern view of step-families, which is substantially the same as that held today.

15 Even if a man supports his step-children, if their mother dies, he is not legally entitled to go on having the children living with him unless their father agrees.

16 See Burgoyne and Clark, 'From father to stepfather', p. 205.

17 The rights of fathers in some societies extend to pawning their children or selling them into slavery. However they do not have the right to kill or maim them, though they may beat them in a manner that would not be approved in Britain today, although it seems to have been more common in the past. See Houlbrook, *The English Family*, and J. S. La Fontaine, 'The domestication of the savage male', *Man* n.s., 16(3) (1980).

18 Disputes over custody and access visits may be the setting for allegations by the mother that the child was sexually abused by its father. While these allegations appear to be fictitious more often than in other contexts, the proportion of reliable accounts found in a careful study by D. Jones and A. Seig was 70 per cent ('Child sexual abuse allegations', pp. 22–36).

19 B. Campbell, *Unofficial Secrets* (Virago, London, 1988), pp. 171–5.

20 Houlbrook, *The English Family*, shows the preoccupation of parents with the need to punish a child for its own good; he shows that the characteristically English custom of sending children away from home for their education was related to the belief that parents' love for their children will result in a child's being 'spoilt' for lack of suitable discipline. The proverb 'Spare the rod and spoil the child' obviously has a long history.

21 Maisch, *Incest*, pp. 63–5, 128; Meiselman, *Incest*, p. 91; Herman, *Father–Daughter Incest*, p. 73; Finkelhor, *Sexually Victimized Children*, p. 26.

22 The state also requires that parents ensure their children go to school or are suitably educated; after a divorce the fulfilment of this obligation is the duty of the custodial parent.

23 Burgoyne and Clark, 'From father to stepfather', pp. 196–207.

24 Ibid., p. 203.

25 Finkelhor, *Sexually Victimized Children*, p. 123.

26 Burgoyne and Clark, 'From father to stepfather', and also Brenda Maddox's account of the difficulties stepmothers face: *The Half-Parent* (Evans, New York, 1975).

27 E. Chesser, *The Sexual, Marital and Family Relationships of the English Woman* (Hutchinson, Watford, 1956), p. 540.

28 Burgoyne and Clark, 'From father to stepfather', pp. 198–9.

29 This does not apply to the stepfathers in the Parkers' study, where all

those labelled stepfather were explicitly stated to have been married to the mother of their stepchildren.

30 See M. Fortes, introduction to J. Goody (ed.), *The Developmental Cycle in Domestic Groups* (Cambridge University Press, Cambridge, 1958).

31 S. Yanagisako, 'Family and household: the analysis of domestic groups', *Annual Review of Anthropology*, 8 (1979), especially pp. 199–200.

6   Brothers and Sisters

But what is important to me and what I will never forget is the look that was in my brother's eyes and my awareness that he simply didn't care how I felt about what he was trying to do to me.

Married woman aged 35–44, Kent

One night I had a nightmare, my brother often used to take me in his bed to comfort me and so he did this night. But it was different. He began touching my body, and he tried to have intercourse with me. He told me to trust him, he wouldn't hurt me but he did hurt me.

Unmarried woman, aged 25–34, Lancashire

Sexual activities between brother and sister have received very little attention, either from those engaging in research on the sexual abuse of children or those concerned with their protection. This is probably because the accepted ideas about such behaviour prevent it being considered as abuse. If the brother and sister are not yet adult then their behaviour is thought of as sexual experimentation. This may be discouraged, more or less severely according to the attitudes of the parents or teachers who may observe it, but it is not believed to be something that children must be protected from. Alternatively, incest between brother and sister is considered to be a rare occurrence, a mistaken but mutual adult attraction, the consequences of which are equally tragic for both partners. Underlying both ideas is the assumption that brothers and sisters are each other's equals and that therefore any sexual element in their relationship is there by consent. In such circumstances it is not surprising that abuse of a child by a brother or sister is ignored.

Sibling incest has much greater relevance for a general under-standing of the sexual abuse of children than the rather small numbers of known cases of it would suggest. In brief, it makes clear that to use the ideas of 'family' and the common notions of its structure leaves out much of what affects actual people living together. Even in the early study of incest behaviour by Weinberg, published in 1955, the very varied circumstances of the sibling pairs he considered are obvious. He wrote that, in some cases, 'The discrepancy in age between the siblings made the relationship resemble father–daughter incest.'[1] In other cases, there was inadequate parenting or the parents had separated. In a few cases, one child, usually the boy, was isolated and his seduction of his sister was an act of hostility. The circumstances of the parents, the age and gender of all the siblings and their relationships with each other and with their parents are all relevant to these variations. But they are still glossed over by the persisting practice of labelling the individuals by reference to their role in 'the family' and particularly by their position, relative to adult members of the family, as 'children'. This latter term includes two ideas: of immature individuals who develop into adults under parental care and supervision, and also the relationship of equality which derives from common parentage. The two stereotypes of sexual behaviour between brother and sister refer to these twin aspects. The consideration of actual relationships between brothers and sisters will show that sibling incest is not a distortion of either of these ideals but a more complex phenomenon which displays some of the same social features that are relevant to understanding the sexual abuse of children by adults.

Sibling Incest in Anthropological Theory

The work of the anthropologist, Robin Fox,[2] has been influential both in some anthropological circles and more widely, so that it is worth considering it in some detail. His general thesis makes use of popular thinking on the subject, which may be why it has been accepted. Fox's view is that incest between brother and sister is very rare, not because it is forbidden, but because it is not desired. His argument is based on the assertion that, unless prevented, young children will engage in sexual play with their brothers and sisters. The fact that they do this at an age when they are not yet fully developed sexually engenders frustration, which 'teaches' them that the other is not a suitable sexual partner. Therefore at a later age, when they are sexually mature, they are not attracted to each other. Thus brother/sister incest is rare, he argues, not as the result of a ban on something that is desired, but because it is prevented by a 'natural aversion' that is the product of childhood development. However, where children are prevented by adults from indulging in early sexual exploration, their attraction for one another will persist into adulthood and it is in such societies that the idea of brother/sister incest causes the greatest anxiety. Equally it is in societies where children are prevented from sexual play with one another that incest between brothers and sisters is likely to occur, because the natural mechanism which produces a lack of attraction is absent. Alternatively, where by chance brothers and sisters are not brought up together from early childhood, they may also feel sexual attraction for each other.

Like many scholars, Fox uses the legal sense of the term incest as sexual intercourse, so the 'sexual play' of young children is not incest. His theory links the two ideas which people have of the possibility of sexual relations between brother and sister in a causal sequence. *Because* sexual play between children is common and not serious, *then* incest between adult brother and sister does not happen, except where they have not been brought up together. Fox sees himself as developing the ideas of Westermarck who first produced the thesis that, as some contemporary remarked: 'familiarity breeds contempt'; Fox adds that in fact it does not breed at all.[3] The witticisms reveal the assumption that incest among human beings is equivalent to inbreeding, an idea which, as we saw earlier, has been present in one way or another in discussions about incest since the earliest times. His theory is that evolution has developed a human aversion to inbreeding, which is implanted in brothers and sisters as they play together. But, as this chapter will show, the facts of sexual activity between siblings, like those concerning incest and incestuous abuse between father and daughter, cannot be explained so simply.

Children's Sexual Play

It is commonly believed that most brothers and sisters in Britain experiment with sexual play, but the evidence for this is weak. Although it is now accepted that children have sexual feelings, we must distinguish between this fact and their sexual knowledge or willingness to engage in mature sexual activity. Not a great deal is known about early sexual development and probably even less about the development of children's knowledge and understanding. There are virtually no studies of children's sexual development and writings on the subject rarely distinguish between the capacity of children's bodies to become aroused or to have pleasurable sensations, children's behaviour and their knowledge or intentions. Bentovim and Vizard point out that much more is known about sexual development at and after puberty than before it.[4] They cite studies which show that the biological capacities for sexual behaviour have been observed in very young infants, but these merely indicate the body's potential.

It has also long been known that masturbation gives physical sensations which are pleasurable to infants and young children. Small children who are neglected or unhappy may comfort themselves in this way. In one study of pre-pubertal children, 55 per cent of boys and 30 per cent of girls reported that they masturbated. The figures are said to be similar to those obtained in retrospective studies with adults.[5] Before puberty this usually appears to be self-stimulation rather than mutual masturbation, which occurs later, in adolescence. Pre-pubertal masturbation is not evidence of children's having sexual *relationships*; it merely shows their knowledge of how to produce pleasurable feelings in their own bodies. The difference between boys and girls is interesting and we will return to it later in this discussion. It could mean that girls are less curious about their bodies or develop this awareness later than boys, but it may also reflect adult discouragement of self-exploration, which probably incurs more adult disapproval where girls are concerned.

Before puberty children may engage in what is usually termed 'sexual play' with one another. This is how adults interpret it, in the same way that adults understand much childish behaviour: by reference to their own understanding. Body contact among adults takes place briefly as greetings between close kin and intimates, but in British society at least it is not encouraged. Women are expected to have close physical contact with babies and children, which is clearly defined as maternal and not erotic. The only bodily contact men experience that is more than formal and fleeting takes place as part of sexual encounters. Perhaps for this reason the sensual pleasure children clearly take in cuddling may be interpreted as sexual. Little girls may be referred to as 'sexy' when they climb on a father's knees and snuggle close to him or imitate adult feminine behaviour. This is an adult interpretation which may say more about the interpreter than about the child's behaviour.

Children's 'sexual' activity involves children of the same sex and/ or the same age; these are their peers, their equals. Although much writing refers to sexual play without being very specific as to what the 'play' consists of, it seems largely to involve mutual inspection and display of the genitals, which is clearly the result of curiosity about anatomical and individual differences. There may also be touching of each other's genitals. Games like 'Doctor and Patient' which allow for exploration of another's genitals may also be played. There is also a certain amount of bodily contact in the wrestling that children engage in, and which they seem to enjoy, but while this may be sensual, it is less obviously sexual in nature. An important element in it appears to be a contest for physical dominance, which gives satisfaction to the winner. Sexual play with peers usually stops before adolescence, although masturbation may continue.

Children's sexual knowledge appears to develop much later. Bentovim and Vizard refer to evidence that children are aware of the bodily differences associated with male and female identity by the age of five. In households with children of both sexes the association of genital anatomy with gender identity seems unremarkable but where there are children of only one sex the children may have fewer opportunities to satisfy their curiosity. However, 'their understanding of the function of genitals is very much more limited'.[6] In particular they are not able to envisage what mature sexual behaviour entails or understand the activities which adults label 'sex'.[7] Even much later, and after attending sex education classes at school, individuals may assert that their understanding of mature sexuality was inadequate.[8] If pre-pubertal children do not have the knowledge or understanding of mature sexuality, their experimentation can hardly be called sexual in the adult sense. Kinsey and his associates remarked in 1948 that 'some of the sex play of younger children seems to be devoid of erotic content'.[9] It is 'sexual' only in the sense that it involves parts of the body and sensations which adult knowledge understands as 'sexual'. Indeed most people distinguish between the two, either by the use of the term 'play' or by putting the term 'sexual' in inverted commas.

Only one British survey of sexual abuse has attempted to investigate childish sexuality by asking adult women to record their pre-pubertal experiences. This survey of readers was undertaken for *19* magazine and attracted answers from 3,000 women.[10] They were not necessarily representative of British women as a whole; in fact, three-quarters of them were between the ages of 17 and 24. Three-fifths of them (61 per cent) said they had taken part in sexual games with other children; most of them started at around the age of four and few continued after the age of ten, although the largest number of answers indicated ten as the age when these games occurred. The majority of the women who reported these experiences did not consider them abusive or damaging.

Unfortunately the published report of the survey gives no information as to what these games consisted of or whether they were played with brothers and/or sisters. Although respondents were given a check-list of possible activities, the list was designed to suggest answers to a series of questions, only one of which referred to childhood. They were asked to report anything that 'might seem sexual to you *now*' (my emphasis); they were not asked to recall their knowledge or intentions at the time. Nor were they asked who played the games with them. The answers cannot therefore give us information on the nature of girls' sexual activities before puberty or on the prevalence of sexual play between brothers and sisters. Kinsey's survey noted that pre-adolescent sexual play with same-sex friends is 'found in more histories, occurs more frequently and becomes more specific than the pre-adolescent heterosexual play'.[11] He and his colleagues report that the reasons for this among boys is that there is socially encouraged disdain for girls and admiration for masculinity as exemplified by fathers and older brothers while girls were relatively inaccessible. Almost all the heterosexual activity consisted of exhibitionism or manual manipulation of the genitals.

The information provided by the magazine survey does provide some evidence to support the general view that children commonly engage in sexual experimentation with one another, although it is rather weak, being based on a single, self-selected survey. It does not, of course, show that this usually happens between brother and sister. It also shows that sexual experimentation between children before puberty is not usually full sexual intercourse; therefore if it occurs between brother and sister, it is not incest.[12] The available evidence shows that between children close in age, where there is no coercion, it is not damaging and therefore is rightly distinguished from sexual abuse.

Gender Differences

There is very little recent discussion of any differences between the sexes in the nature and course of their sexual development. Kinsey and his associates concluded that: 'among most females . . . sexual development comes on more gradually than in the male, is often spread over a longer period of time, and does not reach its peak until a good many years after the boy is sexually mature' and 'the male is conditioned by sexual experience more frequently than the female.'[13] The existence of a male sexual culture which has a strong influence on the attitudes and behaviour of men and boys and which is different from that of women has often been remarked, but differences in the sexual development and ideas of boys and girls before the onset of puberty have been little explored. Descriptions of sexual play often refer to children, rather than boys or girls, as though differences between them emerge only at puberty.

There are indications that the two sexes do differ in their sexual interests and development in a number of ways earlier than that. Masturbation is much more prevalent among boys than girls; the study of pre-pubertal children by Elias and Gebhard cited earlier shows that while over half the boys masturbated, the majority of girls (70 per cent) did not. Boys' early and sustained interest in the comparative size of male genitalia is well known; the less obvious appearance of female genitalia may explain the lack of a similar interest in girls, although later on the development of breasts is a matter of comparison, prestige and anxiety. It seems likely too that boys are subject to frequent sexual overtures, remarks and gestures from older boys and men, which may be exploitative. The men in the CSA Unit's therapy group agreed that such approaches were so common as to constitute a virtually universal experience. Even if this behaviour is not exploitative, it maintains a level of awareness of physical sexuality that is rare among girls of the same age, whose culture makes the ideals of romantic love, marriage and motherhood their central preoccupations.[14] Single-sex boarding schools are characteristically British, rather than a feature of all

Western societies and they may well encourage this divergence between the sexes. Schools or other organizations for girls are concerned to repress and control expressions of developing sexuality, whereas the same organizations for boys appear to encourage it. The atmosphere in a boys' school was described to me as having an overt and persistent preoccupation with sexuality that would not be tolerated in a school for girls. Since my informants were men and two are the fathers of daughters one must take their views into account. The occasional scandal about sexual abuse in schools, whether these are primary or secondary schools, refers largely to boys. The British public school system has a highly ambivalent reputation in this respect. In short, boys are likely to show much more sexual interest in and curiosity about their sisters than the latter are about brothers. This is directly relevant to the subject of incest between them.

The Prevalence of Brother–Sister Incest

If it is true, as Fox alleges, that sexual play between siblings results in a lack of attraction to these early playmates, one would expect very little incestuous intercourse between brother and sister in Western societies where this play is generally permitted. The exceptions would occur when the siblings had been separated in early childhood and met as adults. The latter part of this hypothesis is not supported by the findings of Weinberg, the American scholar, who reported on 201 cases of incest derived from prison records. Thirty-seven cases involved sibling incest. His book, published in 1955, recorded that six of the brother–sister pairs had been brought up apart, 'because of the death or separation of their parents'.[15] This number is less than 20 per cent of the sibling pairs and we do not know at what age they were separated; the others were brought up together. Weinberg describes the sexual play that in some cases led to incest. However, few of his generalizations give numbers and details so that it is difficult to use his work.

There has been little research on incest between adolescent or adult brother and sister since then, particularly in Britain, so Fox's theory has still to be tested. However, articles in two newspapers, the *Observer* and the *South London Press*, provide two British cases. Both stories are sympathetic. In the first, Andrew Wilson describes in poignant terms the case of a young couple 'dragged before a St Albans court'; he describes their respectable characters and devotion to their children.[16] The second account also plays on the theme of innocent devotion under the headline: SHOCK FOR YOUNG LOVERS. Its first sentence makes it clear that the reader's sympathy is being sought: 'A teenage girl is battling against all odds to bear the child no one wants her to have – because the father is her half-brother.'[17] In this second case the pair had no knowledge of each other's existence until introduced by the father of them both; but he was also reported to have told his son that the girl was his sister. Both these stories appear to confirm the Fox hypothesis that the rare cases of incest occur where brothers and sisters have been separated and meet as adults.

A few additional accounts of sibling incest have been published with the results of a survey carried out by *Woman* magazine.[18] They do not resemble the newspaper reports for they concern single incidents with no element of romantic passion. There is no indication that the brother and sister were brought up apart. In one a woman reported: 'My sister and I "slept together" out of curiosity when I was 16 and she was 23. It was fun. I slept with my other brother [sic] when I was 16 and he was 18 – curiosity again. It doesn't worry me.' This remark is an indication that sexual curiosity continues after puberty but we cannot tell whether it was despite earlier sexual play or not. (The mention of the 'other brother' is intriguing but no further information is offered; perhaps it is a mistake for 'older'.) This is certainly an incident of incest but it does not seem to be an incestuous relationship.

Another, much older woman reported one occasion which was much less carefree than that. Both she and her brother, who was staying at her flat, had been drinking there with friends. When the friends left,

> somehow we were in bed. I felt very badly about it at the time but not for the usual reasons. One reason was that I don't like making love to older men – they give me the creeps. The second was that I am like my mother in appearance. He hated her and I felt that he was literally laying the ghost. I know that she made sexual advances to him when he was in his teens. I've rationalized these ideas now and am quite happy about it and him, though I wouldn't do it again.

In this case the woman knew about the advances made by her mother, so it seems likely that the two were brought up together; in the earlier case one cannot be sure, although there is no mention of any separation.

One case referred to the hospital CSA Unit concerned a brother and sister who were very attached to one another. They were aged 17 and 13 at the time of referral and although they admitted to having attempted sexual intercourse, there had been only partial penetration. Not long after the initial referral the boy developed leukaemia and the new crisis pushed the question of possible abuse into the background. This case comes the nearest to exemplifying the romantic myth of sibling incest, but there had been no separation between the brother and sister, who had been brought up together in the normal way, as indeed were the brothers and sisters in *all* the other cases referred to the hospital because of their sexual relationship. The lack of evidence to the contrary forces one to conclude that in Britain mutual love affairs between adolescent or adult siblings who are separated from an early age are either extraordinarily well concealed or very rare, although sexual relations between brother and sister who are brought up together do occur.

A Matter of Under-reporting?

Cases of incest between brother and sister may be reported to the police; Gorry's study records that 11 per cent of the cases reported to the Metropolitan Police involved such siblings.[19] This suggests that although incest of this kind is unusual, it is not rare. It is, however, likely that it is even less reported than father/daughter incest. There are two possible reasons for this. Where brother and sister are adult, no one would question their right to share a house or flat by implying that the relationship might be incestuous. The possibility is not entertained. If they move to live somewhere where they are not known, they can live openly as man and wife. Three of Weinberg's sibling pairs were described as married to each other. The couple described in the *Observer* had apparently lived as a married couple for years without interference; it is not clear in any of these cases how it became known that they were brother and sister.

Where the pair concerned are still children, their parents have the initial responsibility for them. If they wish to deal with the incest themselves and are not willing to report it or to seek help for the children, the incidents may never be made public. Two cases among the eight referred to the hospital suggest that this may be happening. In one a clergyman referred a girl who had allegedly been assaulted by her 16-year-old brother. The assaults consisted of inappropriate fondling and there was also a reference to the boy's showing his sister 'dirty pictures'. Appointments were made for the mother and children but they were not kept and finally a letter from the mother made it clear that she was not going any further with the matter.

In the second case, a woman referred her son and daughter for 'sexual experimentation'. They were eight and seven years old but their mother was particularly sensitive to the issue of sexual abuse since she and all her sisters had been abused by their father. There was some suspicion that the children's stepfather might have been involved but the situation changed before the appointment at the hospital was kept. The couple separated and the children's mother had stopped the children repeating their behaviour. There were no further meetings, since the therapists were satisfied that the children's mother was concerned and able to cope with the matter herself.

Another reason for the small numbers of reports of incest or incestuous abuse involving brother and sister might be that, as many people imagine, 'sexual experimentation' is common but not considered serious. Gorry reports that the police rarely proceed in cases of incest involving siblings.[20] In neither of the cases above was the behaviour extreme. There was no penetration of the girl, so that legally there was no question of incest. In another similar case in the hospital CSA Unit, a little girl of four was referred by a doctor after an allegation from the nursery school she attended that she was showing sexualized behaviour unusual for a child her age. Her parents agreed that she might have been sexually abused and suggested that her elder brother might have been to blame. However her father said it was normal for children in the same family to be interested in each other and stated that he had consulted other parents with children of both sexes who had agreed with this. Both parents gave the impression that since the boy was now away in boarding school the whole matter was solved. Without their co-operation the case could not be pursued.

Although the evidence is sparse, and more careful research on sibling incest is needed, what information there is suggests that Fox's explanation is untenable. The evidence shows that the majority of adults surveyed have indulged in some form of sexual play; there is little to indicate that their playmates are their siblings. Given the differences in male and female sexual development and sexual attitudes that the rather sparse research on the subject seems to indicate, it is likely that even brothers and sisters who are close in age are rather different in their sexual development, so that their sexual curiosity is satisfied with friends and age-mates, not each other. There is nothing to suggest that in British society brothers and sisters are kept strictly apart for fear of incestuous relationships, which might encourage sexual attraction between them. However, they are expected to be given separate bedrooms at puberty. Yet one father was inclined to believe that sexual interest between brothers and sisters was perfectly normal and was unconcerned. Being brought up together does not seem to be the reason why brothers and sisters do not engage in sexual relationships. Incest between brother and sister, while uncommon, is not the rarity that Fox's hypothesis would predict or that popular wisdom would suggest. The CSA Unit cases suggest that it only rarely takes place by mutual consent between equals.

The general assumption that brothers and sisters are equals is unrealistic. They may be of the same generation and all subject to the same parental authority but differences of age among them, which entail differences of sexual development and of strength, generate inequalities among them. In addition, the status which their gender identity as boys or girls assigns them may differentiate among them, giving the boys higher status than their sisters. The relationship between an older brother and younger sister is so unequal that sexual activities between them resemble the sexual abuse of a child by an adult.

Sibling Violence

Violence as a part of sexual behaviour between siblings, that makes the relationship quite unlike the popular conceptions of it, appears in the retrospective accounts of women in self-selected surveys, such as that undertaken for *19* magazine, or for the BBC as a preliminary to the ChildWatch programme. The perpetrators of the abuse are brothers who are older, sometimes consideraby older, than the victim and they may use force to ensure her compliance. The women quoted at the head of this chapter, who took part in the BBC postal survey, were about six when they were abused by a teenage brother. Cases where there is a difference of ten years are not uncommon: the girls in two of the cases already mentioned were six and four years old and their brothers 16 and 13 respectively. Such experiences are clearly abusive. In these cases the sexual activities appear to be undertaken in no spirit of love. The older sibling may be experimenting but with an uncomprehending and unwilling partner. These are traumatizing experiences, generating fear, misery or hatred in the victims; the victims make it clear they felt bullied and exploited.

It is probable that this type of incest or incestuous abuse is rather common, although the evidence is equivocal. Surveys of adults asking them to record their childhood experiences regularly show much higher rates of sexual contact between brothers and sisters than the figure produced by either the courts or the child protection agencies. Finkelhor's survey of Boston students shows it to be by far the commonest form of childhood sexual experience for girls. Of the women who reported sexual abuse in his survey, 39 per cent or nearly two-fifths blamed their brothers, and so did 12 per cent of the male students.[21] The BBC national survey found more respondents who claimed to have been sexually abused by their brothers than by any other close relative except fathers.[22] On the other hand, ChildLine's report for three months of 1987 showed that only 6 per cent of the sexual abuse reported by girls to them and only 2 per cent of that reported by boys was perpetrated by their brothers. It is difficult to draw any definite conclusions about its prevalence from the contradictory evidence.

However, it is unlikely that the respondents were referring to consensual activities in which they were willing partners. Both the BBC surveys, postal and national, asked questions referring explicitly to sexual abuse. In both surveys, too, the brothers and sisters who are involved in incestuous abuse are not close in age. The Boston survey defined as sexual abuse activities where the perpetrator was five years older than the victim, ignoring those cases where the two were closer in age. All these cases, then, were instances of sexual activities initiated by an older brother; the probability that there had been coercion was high.

Two cases of this nature that occurred among the rather few cases in the hospital CSA Unit are reminders that sibling relationships can include negative emotions such as jealousy, anger and hatred. In one of them two little girls of five and seven were alleged to have been 'molested' by their half-brother, aged nearly 16. He had been attending a child guidance clinic to which his mother first reported the incidents. In the second case, another teenage boy, aged 15, was alleged to have sexually assaulted his half-sisters, aged six and seven. The girls were behaving in a sexually provocative way which made it clear that they had been abused. Their brother denied it; his stepfather was recorded as somewhat over-eager to put the blame on his step-son. His own behaviour with his daughters added to the suspicions in the therapists' minds, but the identity of the abuser was never clearly established as the girls' parents separated. The girls stayed with their mother and their half-brother was taken into care where he could have treatment for a psychiatric illness. His mother had declared to the court that she could not have him at home because she could not control him and none of their relatives would have him with them. In both cases there was a background of divorce and violence, with the boys, as the eldest children, having perhaps borne the brunt of the effects of the instabilities of their home background. Both boys were violent and aggressive and the assaults seem to have been quite as much punitive as sexual in intent.

The study of rape has shown that anger and hatred can motivate sexual assault. This knowledge is often excluded when incest is considered, although some authorities, such as Finkelhor, have remarked on the element of anger and aggression in American cases where children have been abused by brothers.[23] The brothers are almost all older, sometimes a good deal older, and there is an atmosphere of bullying, with the use of force quite common. This account from a woman who filled in the BBC preliminary postal questionnaire is typical of the British cases in many ways:

> I was the sixth of seven children. My father left home when I was about five years old. I remember him making me feel very loved but not much more about him. After my father left my mother didn't bother with us at all. When I was six years old

my three elder brothers took me into their bedroom and made
me take off my clothes and they took off theirs. I had to touch
them and let them touch me. I felt very frightened because two
held me down and one kept touching me. I told my mother
and she didn't believe me. She sent me to live with Mrs Bates.
After a year I started going home for weekends and everything
was all right until I was nine years old and it all started again
and now I was forced to have sex with them. I told my sister
and her husband as well as my mother and they told me I was
only trying to cause trouble. This only made things worse as
my sister's husband then started saying if I let my brothers do
things to me why wouldn't I let him and instead of helping
me, he joined in. They hurt me so much. This went on until I
was 15.

This case history also reveals other significant features which
added to the girl's vulnerability. They occur in other forms in other
case histories. Either the mother or the father are actually or
effectively absent and not available to protect the weaker children:
'after my father left, my mother didn't bother with us at all.'
Where they are present, they may not redress the balance between
siblings or protect their daughters and younger children. It is
common for parents to have favourites among their children,
supporting them against accusations, or alternatively children they
are unsympathetic to, whom they disbelieve. The relationship
between the siblings thus depends a good deal on the behaviour and
attitudes of the parents.

In addition, boys are often favoured above their sisters, particularly
by mothers; not uncommonly a mother is not prepared to listen to a
girl's complaint against her brother, or the girl believes she will not.
Sometimes a brother will say that their parents or mother will not
believe her or that they will blame her rather than him. On
occasions telling may have painful consequences: in the case just
cited, it seems likely that the mother believed her daughter's
complain but the little girl was sent away to live with someone else
as though she were to blame. Consequently, when it happened
again, she did not tell her mother. One social worker, referring a
case to the CSA Unit, one in which the three girls had all been
abused, either by their father or their two elder brothers, remarked:

'Mrs Williams has clearly decided in favour of her husband and the boys rather than the girls.'

In other cases, the results may be even more shocking to the child, as in the following case history:

> I remember when I was about five to five and a half years old, my brother who was then about 14 or 15 years old pulled my underwear down and started playing with my privates. I thought I'd better tell my mum, all she did was rant and rave at me then take a belt to my backside. So when he did it again I didn't say anything so when I was about seven years old and he started to do more than just touch I was too frightened to tell her. Before I was seven and a half years old he had full sexual intercourse [he was then 16 or 17]. Luckily he was a small man or I think he could have done a bit of damage.

In such households it is clear that the girls take second place to their brothers.

The Abuse of Boys by Siblings

So far this chapter has considered mainly girls who have been the victims of incest or incestuous abuse perpetrated by their brothers. However homosexual relations between brothers are also reported, although very few between sisters. Surprising numbers of the former type of cases were revealed in the Boston survey by Finkelhor. Only one man in the BBC national survey claimed to have been abused by his brother, but since only 12 men in all admitted to having been abused this figure can hardly be taken as significant. *Woman* magazine's second survey, of the male relatives and friends and husbands of its readers, refers, but without detail, to abuse by older brothers and gives one or two instances of abuse by older sisters. One is worth quoting because it reverses the normal pattern: the man was then aged 12 and his sister 16. Jerry, a civil servant, is recorded as reporting: 'At first I wasn't forced into it . . . Towards the end she started bullying and teasing me. She became too rough with me, as if despising me and demeaning me, making me do things I didn't want to do. It just felt so wrong and bad.'[24]

There was only one instance of brother–brother sexual relations among the cases in the hospital child sexual abuse unit. Twin brothers of 14 were referred. One of them, Terry, was alleged to be acting as a male prostitute; the other, Guy, had been sexually abused but it was not clear whether this was sexual experimentation with his twin or the action of a man to whom Terry had introduced him. The boys were very attached to one another and had been left alone a lot. Their parents were divorced but before that they had led a hectic social life with little time for the boys. (During therapy their father revealed that he had had a similar experience which he had kept secret from everyone until that time.) There were also reports that they watched pornographic videos. The police prosecuted a man who admitted abusing Terry. At the follow-up two years later, Terry was still disturbed and had been in trouble again for prostitution and absconding from the children's home where he had been living. In this case, the element of exploitation occurred in Terry's relation with the older man, which probably preceded his activities with Guy. Accounts by adult men recorded in American studies indicate that when boys are involved as victims in an abusive relationship with a brother it is an older brother, which is not surprising, given the advantage of physical strength that age confers.

The impression left by these case histories is of the essential *in*equality of children in one household: there are inequalities of age, of strength and size, and of gender. The myth of mutual consent which underlies the generally accepted picture of sibling incest implies that each child has the possibility of participating or not. Clearly in these families, as in most others, children are not equal in that sense.

Parental Authority and Sibling Incest

Children are, ideally, equally subject to parental authority. Parents, particularly mothers, are expected to intervene; relationships between the children are normally controlled by parental authority. The mother of the girl in the first case history separated her from her brothers by placing her with a foster mother. In the second, the victim's mother clearly subscribed to the idea that girls are responsible for their own abuse; the way in which she reacted to the abuse merely made it more certain that she would not hear about it of it continued, as it did. In a case among those that have been cited a woman brought her two children for professional advice when she found them sexually experimenting. In many other cases, no doubt, intervention by either parent stops abuse and nothing is ever heard of it.

Parents' authority can influence their children in more negative ways as well. The hospital CSA Unit cases contain many instances of sexual involvement between brothers and sisters which are not merely the result of neglect, lack of supervision from parents or ineffective intervention but of prior sexual abuse by their father or stepfather. In fact, more than half the hospital cases of sexual involvement between brothers and sisters or brothers implicate the children's parents. On 19 July 1988 there was a report in a national newspaper that the Court of Appeals had heard a case involving allegations against 15 adults of abusing 17 children aged up to 12. The President of the High Court Family Division was reported as saying that 'The adults and the children were all members of what may be described as an extended family and its associates.'[25] Cases involving multiple abusers and multiple victims form a type of case which is largely neglected in the literature, although a study by Smith and Israel in the United States provides confirmation that the pattern is found there too.[26] These cases imply that the sexual exploitation of young girls may be learned from example or occur as a reaction to the abuser's own sexual abuse.

Smith and Israel found that in nearly a third of the 25 cases of sibling incest they studied, father–daughter incest had preceded it; in nearly half, the abusing sibling had previously been abused by an adult. Similar antecedent abuse is shown in many of the hospital CSA Unit cases as well. Alison, aged 17, went with her uncle to the police with allegations against her father who had been having intercourse with her for three years. Shortly after that her twin brother told an aunt that he too had been abused by his father and that he and his sister had slept together. Annie, who had been placed in care when she was 13, told her foster parents that she had been sexually abused by her father and then her older brother for several years before she came into care. Richard was referred to the hospital for the sexual abuse of his two younger sisters and a neighbour's daughter; it transpired later that his stepfather had sexually abused Richard as well as his sisters. In four other cases there was multiple abuse of children of the household by one or more of the adult men living there and sexual activities between brothers and sisters.

In all, there were 15 households referred to in the CSA Unit cases in which there was either sibling incest or incestuous activity among the children. In six of them there was no clear evidence that the father or stepfather had sexually abused either the brother or sister, but in only two was there no suspicion that prior abuse by some adult had not occurred. One of these has already been referred to; in both there were particular stresses on the adolescent and the abuse was angry and an expression of jealousy. In three of the other four cases there was evidence that suggested a sexual involvement by the father or stepfather with the girl; the fourth was the case involving twin brothers which has already been mentioned. In the rest of the cases, that is, in three-fifths (nine) of all the cases of sibling incest, there were clear allegations or admissions that the sexual activities within the household had begun with the adult men.

The following case history given at more length is an example of these complex cases and shows the sequence of relationships that may develop:

Mr Hill was the night porter in a hotel where his wife was a chambermaid. Their five children, two boys and three girls, ranged from 19 to 11 when the case was referred to the hospital unit in 1982. Mr Hill's incestuous abuse of his two eldest daughters had been discovered by their eldest son, Patrick, in 1979, when the girls were 11 and nine respectively. He told his mother but she was unable to believe him. After that Patrick, then aged about 16, began sexual assaults on the older of the two girls, Emma, who continued to be abused by her father as well. In 1982 the whole matter was reported to the police by Mrs Hill's sister-in-law who was staying with them. Mr Hill's daughter by his first marriage, by then grown-up and married, then revealed that she had also been abused by her father when she was 14. Mr Hill was convicted and imprisoned. Some time later Patrick went to the police with an accusation of incest between his younger brother, Simon, and Emma. However, when questioned by the police, Emma, who was fond of Simon, denied the accusation against him, although she agreed she had said this to Patrick; but, she said, it had actually been Patrick who had abused her. He subsequently admitted it and was put on probation.

In this, as in the other cases, the sexual activities of the children, which culminated in sibling incest, began only after the abuse of two of them by their father. In some of the other cases both the boys and the girls had suffered abuse by their father. The breach of the sibling taboo in these cases seems to be consequent on, and the results of, an initial breach by the father.

As we have seen, it is not uncommon for perpetrators of the sexual abuse of children to have been abused themselves as children. The early history of abusers contain episodes which resemble events in the lives of abused boys. Dan Grimshaw, the abuser of his daughter and stepdaughters whose case was described in the last chapter, was the son and grandson of men who had been convicted of rape and incest and subjected their children to fearful beatings. It seems not unlikely that in many cases of brother–sister incest the same mechanisms are at work. The boys are identifying with their abuser; they are only different from those who later in life abuse their own children in that the repetition of the pattern is relatively immediate. Anal intercourse is seen by men as symbolic of domination and is understood as humiliating by abused boys, who often express their distress at being made to feel weak and helpless.[27] Many worry over their sexual identity. A sexual assault on a sister may seem to wipe out the humiliation and establish masculinity beyond doubt.

Other adolescent boys, like Patrick in the case history given above, are reacting to knowledge of a sexual relationship between their father and sister. In the case of the Hills, none of the relationships were violent and the father was not physically abusive, but in several of the others the daily life of the household was full of unpredictable rages and the unbridled use by the father of his superior strength to enforce his will or punish those who flouted it. The effect of paternal violence can be very varied, however. A father in one of the CSA Unit cases made an angry scene at a hospital meeting, insisting that his daughter apologize for causing him to be tried for incest. He had abused both her and her brother but he demanded that she accept that it was her fault; when she was silent he stormed out. Yet there seemed to have been little violence in the brother–sister relationship; their parents had been separated and they were each other's only source of comfort for a long time. One brother, his sister reported, abused her when he was angry with their father; other adolescent boys showed the same aggressiveness as their fathers in their attitudes and behaviour.

Whether there is a great deal of physical violence or not, boys who are abused themselves or know that their sisters have been abused by their father, have been given a practical lesson by an adult in the association between masculine power and sex. Where a father/stepfather abuses a boy, his power is associated with a difference in generation and adult male strength. In seeking a sexual relationship with a sister, the boy is also exploiting the power associated with masculinity and, usually, age. Girls in cases of sibling incest are almost always younger and hence physically weaker than their brothers. Where they have also been abused by a father or stepfather they are confused, unable to assert themselves, or resigned to what has become normal in relations with the males of the family. The sexualized behaviour they have been taught to use with them may even seem to be an encouragement of their brothers. Often they take second place in the family to their brothers and parental authority may be no protection for them. They are easily exploited by their brothers, who use them as a means to assert their superior masculine status and, perhaps, wipe out their own unhappy memories.

In cases where there are multiple sexual relations between the children and one or more adults as well as among the children themselves, the sibling incest seems to be considered merely a part of the overall disorganization within the household. Such cases appear to exemplify the anthropologist Malinowski's assumption that one breach of the incest taboo results in the collapse of them all. Yet it seems more accurate to see them as cases where the children are initiated early into sexual activities by an adult, usually a man who lives with them; their subsequent behaviour appears to be attributable to an imitation of adult behaviour, to the effect of an adult abuse of authority rather than to any display of spontaneous mutual attraction. But earlier events of abuse by adults are not searched for or, if volunteered, are given little attention.

It is not uncommon to find, in the background of men who abuse children, an early history of sexual abuse where they themselves were the victims. Some boys react to their abuse with reactions similar to the girls; they lack self-confidence, have no sense of their own worth and, in addition, have added anxiety about their own sexual identities. Some of them then later go on to abuse their own or other children. The only man in the BBC national survey to accuse his father of having had intercourse with him as a boy also reported himself for three counts of sexually abusing a child. In such cases there seems to be an identification with the original abuser, but it takes the form of an adult/child relationship when the former victim is himself adult. Other boys, however, may react with more immediate sexual activity and this may take the form of sibling incest. More research into the effect of antecedents in the histories of abusing boys is badly needed.

Sibling incest is little studied, partly because the greatest threat to children is seen to come from adult men, whether these are father figures or unrelated, and in addition sibling incest is seen either as childish or a matter of mutual consent. There is a dearth of reliable information on most aspects of sibling incest and the incestuous abuse of children by older step- and foster brothers and sisters. The hospital cases from which these conclusions are drawn are very few and cannot be said to be representative of all cases of sibling incest. Nor are they a large proportion of the total number of cases. However, many of the elements which can be seen in them are mirrored in the much larger number of retrospective reports by women of their abusive experiences with brothers. They show that the reality of sibling incest is neither childish play nor doomed love.

The two forms of incest that have been considered in this chapter and the last seemed at the outset to be very different. Actual cases of incest as distinct from stereotypes of them show that the two forms of incest, paternal and sibling, have much in common. The most obvious feature that they share is the use of coercion. This may be the exercise of superior status, using the prestige of seniority, of age or generation but it also takes the form of physical force exercised or threatened by adult men and adolescents. Their superior strength is a quality that gets little recognition, yet it may need very little demonstration of this physical power to convince a child that it is impossible to resist. What is different in the two forms of sexual abuse is the social definition of the abuser's position, as father or brother, and it is this which prevents us seeing sibling incest for what it often is. Like father–daughter incest, incest between brother and sister must be seen in the context of actual relationships and in the light of how households are actually organized: the use of rooms which makes privacy possible, the normal routine of activities which includes the predictable absences of adults and the patterns of where and when the various members of the household go to bed and get up. There may be a conflict of interests between members of the group, as when a father or brother wishes to use a daughter or son, a sister or brother, for his own sexual purposes against his or her wishes. The power of the different individuals to obtain what they want against other members' wishes or interests is a vital factor in the actual relationships in any household, not just those in which the force is misused.

Discussions of 'the family' usually ignore this vital ingredient, especially among those who are its junior members, the children. The social roles of brother and sister make them subordinate to parents, who have the right to intervene between their children and are expected to do so. Ideally, parents should be responsible for maintaining proper relations among their children, including their equality. In the actual day-to-day life of the household, the social value that masculinity is afforded in society generally may give brothers a position superior to their sisters. A difference in age as well endows them with the physical power to enforce the authority this gives them. Seniority of age and generation affects the position of women and girls as well. On rare occasions an older sister may exploit her seniority, although girls are normally taught to be more maternal to younger siblings. Where a mother is concerned, the growth of her sons weakens her ability to enforce their obedience to her; she may not be willing to put her paternal authority to the test with powerful near-adult sons and, as some of the cases quoted in this chapter make clear, there may be no one else in the household who offers the weaker children any protection.

Feminists have already pointed out[28] that those who abuse children sexually, whatever the social identity they are given, have the power to coerce.

However, many of these writers have been so concerned with the power of fathers and the power dimension of relations between adults that they have failed to see that relative to children, all adults and most adolescent boys are stronger and have the potential to abuse their strength. Children are vulnerable to men and to women, particularly when they are young which is why one must expect to find female abusers as well as male. Adolescents also far outweigh children in physical power, social prestige and experience. These strengths relative to children are found in many individuals, inside and outside their homes, although the circumstances of domestic life define the area of their greatest vulnerability. Although their homes are not the only areas of socially organized activities where children may be abused they are the most common. The privacy of the family and the unquestioned dogmas defining family relationships as protective hide the fact that the organization of domestic life may also provide opportunities for this kind of exploitation of the weak.

The unequal distribution of power among individual members of a household is rendered invisible by referring to it as a family. The idealized, partial nature of this concept also makes it impossible for many people to accept the reality of the sexual abuse of children at home. To maintain this ideal of the family as a picture of reality, the main recourse must be to deny that children are abused and to attack those who imply the contrary. But even those that do accept the possibility of children's being sexually abused may be influenced by the ideas contained in the dogma of the family. Their roles may be to support the family and their intervention is required when parents are manifestly unable to cope; their information is therefore biased towards seeing children only as part of a 'family problem' with the parents as part of it. While there is undoubtedly evidence that the most common relationship within which abuse may happen is that of a man and a child in his own home, the influence of the social ideal may make the protectors of children unwilling or unable to see the victims of sexual abuse in the context of children's participation in a social world which is centred on their home but not always confined to it.

The relative indifference to sibling incest which is to be found among clinicians, social scientists undertaking research and the general public, as well as the romantic myth of sibling incest, serve to hide the unacceptable realities of sibling incest in the same way as the myth of *Lolita*, Nabokov's novel, in which a knowing and nubile adolescent seduces her stepfather, obscured the facts of father–daughter incest. Just as genetic connection between parent and child is believed to entail close and loving relations that prevent paternal incest, so the ideas of sibling incest held in the West constitute a myth: in this case, that growing up together in one household, that is under the same parental supervision, turns childish sexual exploration into mature sexuality and establishes the incest taboo. The widely held notions that sibling incest is the result of sexual immaturity or of genealogical ignorance imply that the role of parents is to restrain the impulses of children and instil into them the necessary knowledge of social mores, including the ban on incest.

The distinction drawn between incest and the sexual abuse of children, both by the law and in public opinion, serves to reinforce the difference between relationships which are defined as family ones and all others. The general concept of fatherhood as a 'natural' quality which makes a man protective does not prevent men abusing their natural daughters. The relatively high proportion of stepfathers who are abusers cannot be attributed to the lack of a genetic connection with their victims but to membership of a particular kind of household. This draws attention to the other factors, physical and material, which affect individuals living together and which affect the way 'real' fathers and 'real' brothers behave. The concepts which define the family select for emphasis those features that define and give legitimacy to the expected household pattern and ignore the circumstances of individual lives, the sources of power available to members of a household and the possibilities of exploitation this provides. The disjunction between the ideal family and the complexities of actual household structures focuses attention on the mythical, or, in some writers' terms, 'ideological' qualities of the concept of 'the family'. However, to describe it as a myth or an ideology is not sufficient to explain its influence; the next chapter will have to consider the components of the ideal in an attempt to explain its persistence and the strength of its hold on people's thinking.

Notes

1 S. K. Weinberg, *Incest Behaviour* (Citadel, New York, 1955), p. 79. The section of the book on sibling incest is on pp. 73–85.
2 R. Fox, *The Red Lamp of Incest*, (Hutchinson, London, 1980), and an earlier paper, 'Sibling incest', *British Journal of Sociology*, 13 (1962).
3 *Red Lamp*, p. 24.
4 Bentovim and Vizard, 'Sexual abuse', p. 2.
5 J. Elias and P. Gebhard, 'Sexuality and sexual learning in childhood', in

R. S. Rogers (ed.), *Sexual Education – Rationale and Reaction* (Cambridge University Press, Cambridge, 1969), cited in ibid.

6 Bentovim and Vizard, 'Sexual abuse', pp. 7–8. But see the discussion of the difficulties of assessing young children's knowledge and understanding in C. Henshall and J. McGuire, 'Gender development', in P. Light and M. Richards (eds), *Children of Social Worlds* (Polity, Cambridge, 1986). This book is an indication of a changed approach in new studies of child development. This collection of essays written by a number of scholars engaged in research in the field demonstrates a view of children's development as a process of interaction with adults.

7 Ibid., p. 8.

8 D. Sanders, *The Woman Book on Men* (Sphere, London, 1985), pp. 172–3.

9 A. Kinsey, W. B. Pomeroy and C. E. Martin, *Sexual Behaviour in the Human Male* (Saunders, Philadelphia, 1948), p. 157.

10 *19* magazine, May 1983.

11 A. Kinsey, W. B. Pomeroy and C. E. Martin, *Sexual Behaviour in the Human Female* (Saunders, Philadelphia, 1953), p. 168.

12 The question of the age at which a boy normally becomes capable of full sexual intercourse has not been established. The law puts it at 14 but there is evidence that it may occur earlier than that. See the case of Sally, impregnated by a boy of 13, referred to in A. Elton, 'Treatment methods and techniques', in Bentovim et al., *Child Sexual Abuse*, p. 193.

13 Kinsey et al., *Sexual Behaviour in the Human Female*, p. 687. See also J. H. Gagnon and W. Simon, *Sexual Conduct: The Social Sources of Human Sexuality* (Aldine, Chicago, 1973), excerpted in M. Brake (ed.), *Human Sexual Relations: A Reader* (Penguin, Harmondsworth, 1982).

14 See J. Sarsby, *Romantic Love and Society: Its Place in the Modern World* (Penguin, Harmondsworth, 1983), especially pp. 99–112.

15 Weinberg, *Incest Behaviour*, p. 78.

16 *Observer*, 4 August 1974 and 2 November 1975.

17 *South London Press*, 30 September 1986. Various inconsistencies make one suspect that the full story was somewhat more complicated and equivocal than it appeared to be in the newspaper report.

18 Sanders, *Woman Book of Love and Sex*, pp. 172–3.

19 Gorry, 'Incest', p. 24.

20 Ibid., p. 24.

21 Finkelhor, *Sexually Victimised Children*, p. 89.

22 *ChildLine – The First Year*, report for 1987 issued by ChildLine, London, unpublished.

23 Finkelhor, *Sexually Victimised Children*, pp. 90–2.

24 Sanders, *Woman Book on Men*, p. 166.

25 *Independent*, 19 July 1988.
26 H. Smith and E. Israel, 'Sibling incest: the study of the dynamics of 25 cases', *Child Abuse and Neglect*, 11(1) (1987).
27 Gagnon and Simon, *Sexual Conduct*, excerpted in Brake (ed.), *Human Sexual Relations*, p. 205.
28 See, for example, Herman, *Father–Daughter Incest*, Russell, *One Secret Trauma*, Nelson, *Incest*.

7 Sexual Abuse at Home

The family is normally regarded as something sacred; incest, like patricide or matricide, is sacrilege.

A. R. Radcliffe-Brown, *African Systems of Kinship and Marriage*

I hate all the people I grew up with, as far as I am concerned I don't have a family, they are just people whose lives I had to pass through to get to Adulthood.   London woman aged about 30

The public concern with the sexual abuse of children as well as the vigorous efforts to deny that it happens are both reactions to violations which threaten the myth of the family. As the British anthropologist Radcliffe-Brown pointed out as long ago as 1950: 'Incest . . . is not merely disruptive of the social life of a single family, it is disruptive of the whole system of moral and religious sentiments on which the social order rests.'[1] His point was reiterated more recently by the American anthropologist, D. M. Schneider: incest, he wrote, 'stands for the transgression of certain major cultural values, the values of a particular pattern of relations among persons'; it is 'desecration'.[2]

At first sight, these conclusions appear to be at variance with the relative indifference to the idea of incest which, it was claimed earlier, characterized British ideas. The distinction between incest and other sexual offences, found not only in the criminal law but also in public opinion, reflects what is believed to be the rarity of the former. This is one of the reasons for general indifference. The other is to be found in a cluster of other beliefs which surround the notion of incest. Incest is normally associated with forbidden marriages and inbreeding, which allows the assumption that incest concerns sexual relations between mature individuals. It is the idea of sexual relations between an adult and a child that provokes serious, even violent, condemnation. The distinction between the idea of incest and that of the sexual abuse of a child is maintained by the common belief that a genetic connection between parent and child is a guarantee that the relationship will be one of trust and care. It is then axiomatic that incest cannot involve children.

Information on the sexual abuse of children has made it undeniable that incest involving children does occur. Fathers may commit incest with daughters who are quite young, or abuse them sexually; brothers may force their sisters into sexual activities that are very different from the kind of sexual experimentation that is regarded with a certain tolerance. Moreover, as we have seen, incest and the sexual abuse of an unrelated child are very similar. The age and sex of the victims and the nature of the sexual activities which occur do not show differences that can be attributed to the relationship between abuser and victim. The fact that people may also use 'incest' to refer to all sexual abuse in the home shows that it is domestic intimacy involving adults and children that is significant. It was the recognition that incest involved small children not adolescent girls, rather than the idea of incest itself, which contributed to the public furore over the Cleveland affair. Whether individuals were outraged at what had happened to children in their own homes or supported the idea that innocent parents were being accused, their reactions to the issues raised there show that 'desecration' is not too strong a word.

It is the idea of the family that is desecrated by incest. In Western societies, 'the family' is an obvious example of what Schneider means by a 'major cultural value'. The term carries heavy moral overtones and arouses strong feelings. This widespread and deep attachment to the concept indicates that it involves key values and beliefs. The concept of 'the family' encapsulates and symbolizes these more taken-for-granted assumptions. They do not necessarily combine in a clear or coherent set of ideas; like many other key cultural values in other societies, 'the family' contains multiple ambiguities, even contradictions, within the whole complex of notions it represents. The multiple meanings evoked by the term are an indication of its fundamental symbolic nature.

To begin with, 'the family' is thought of as a traditional institution, that is social behaviour which is intrinsic to 'our way of life', a part of national identity. Other societies may live differently but to most British people the family is the foundation of their social life. This implies that 'the family' is a social institution particularly characteristic of certain peoples, that is of Western

Europe.[3] But the family is also held to be the institutionalization of a natural unit, the result of the biological process of re-creating the physical individuals who will be the succeeding generations and of bringing them up to be members of society. In this version, parental behaviour and feelings are instinctive, based on protective altruism, part of the genetic connection between adults and 'their' offspring. The implications of this view are that since human reproduction is everywhere the same, the family is also a universal social group. 'Family life' is often seen as the basis of society, which is then thought of as a collection of 'families'; the independent family then may be described as the building block from which society is built.

In apparent contradiction to this, the family is also opposed to other social institutions such as the workplace, or political life. This difference is expressed in the contrast often drawn between 'the family' and 'the outside world' of work and of political life embodied in the state, both of which exercise control over the lives of individuals. 'The family' may seem a haven from a world of competition and rivalry: at home in it, people are relieved from the stresses of 'public life', they are free to 'be themselves'. 'Home' is a secure retreat under the individual's own control; the proverb, 'the Englishman's home is his castle', expresses these ideas. It follows from this set of ideas that a strong and independent family may be seen as the guarantee of personal freedom against the intervention of the collective powers of the state, or as the support of each individual in a hostile and competitive world. Yet if 'the family' is private and the rest of society consists of 'public' institutions, the family cannot be the basic unit from which society as a whole is constructed, for it is qualitatively different from the other institutions of society.[4] However, these logical contradictions in the various ideas that are held about it, often by the same individuals, do not weaken the general acceptance that the family is fundamental to social life.

The influence of this image of domestic life has been profound and widespread. It is to be found in political speeches, moral exhortations and in everyday conversation. It has also affected academic thinking. Although there has long been recognition that most families do not fit the ideal pattern, many sociologists have studied 'the family' without questioning the nature of what they are studying. Some earlier anthropologists sought to demonstrate that the family was a universal, because a natural, social unit.[5] Although their efforts were heavily criticized within the discipline, the concept of the family has continued to be used in studying other peoples whose way of living is different from those who claim 'the family' as the basis of theirs. It has even influenced the study of animal behaviour. The concept of the family forms the basis of the psychological disciplines. In practical affairs, concern for the family appears in the institutions, public and private, which exist to support and maintain an approximation to the ideal; for example, the training of social workers makes the protection of 'the family' a central priority.

Family therapy, the form used in the hospital CSA Unit I studied, also seems to be based on the concept. The approach offers an explanation of the sexual abuse of children in terms of the distortion of relationships within particular families.[6] The implication is that it is the whole 'family' that is responsible, as though the system were a malfunctioning machine and the sexual abuse of children its faulty product. The parts of the machine are relationships between the positions in a 'family'; malfunctioning in one affects the others. However, family systems therapists usually[7] consider the relationships among a set of individuals living in the same house, a household, and measure them against an image of the system as it should 'work'. In doing this they assimilate a household to the ideal model of the family. The structure of the healthy family to which those with serious malfunctions are implicitly compared owes more to the social ideal than is often recognized. Yet the relationships among people living together cannot be understood solely in terms of the ideal of 'the family', as I have argued, for although the practice is consistent with general usage, general usage leaves much out of account.

The ambiguity in the meaning of the term 'the family' and the proliferation of contradictory images associated with it are indications that the concept is not a unitary one but a cluster of ideas which represent in condensed form a range of assumptions about the world. They include moral dogmas about why certain persons (parents) *should* be obeyed, rather than descriptions of the power they dispose of to ensure that their commands are followed. What is left out of the ideal of the family is as significant as what is included: it ignores the physical, legal and economic powers of the adults and, despite the reproductive function the family is deemed to serve, it largely ignores the children except as products of a marriage.

It is important to remember that the family is an ideal model of what domestic groups should be, not a description of their general or normal features. While the terms 'family' and 'household' are commonly used interchangeably, they have different implications. In order to understand the sexual abuse of children in their own homes, it has been necessary to emphasize the distinction between the ideal of 'the family' and forms of 'the household'. So far it has been possible to do this without examining the ideal more carefully than was needed to show the difference between what certain relationships are thought to be and the very different forms they can assume. Now, however, we should consider it more closely.

The internal structure of the family is based on two distinctions, each of which sustains a form of superiority and justifies the exercise of authority. The division between the generations gives parents authority over children and the distinction between genders gives males superiority over females. Both pairs of categories link social roles with 'natural' differences: of maturity in one case and sexual difference in the other. Individuals classed together are perceived as the same and are therefore equal: parents are equal partners and children are equally their dependants. The intersection of the two paired concepts establishes the various family roles. Each of these positions implies a relationship between generations or between genders: to speak of a mother implies the existence of a daughter or son, to refer to a daughter involves her parents. The adult couple are both parents and spouses. The whole set of relationships together makes up 'the family'. Partly as a result of the rising rate of divorce and partly because of feminist writing, most attention has been given recently to gender relationships. In fact, the salient distinction on which family roles are based appears to be that of generation not gender. Although parents usually treat their daughters differently from their sons, male children do not have either the authority or the actual powers of men. Any analysis of the values which support the ideal of the family must start from its generally accepted basis and *raison d'être*: the relation between parents and children.

Parenthood, Altruism and Society

The authority of parents is based on their protective nurturant role. The parent is the essential symbol of altruism in Western culture;

parents are assumed to put the interests of their children before everything else, including their own needs and wishes. This altruism is believed to be innate in parenthood; the self-sacrifice of parents is seen as 'natural'. It is the prime example and, by implication, origin of the mutual help and loyalty of people who are related. There may be an explicit contrast with relationships 'outside' the family, were self-interest, competition and rivalry are seen as the norm.

But parenthood is also perceived as a matter of controlling the impulses of the young, training them to respect rules and become members of society. The view of human beings as having an essentially egotistical, animal nature, which is restrained by the requirements of social living is reflected in this notion that children must be taught to participate in social life. In effect children may represent the raw material of society, parents the finished product.[8] In former times disciplining children was seen as a social duty which parents would find difficult because of their natural affection for them.[9] Although the idea of a beating as good for a child would find little general support today, parents are still entitled to use corporal punishment on their children.

Children are recognized as socially and physically dependent; they are also expected to be subordinate to their parents and to obey them. While parents represent the altruistic self-controlled adult, children are expected to be selfish, competitive and lacking in self-control or consideration for others because they are not yet fully competent social beings. Children may thus serve as a model of qualities which are the direct opposite of those expected of adult members of society. Parental authority and guidance should teach them to share and to help each other and should give them examples of their gender-specific adult roles. The way the children 'turn out', their success or failure as adults, is attributed to their parents, provoking the praise or blame of other people. It is the essence of this process that a 'natural' human being is turned into a member of society, by parental control, which in the adult becomes self-control. Children are, so to speak, the material out of which social beings are constructed. To be a parent oneself is the mark of full adult status in Western societies, as in most others.

The family then is a microcosm of society. The picture above represents a Hobbesian view of humanity, in which parents as agents of society moderate the self-interested behaviour of natural human beings, their children; in both the family and society restraints on individual behaviour make living together possible. Yet the contrast between adult and child does not depend on this particular view of society. The opposite view that is associated with the name of Rousseau represents childhood as natural innocence, uncorrupted by society. It gives the terms of the opposition different contents but reflects the same basic idea: that children are not initially the social beings they become when they have undergone the process of 'bringing up' and have reached social maturity.

The roles of parents *vis-à-vis* children may also be differentiated by gender. The two aspects of parenthood, control and nurture, are seen in some contexts as pertaining to the gender of parents: fathers are the source of discipline and control, the link with wider social life and public affairs; mothers are the protective and nurturing parent, the provider of food and comfort. The characterization of their parenting roles is consistent with gender stereotypes which attribute more rational powers and control of their feelings to men than to women. Mothers are often accused of 'spoiling' their children by giving in too much to their demands, a failing which was noticed even in early modern England.[10] Mothers and fathers have different roles, although as parents both have authority, and as adults they may wield considerable power over their children, particularly when they are young. However, a mother loses her physical domination of her children as they grow older, whereas a father may be expected to retain it much longer. He also disposes of economic power over his dependants. Individual men and woman may, of course, behave in ways contrary to the social stereotypes; if they are very deviant they may be labelled unnatural. Paradoxically, however, the 'natural' mother or father is the individual whose behaviour approximates to a socially defined role, who controls his or her 'natural' selfish impulses and does what is best for their child.

The equality of children as dependants leaves out of account the superiority of brothers over sisters, the authority of relative seniority and also the differences in strength which are determined by age[11] and sex. The eldest child is often regarded as a subordinate authority, intermediate between parents and children, but the emphasis is more often placed on an ideal of equality among the children and mutual support of each other. As research has shown, the significance of gender differences have their effect on children very early; the treatment of boys and girls, by their parents, outside the household and in school, reflects the general social construction of masculinity as superior.[12] The rights of seniority and the relative physical strength of a male can make the relationship between brother and sister a totally unequal one. As the last chapter demonstrated, it is this unrecognized element of their relationship which may be responsible for the sexual abuse of a girl by her brother.

The exercise of parental authority and relations between parents and children are also modified in practice by the differences of gender. The variations in relations between parents and their children result from the different values society attributes to gender, but also from differences in the physical powers of males and females. Where father and daughter are concerned these two factors increase the inequality in their relationship and make the daughter doubly vulnerable; it is not really surprising that this is the most common form of incest. However, the growth of children may alter their relations with their parents. Many victims of sexual abuse which has started in early childhood find courage to tell someone as they grow older; often it is a boyfriend in whom a girl confides and who supports her when she does this. As a youth gets older he also becomes stronger physically and this may change his relationship to his parents. He may also benefit from the higher status of being a man. A mother's ability to enforce her authority over her son decreases as he grows to manhood, which may render her powerless to protect her daughter from him and, on rare occasions, even put her at risk herself. One case of mother–son incest reported by Gorry concerned a young man's brutal rape of his mother. This is a dramatic and violent example of the reversal of their respective powers.

In this complex of constructs, the role of father is the apex of the structure. It represents authority as a parent and as a man. A 'family man' is also the symbol of what it means to be fully adult, that is self-controlled in obedience to social norms. A man also exercises the greatest power in his household in that it is based not merely on his physical dominance but on his economic strength as wage-earner. In his role as head of the family, a phrase used less often today but not completely abandoned, a father is the representative of society. His public role as wage-earner and rep-resentative of the family in political and legal contexts supports his authority within it. The attribution of childlike qualities to women in many contexts lends additional authority to him as male parent. His combined authority as husband and father is based on his superior social understanding and particularly his ability to take responsibility for and protect the interests of his dependants. Male power and paternal authority reinforce each other.

The sexual abuse of a child is the negation of responsibility; it is an entirely self-interested act. In descriptions of sexual abuse, whether by a father, stepfather or brother, the main motivation appears to be the abuser's own gratification, whatever the accompanying emotions. It is pursued despite the victim's wishes, physical well-being or any attempts to resist. The disclosure that such selfish objectives are satisfied, in ruthless disregard of the child's feelings or welfare, by people whose attitudes and behaviour are assumed to be motivated by natural affection and protectiveness is one of its most socially disruptive features. If parents, who represent socially responsible adulthood, are seen to be merely pursuing their own selfish interests at the expense of those for whom they are responsible, then adults are as self-interested as children.

The evidence that children are abused by their parents casts doubts on the general belief that adults acquire an ability to exercise self-restraint in social life and that they display this altruism most strongly to their children. The regulation and continuity of social life rests on this vital quality and the corollary that its basic tenets can be transmitted in child-rearing. The distinction between human beings and animals is believed to be based on the presence or absence of culture, the language, knowledge, beliefs and codes of behaviour transmitted from generation to generation. This process assumes that adults are the finished product and are thus able to induct natural human beings, their children, into social life.[13]

The assumption that, among adults, it is men who are more rational by nature and possess more control of the personal emotions and desires that underlie breaches of social norms makes paternity the key symbol of ordered society. Paternity may be generally assumed to derive from a genetic connection between father and children, but in fact it is entirely socially constituted.[14] Maternity is visibly demonstrable, but paternity is not. In fact, fatherhood depends on a social mechanism which determines the paternity of children, that is, their legitimacy. Legitimate paternity is the result of marriage. Marriage entails the assignment to her husband of a woman's sexuality so that any children she bears are the legitimate offspring of her husband.[15] As Fortes puts it: 'Fatherhood is a creation of society, a social status marked out to serve, figuratively speaking, as the fount of the rule making and rule-following that is the basis of social organisation.'[16]

The incest taboo encapsulates this cluster of fundamental tenets which underlie not only 'the family' but many other aspects of Western society. The idea that it is instinctively followed supports the dogma that adulthood, parenthood and paternity are natural attributes of individuals. The corollary: that incest is only committed by those who are not fully social, because they are 'different', mad or bad, reinforces confidence in the taboo. It is not surprising therefore that the existence of incest is denied. The association of households with families ensures that the vulnerability of children to sexual abuse is also denied.

The Complicity of Women

Family roles are often referred to as though they described actual people; feelings and motives are attributed to mothers or brothers, for example, as though the individuals played only a single part in the family. In fact children may combine the roles of child and sibling, and adults are both husband and father or mother and wife. The tendency to talk about men and women instead of distinguishing between their roles as parents and as spouses obscures the fact that the two roles may conflict. This is particularly true for women: in their maternal role they are expected to protect their children but in the role of wife they are expected to show loyalty to a husband. Their two roles, as wives and mothers, may relate them to both abuser and victim; the disclosure that her child has been sexually abused by her husband poses a severe coflict of loyalties for a woman. Women do not always resolve these dilemmas in favour of the child; some of them choose to give priority to the role of wife rather than mother; others may be forced to do so.

As mothers, women have been accused of collusion in incest or the sexual abuse of their children.[17] This may be expressed either by arguing that mothers know about the abuse and keep silent, or in stating that they actively encourage it by absenting themselves from the house, making an opportunity for abuse to occur. The concern of family systems theorists to allocate some responsibility for the events of children's sexual abuse to women has been seen as implying that women should share the blame if their child is abused. Feminists have reacted strongly against these conclusions, arguing that they are an attempt to shift guilt from men on to their wives. They argue that women with violent husbands, who have grown up with the idea that to be a wife is a woman's main role in life, are powerless to control a husband who is really determined.[18] The earning capacity of women with children is low and often will not pay for child-care to allow lone mothers to take paid work. It is well known that many mothers are faced with poverty as the only likelihood if they leave their husbands. The children would suffer equally from the sudden diminution of household resources, so that a decision to ignore what is happening may not be an entirely selfish one. In addition, a woman whose absence from the house becomes an opportunity for her child's abuse by its father may have reasons to go out which resemble those of many other women who leave their children with no ill effects. She may be at work in order to supplement resources which are under the husband's control and where his allocation of them to her may not be reliable or sufficient. Alternatively, she may be shopping or visiting elderly relatives, both activities which are held to be women's tasks. Staying with the children while his wife goes out may be a man's sole contribution to the work of caring for the house and children. It may only be hindsight that shows that it was not safe to leave the children with their father, stepfather or brother. The feminist analysis thus looks behind the myth of family structure to the allocation of power in the household.

While this is an advance on earlier attempts to explain either incest or sexual abuse, it too has its limitations. In their indignation some feminists come close to arguing that women never know of the abuse and never have any responsibility, because they are always powerless. Where actual cases of children's sexual abuse are concerned, this is not so: the women in the cases in the hospital CSA Unit represent a series of individuals whose expressed feelings ranged across a wide spectrum. Some had walked out as soon as they found out what was happening and expressed furious anger;

the vengeful fantasies of some mothers of abused children about appropriate punishment for the offenders are described by the former Great Ormond Street therapist, J. Hildebrand.[19] There were mothers of patients in the CSA Unit cases who had not been able to understand or believe what their child was saying; others had suspected but done nothing, hoping that the problem would resolve itself. A few had participated in group sexual activities in which the children were involved.[20] These last cannot be absolved of all responsibility. But there are women too who know of a child's abuse and whose independent sources of finance make them better placed to act. Women are physically powerless relative to men and economically at a disadvantage; but they do not lack the capacity to act to protect their children. Women living in refuges for battered wives may reveal that their children had been sexually abused by the man who battered them.[21] We know little about how many marital breakdowns are provoked by the discovery of sexual abuse of the children, although there is anecdotal evidence, confirmed by the accounts of survivors, that this may appen. Allegations of sexual abuse may be made in disputes over custody and access; a study of 20 of such cases in America by Jones and Seig showed that 70 per cent of them were substantiated.[22] Although much greater publicity has been given to the state's role in removing children from their homes for their protection and 'breaking up the family', little has been heard of the action women take to protect their children that has the same effect.

Marriage, Sexual Relations and the Sexual Abuse of Children

Marriage is still critical to the way in which sexual relations are conceptualized. The Christian Churches' tenet that sexual relations outside marriage are sinful has probably disappeared except as a minority view but certain related attitudes have not. It is a basic assumption of Western societies that marriage transforms a relationship based on personal (i.e. sexual) attraction into a conjugal relationship which has other more permanent social functions: the bearing and rearing of children and the organization of domestic life. Sexual relationships outside marriage are seen as individual relationships, concerning personal feelings and therefore private affairs. Marriage is public and the basis of the family.

The views of incest which see it as destructive of the family make an implicit contrast between a purely sexual relationship and family roles. Good illustrations of how the former is thought of are to be found in the writings of earlier scholars such as the great French sociologist, Durkheim, and the anthropologist, Malinowski.[23] Durkheim was explicit in his use of pre-marital courtship as the model of unregulated sex in order to discuss the incompatibility between sexual relationships and close family ties. Malinowski's argument that incest would make it impossible for the family to continue as a domestic organization was based on a very similar view of sexual relations. Both envisaged sexual relationships as a matter of rivalry and competition between individuals of the same sex and of unstable relationships between the sexes. An important but implicit element in this view is the absence of constraints on the individuals concerned: they appear as free and equal players in the game of choosing partners.

The picture is one that is still current today. Despite the increasing use of contraceptives, the definition of marriage as the foundation of 'the family' ensures that sex is defined in relation to reproduction. The general definition of sex as normal only when it makes conception possible, that is when it is mature, heterosexual and vaginal, is part of this concept. The comparison of human sexual relations with the mating patterns of animals that has been undertaken by ethologists is also a product of this view. It is a normative definition which selects part of the whole range of human sexual behaviour to define the socially acceptable. The disapproved elements of human sexual behaviour: rape, homosexuality, the sexual abuse of small children, and bestiality are discarded as abnormal and deviant[24] and then ignored as though they ceased to exist. This picture implies no other motive for sexual relationships than heterosexual attraction or the urge to reproduce and merely contrasts the impermanence and competitive nature of sexual pairing with marriage.

An important aspect of marriage is the expectation that it will provide for the sexual satisfaction of both partners. While in the past this was largely seen as sexual satisfaction for the husband and the fulfilment of the desire for motherhood in women, it is now generally conceded that women have sexual needs as well. There is a folk notion that a man must have 'enough' sex and that frustration of his needs leads to his making use of available outlets, even abnormal ones. Sexual frustration may be used as an explanation for homosexual relationships among adolescent boys and for the prevalence of homosexuality in such all-male institutions as prisons.[25] It is common to find it suggested that a man's lack of sexual satisfaction in his marriage is a contributory cause of the abuse. Often the wife is ill or pregnant when the first episode of abuse takes place or she appears uninterested in sex.[26] The husband, feeling rejected and frustrated, turns to his daughter for emotional comfort and sexual satisfaction. The idea that sex is a need like other bodily needs is expressed in a variety of ways: by abusers who blame the abuse on their sexual frustration and even tell their victims that it is their duty to help satisfy the man of the family; by women who see their own lack of sexual enthusiasm as a cause of the abuse; and even publicly by a judge who caused a public uproar in December 1988 by suggesting that a young man's abuse of his step-daughter was caused by the sexual coldness of his wife during her pregnancy.[27] As well as forming part of the stories in many men's magazines, the same idea appears in serious journals and books.[28] In all these places the wife/mother is described as colluding with the sexual abuse in order to avoid sexual relations with her husband. The notion places responsibility both for the man's sexual frustration and his subsequent abuse of the child(ren) on his wife. It seems as though there is an implicit recognition that his sexuality may have a negative side unless controlled by her sexual submission on demand.

Although sexual frustration cannot be said to be an acceptable *excuse* for sexually abusing a child, like drunkenness, it is considered a convincing *explanation* of male sexual misdemeanours. Frustrated women may also be said to show disapproved behaviour such as shrewish bad temper or they may be unfaithful to their husbands. There is a general (largely male) belief that frequent sexual intercourse ensures that a wife remains submissive and pleasant to her husband: it is a means of controlling her. But women do not legitimately claim sexual frustration as their justification for deviant behaviour, sexual or otherwise. Certainly, female frustration is not expected to break out in seriously deviant sexual acts; the few women who are found to have sexually abused their children do not claim frustration and would not be excused if they did. It is male sexuality that is believed to be liable to become uncontrollable if not given a legitimate outlet.

It cannot be assumed that other societies have the same view of gender differences in sexual appetites or even that ideas on the subject are uniform throughout the Western world. A study in a Spanish village showed that women were thought to have a much greater sexual appetite than men; men on the other hand were thought to be debilitated by too much sexual intercourse and women might even be accused of killing their husbands in this way.[29] The biological basis for human sexual behaviour is shaped by the general assumptions about what it is and the rules which circumscribe it that are accepted as valid in a community.[30]

The assertion that sexual frustration is a contributory cause of the sexual abuse of children in the household is based on the study of households where there has been sexual abuse. The absence of all control groups and indeed clinicians' lack of experience with 'normal' families casts a considerable amount of doubt on these findings. Chesser's study of marital and family relationships among English women, published as long ago as 1956, showed a close correlation between alleged unhappiness in marriage and the admission that a husband was sometimes refused intercourse.[31] There was also a clear correlation between the women's marital unhappiness and their own lack of sexual satisfaction. So, if there are emotional or sexual difficulties in the marriage, both partners are likely to be frustrated. This may add to both partners' dissatisfaction with the marriage but it hardly supports the idea that sexual frustration in marriage is only the lot of men. To judge from divorce statistics, unhappiness in marriage and lack of sexual fulfilment must be far commoner than the sexual abuse of children but the common pattern in most such situations is for one or both partners to start an affair.

There is a tendency in some writing about the relationship between an abuser and a victim who is a daughter or step-daughter to see her as a younger mistress and stress the attractions of her newly-developing sexuality and his jealousy of her boyfriends. The common tension between mother and pubescent daughter may also be seen as sexual jealousy or as facilitating the latter's abuse. Some women do react with jealousy to the news that their husband and daughter have had sexual relations; one woman in a case in the hospital child sexual abuse unit refused to have anything further to do with her adolescent daughter, telling her, 'You stole my man.' The girl had been involved in sexual relations by her relatively recent stepfather. It is not, however, a ubiquitous feature of these relationships, and probably should be seen as one of a variety of ways women resolve the particular conflict between the roles of wife and mother in which they find themselves as a result of the abuse.

However, Herman argues that 'careful interviewing of incest offenders, moreover, reveals that even in very disturbed marriages, the father is usually able to command sex from his wife.'[32] She quotes Groth, whom she describes as having considerable experience of treating sex offenders, as reporting on a series of incestuous fathers in the following terms: 'The men were having sexual relations with their daughters or sons in addition to, rather than instead of their wives. Those offenders who confined their sexual activity to children did so through choice. There was no one for whom no other opportunity for sexual gratification existed.'[33] There was no consistent information on the sexual relations of offenders among the cases in the CSA Unit but in more than one case the wife volunteered the fact that they had been having sexual intercourse regularly.

The attitudes to their victims that are evinced by some abusers of children make it clear that sexual acts do not have simple motives. The anger and even hatred, the wish to punish and control and the physical abuse that may accompany the sexual abuse of children are reminders of the sadism and the wish to dominate that may also be aspects of sexuality. Finkelhor has summarized the research findings indicating that the sexual abuse of children may represent a variety of emotional needs.[34] Prominent among them is the need to feel powerful and to control others. In commenting on them, he argues that the discussion of emotions accompanying the sexual abuse of children has distracted attention from the main issue: 'If the abuse were merely an expression of a need for dominance or affiliation, the adult should be content to bully or befriend the child . . . The sexual act and the sexualization of the child were important to the expression of the need. This sexualization is something that needs to be explained too';[35] his multi-factorial explanation of sexual abuse attempts to provide for this.

However, Finkelhor also remarks that 'all sexual behaviour, not just child sexual abuse, is laden with nonsexual motivation.'[36] The general attraction of powerlessness to men has already been mentioned. If the urge to dominate and control is common to a wide range of sexual behaviour, as indeed it seems to be, then it is arguable that these elements are not merely additional motivations for a sexual act but intrinsic to it. This must lead to our questioning the assumption that it is solely a natural urge to reproduce.[37]

A sexual attraction to children is described as a sexual preference by some experts and as an addiction by others.[38] Abusers themselves may argue that it is a compulsion they cannot control even if they try to do so. In either case, it seems unlikely that it is an appetite that would be assuaged by sexual intercourse with an adult woman, so that to speak of a man replacing his wife with his daughter or son seems to ignore many of the salient features of this behaviour. However, it may well be that what a wife refuses to participate in, a child is forced to do. One cannot place too much weight on a single individual case but it is interesting that Beatrix Campbell's informant, a Cleveland mother, told her that the police 'wanted to know about his sexual behaviour, and I told them that there was lots that was unusual about it'.[39] There is a general reticence about mentioning sexual activities which are considered abnormal. The details of what happens to children when they are sexually abused are not generally made public or discussed, even if they are known. Even newspapers which do not normally show any reticence in their columns do not indulge in full descriptions of what happens in the sexual abuse of children. The information is considered too shocking. It is also true that sexual activities with a child are so strongly disapproved of by the majority that there is a reluctance to know the full facts. If a child can bring itself to describe what happened, which is not always the case, the description is usually only thought relevant to the prosecution process. Reports of such trials use the phrase 'sexual abuse' to avoid outraging their readership with information about sexual practices that are strongly disapproved of. The exact forms of sexual abuse and sexual experimentation in which children are involved may not be relevant to the care and therapeutic support of the child and are often not recorded in the hospital files. The questionnaire used in the BBC survey asked respondents to record their experiences under headings which specified kissing and touching, attempted intercourse, intercourse and two categories which were very vague: 'being made/forced to do something sexual' and 'suffered something else'. Under the latter there was space to write in a more precise description but few respondents did so. Even a frank and full account from a survivor may be unable to be specific.

There is thus little systematic evidence on what sexual abuse usually entails. However, events in Cleveland made clear that both boys and girls may be subjected to anal intercourse at a very young age. The Cleveland disclosure referred to above was precipitated by a mother's taking her two-year-old daughter to hospital because she was bleeding from the anus.[40] In other cases there is oral sex, both cunnilingus and fellatio, and on occasions rape. Dreadful injuries may be inflicted which require surgery and may result in permanent bodily damage. There may also be occasions of group sex, sadism and pornographic photography. The controversy in Cleveland over the interpretation of anal dilatation stemmed in good measure from the fact that it indicated that buggery of small children was not uncommon. The refusal to accept this fact, and the subsequent acknowledgement by some paediatricians and child psychiatrists that they had not looked for signs of such abuse, indicates the degree to which 'sex' is defined in the minds of the majority of people by the accepted social norms. In the public view, acceptable sex consists of heterosexual, vaginal intercourse between adults.[41]

While homosexuality is no longer illegal, it is still considered deviant and there is a wide range of attitudes to it, from tolerance to outright condemnation. In general it is assumed that anal intercourse is a homosexual deviation from 'normal' sex; there is also a general belief that boys who engage in this activity will become homosexual themselves, or are being recognized as incipient homosexuals by others. Hence there is strong disapproval of the abuse of young boys by men (the age of consent for boys is five years older than for girls to ensure they are old enough not to be influenced in the matter) in case they may turn them into sexual deviants. Men may be too embarrassed to ask wives or girlfriends to engage in anal intercourse, for fear of being thought gay or unacceptable.[42] Some of them turn to more compliant partners. The buggery of small children by apparently 'normal' men disturbs all the accepted ideas of sexual behaviour, by implying that male sexuality is not 'normally' what it is accepted as being.

The horror of child molestation and the characterization of offenders as 'strangers' both imply that engaging a child in sexual activities is outside normal human behaviour. Strangers are people 'we do not know', without a known social identity or normal relationships; like the monster or the witch they represent the alien and the inhuman. The conception of adults, and particularly men, as socialized human beings whose destructive impulses are brought under control by their upbringing is contradicted by the evidence of their lack of control. The common attempts to label the victim as seductive, like the suggestions that victims of rape have provoked it, can be seen not merely as an attempt to shift responsibility but as a refusal to consider the implications of the act. Sex forced on unwilling and inappropriate partners shows the fragility of the self-control that is the cultural foundation of adult male superiority and also threatens the generally accepted understanding of what male sexuality is.

The myth of the family is based on a culturally specific definition of what is normal in sexual relations. Cultural values may influence human sexuality more fundamentally than is generally realized. Attributes which are assumed to be the result of human physical functioning may, in fact, be culturally determined. Heider has described the low level of sexual interest and activity among the Dani of New Guinea and argues that it can only be ascribed to their culture.[43] The fact that there is much variation between societies in what is considered inherent in the physical nature of men, women and sexuality indicates that in any one society that character of male and female sexuality there is culturally specific. In any group, commonly accepted expectations of adult sexuality define the limits of acceptable behaviour, establish sexual identity and determine how the attractiveness of individuals, including children, is perceived. Age differences between sexual partners may be accepted or frowned on; homosexuality may be accepted, regarded with horror or, alternatively, with tolerance as a transitional phase of development or as a matter of individual choice. Human sexuality is always given a cultural form.

Finkelhor has argued that men are more likely to abuse children sexually than women because the sexes are given different orientations to children by their upbringing.[44] The high value now placed by many Western societies on youth as the basis for feminine beauty is likely to influence men to perceive children as sexual objects. The ideal picture of lovers depicting a man slightly larger, taller and older, that is more powerful, than the woman is common to Britain and America where men are expected to take the

initiative in sexual matters. An affair or marriage between a much
older man and a young woman occasions little surprise in Britain,
particularly if the man is wealthy or successful, or she is a second
wife. A couple in one of the parents' therapy groups I attended
provided a typical example: he had apparently fallen in love with
her when she was 14 and used to come to the shop where he
worked to buy things for her mother. He later broke up his
marriage to marry her; their daughter was the victim whom he had
abused. (There were allegations by his adult daughters from his first
marriage that he had abused them too.) There were two other CSA
Unit cases in which comments in the files noted that the victim's
mother looked more like her sister, dressing as though she were
very young and behaving in a rather immature way. One may guess
that this apparent childishness had been the attraction for her
husband in the first place. Others have remarked that the image of
the desirable woman is physically child-like; Coward, the author of
a book on sexual desire, comments that 'this sexual ideal is an
image which connotes powerlessness.'[45] If this is so, then it
is the powerlessness of children which may make them sexually
attractive. This is part of a growing body of evidence that suggests
that elements in Western concepts of sexual desirability and of
inequalities of gender encourage rather than restrain the sexual
abuse of children.

Despite these implicit associations of sexual attractiveness with
physical weakness, sexual relations with children are explicitly
condemned as an abhorrent deviation from 'normal' sexuality.
'Normal' or 'natural' sexuality is generally still associated with the
birth of children and assumed to be demonstrated by marriage so
that married men and women are least likely to be suspected of
deviant sexual activity, let alone the sexual abuse of children.
Departures from the general definition of what are normal partners
and normal sexual acts were once considered rare aberrations, and
associated with other disapproved behaviour, but we now cannot
ignore the fact that they are more common than they are believed to
be even now. Acceptance of this fact inevitably challenges our
understanding of what is 'natural' sexual behaviour.

Equally important to our comprehension of how children may be
sexually abused is the recognition that being a parent is not simply
'natural' and 'instinctive' but a matter of occupying a socially
recognized position, playing a social role. Parenthood is, moreover,

a position conferring authority over children on adults who, merely by being adults, have a good deal of power at their disposal. The legitimate exercise of power by someone with a socially recognized right to do so is always conditional on its proper exercise. Rights are associated with responsibilities so that those who hold authority are held socially accountable for its exercise.[46] Parental authority, like other forms of authority, is circumscribed by conventions and rules that limit parents' use of power and proscribe some form of it as abuse. The most fundamental of these is what we may call the axiom of altruism.[47] The belief that parents will put the needs and well-being of their children before their own is best seen not as the description of an innate disposition but as an absolute social requirement that makes their control of their children legitimate.

Any position of authority may also be abused on occasions, despite controls which are designed to prevent it, and penalties to punish offenders when the checks fail. Where parents are concerned, the deep conviction that they are 'naturally' altruistic and responsible prevents their authority from being subject to the same kind of public scrutiny that may be focused on other positions of legitimate power. The abuse of authority is often difficult to check, despite provision for sanctions to ensure compliance with the rules. The problem of enforcement is particularly acute with the misuse of domestic authority. Analyses of conjugal relationships have shown how men's command of physical force and their access to economic resources allows them to dominate their wives, or even maltreat them, with little fear of being restrained; neither the police nor the neighbours are eager to intervene between husband and wife. The abuse of children is even more easily concealed. The deep conviction that parents are naturally responsible and thus unable to abuse their powers prevents their being subject to the same kind of public scrutiny as other authorities.

All adults who look after children are considered parental figures and therefore have, to greater or lesser degree, similar autonomy in their exercise of authority. The altruism and control of their own behaviour that 'real' parents are believed to be endowed with by a combination of innate love and parental training ensures that this is greatest in 'the family'. However, the fact that the largest single category of sexually abused children is formed by those who have been abused in their homes, by the exercise of domestic (familial) authority calls this into question. If, as has been argued here, parenthood is not innate but socially constructed and maintained, then the explanation of why children are sexually abused is made much easier. It is not that the abusers are monsters or that 'the family is breaking down' but that some adults, mostly men as far as we know now, lack the responsibility towards children and the self-control that is socially demanded of all adults but particularly of parents.

All parents must fail to live up to the ideal in some respects but the majority manage to be good enough not to violate the most important rules. The reasons for the inability of a minority to keep even the most basic rule of parenthood, that is to give the welfare of their children priority over their own satisfaction, are neither simple nor uniform. For many of them, the experiences of childhood have shown how unreliable these are as a form of training for parenthood; those who have been abused themselves as children have had no positive example to follow. Their deficiencies must not be ignored but condemnation by itself is not helpful. Some of them may be able to change with therapy and counselling; others may have to learn to keep away from children altogether. However, the strongest argument for optimism is based on numbers: not all of those who have been abused end up abusing their own children. The chain of damaging behaviour across the generations is not unbroken nor unbreakable.

Notes

1 A. R. Radcliffe-Brown, introduction to his *African Systems of Kinship and Marriage*, International African Institute (Oxford University Press, London, 1950), pp. 6, 70.
2 Schneider, 'The meaning of incest'.
3 C. Harris, *The Family and Industrial Society* (Allen and Unwin, London, 1983).
4 See ibid., p. 39, for an excellent discussion of the multiple meanings of the family; see also J. S. La Fontaine, 'Public or private: the constitution of the family in anthropological perspective', *International Journal of Moral and Social Studies*, 3(3) (1988).
5 For example, G. P. Murdock and T. Parsons, both internationally known, the first as an anthropologist, the second as a sociologist. See G. P. Murdock, *Social Structure* (Macmillan, New York, 1949), and

T. C. Parsons, 'One incest taboo in relation to social structure and the socialization of the child', *British Journal of Sociology*, 5 (1954).

6 A. Bentovim, 'Understanding the phenomenon of sexual abuse – a family systems theory view of causation', in Bentovim et al., *Child Sexual Abuse*, and T. Furniss, 'Conflict-avoiding and conflict-regulating patterns in incest and child sexual abuse', *Acta Paediatrica Scandinavica*, 50 (1984).

7 Sometimes they also include other relatives such as grandmothers if they play a significant part in the child(ren)'s life. While I am not disputing the therapeutic effectiveness of this approach, which I am not competent to judge, the theory itself is inadequate. It cannot offer an explanation of why sexual abuse rather than some other form of malfunction should be the result of the disordered relationships. Nor can the theory deal with sexual abuse that occurs between people who are not related as members of one family. Children are vulnerable to adults, not merely to members of their household, although the circumstances of domestic life define the area of their greatest vulnerability. Any attempt to explain children's sexual abuse should also be applicable more generally.

8 Modern developmental psychology takes children to be social beings from the start. See Henshall and McGuire, 'Gender development', p. 142. I refer here also to popular conceptions.

9 Houlbrook, *The English Family*, pp. 140–53.

10 Ibid., p. 141.

11 Relative age may also influence the relationship between husband and wife but there is little research that I know of to show how it might affect it.

12 E. Goody, 'Why must might be right? Reflections on sexual Herrschaft', *Cambridge Anthropology*, January 1987; see also M. D. A. Freeman (ed.), *State, Law, and the Family* (Tavistock, London, 1984)

13 Teachers have a very specialized part to play in the upbringing of children, but they are not expected to be fully responsible for the child's moral i.e. social education, although the process of teaching is more than a mere imparting of technical skills. Teachers and parents may come into conflict over what they think is best for the child, or teachers criticize the way the parents bring up their child, but the latter's prior rights are still acknowledged.

14 It is popularly believed that blood tests can demonstrate paternity; this is not so. Blood tests can sometimes establish who is *not* a child's father. Genetic 'fingerprinting' will be able to determine paternity in the future but our idea of fatherhood cannot be said to be based on such a recently developed technique. See J. A. Barnes, 'Genetrix: genitor:: nature: culture', in J. Goody (ed.), *The Contexts of Kinship* (Cambridge University Press, Cambridge, 1975).

15 L. Mair, *Marriage* (Penguin, Harmondsworth, 1971). Legitimacy also depends on the wife's fidelity, for her adultery threatens his paternity of her future children. It is intelligible therefore that women's adultery is considered a more serious breach of conjugal responsibilities than a man's infidelity and that unmarried mothers are regarded as a social problem and there is concern if their numbers increase.

16 M. Fortes, *Rules and the Emergence of Society*, Occasional Paper 39, Royal Anthropological Institute, 1983.

17 For examples see: Kempe and Kempe *Child Abuse*; Finkelhor, *Child Sexual Abuse*; Bentovim and Boston, 'Sexual abuse – basic issues'.

18 Nelson, *Incest*, pp. 62–74; also Herman, *Father–Daughter Incest*, and D. Russell, *Sexual Exploitation: Rape, Child Sexual Abuse and Workplace Harassment* (Sage, Beverly Hills, 1984).

19 J. Hildebrand, 'Working with mothers of abused children', in Bentovim et al. (eds), *Child Sexual Abuse*, p. 214.

20 Diana Russell in her survey of San Francisco women reports 3 per cent of mothers who were alleged to have participated in the sexual activities. Russell, *The Secret Trauma*.

21 This information was given me by J. Kissinger who is planning a study of women in refuges whose children have been sexually abused.

22 Jones and Seig, 'Child sexual abuse allegations'.

23 E. Durkheim, 'Le problème de l'inceste et ses origines', *Année Sociologique*, 1 (1896–7); B. Malinowski, 'A sociological study of the rationale of the prohibited degrees of marriage', in *Kindred and Affinity as Impediments to Marriage* as appendix 3 (Church of England Commission, London, 1940).

24 For a discussion of the cultural basis of sexuality see P. Caplan (ed.), *The Cultural Construction of Sexuality* (Tavistock, London, 1987), particularly articles by J. Weeks, V. J. Seidler and G. Shepherd.

25 Accounts of these make it clear that dominance and informal hierarchy are intrinsic elements in the ideas and behaviour involved, at least for the majority; see Coggeshall, 'Ladies behind bars'.

26 Finkelhor, *Child Sexual Abuse*, p. 26.

27 Reported in the *Sunday Mirror*, 20 November 1988.

28 For an example see Kempe and Kempe, *Child Abuse*, p. 66.

29 S. Brandes, 'Like wounded stags: male sexual ideology in an Andalusian town', in S. B. Ortner and H. Whitehead (eds), *Sexual Meanings* (Cambridge University Press, Cambridge, 1981).

30 J. Weeks, 'Questions of identity', and V. J. Seidler, 'Reason, desire and male sexuality', both in Caplan (ed.), *Cultural Construction*.

31 Chesser, *Sexual, Marital and Family Relationships*, pp. 439–40, 472.

32 Herman, *Father–Daughter Incest*, p. 43.

33 Ibid.

34 Finkelhor, *Child Sexual Abuse*, pp. 33–5.

35 Ibid., p. 34.

36 Ibid.

37 Yanagisako argues that the assumption that the function of the family serves a reproductive function has prevented anthropologists making advances in cross-cultural analysis. Yanagisako, 'Family and household'.

38 But see also S. Frosh, 'Issues for men working with sexually abused children', *British Journal of Psychotherapy*, 3(4) (1987).

39 Campbell, *Unofficial Secrets*, p. 174.

40 Ibid., p. 172.

41 Caplan, *Cultural Construction*, introduction, p. 2.

42 A well-known radio 'agony aunt' told me that many of the letters she had from young men expressed a wish to have anal intercourse with their girlfriends. They had either been refused or were afraid to ask in case this would be the response.

43 Heider, 'Dani sexuality'. See also G. Shepherd, 'Rank, gender and homosexuality: Mombasa as a key to understanding sexual options', in Caplan (ed.), *Cultural Construction*.

44 Finkelhor, *Child Sexual Abuse*, pp. 12–13.

45 Cited in Ennew, *Sexual Exploitation*, p. 132.

46 M. Fortes, 'Ritual and office', in M. Gluckman (ed.), *Essays on the Ritual of Social Relations* (Manchester University Press, Manchester, 1956).

47 M. Fortes, *Rules and the Emergence of Society*, Occasional Paper, Royal Anthropological Institute, London, 1983.

8 What Can Be Done?

Adults mistreat children largely because they simply do not accept
that children are people instead of property.
                                   Male civil servant aged about 40

It is the nature of British society that makes it possible for children
to be abused. The reasons for this conclusion have been spelt out in
the preceding chapters. The type of domestic organization: small
groups which are defined as natural, autonomous units, creates
situations in which it is easy for people to take advantage of
children and abuse them sexually. The buildings that house
children – children's homes, schools and nurseries with their many
rooms – provide opportunities for privacy. Certain relationships
between adults and children encourage intimacy between them.
The possibility of being alone with a child without raising adult
eyebrows comes to teachers, babysitters, neighbours and youth
workers of many kinds, as well as to fathers and other male
relatives.

Children respond easily to adults who are interested in them and
spend time with them. Adults also have powerful positions relative
to children and this usually procures obedience from them; their
authority allows adults to enforce secrecy and so hide the abuse and
even facilitate its repetition. If a headmaster exercises his authority
to call children into his study alone, his staff will almost certainly
not put an adverse interpretation on the fact. All the children may
know what is going on but how can they also know that what
happens there does not happen in all schools, especially if he tells
them that it does? Adults not only have the power of their maturity
but the authority society confers on them by virtue of their being
fully social persons, while children are regarded as merely
dependent beings, with no rights of their own. There are many
social roles which confer authority over particular children but the

ones that involve the largest number of adults and children are domestic, those of parents and stepparents. As far as we know today, the majority of children who are sexually abused suffer this trauma at home. This is no coincidence since the great majority of children live at home with one or both of their parents and this is where the possibilities are greatest; but ideas about the incest taboo make it difficult for people to accept that this is so. The sexual abuse of children in Western society is hidden from general recognition by ingrained assumptions about human nature and parenthood that are integral to the idea of the family and fundamental to social life.

The questions this line of reasoning raises are comparative ones. Are children more likely to be abused where the idea of the family is strongest, that is in Western societies (although this label covers some variation from place to place)? In many other societies domestic organization and the relationships between people who consider themselves related are very different from our own. Does this protect the children? Alternatively, are some of the customs reported from very different societies themselves a form of sexual abuse of children? In many societies girls are married very young, sometimes before they reach puberty; in others they are subjected to painful and humiliating rites of initiation. Even where neither of these customs exist there may be ways of treating young children that involve touching their genitals in a manner like that which caused one young mother among the cases in the CSA Unit to be reported for sexual abuse.[1] Answers to all these questions will take time to obtain and they will certainly change our view of 'human nature'.

These are complex issues. There is virtually no good evidence about the sexual abuse of children, as it is defined in the West, that occurs outside the United States and Britain; there are a very few cases of incest recorded by anthropologists[2] but none that I know of which concern sexual abuse other than incest. However in many other societies men have much greater authority over children, particularly girls, than they do in Britain or America; in some they even had the right, traditionally, to sell them into slavery or give them as pawns for a debt. Some of those men might well abuse their position and use a child for their own sexual gratification. There is child prostitution in other societies, although in some of them the customers are largely European.[3] There is good reason to suppose that British or American victims have their counterparts in other societies but we know virtually nothing about them.

There are also grounds for the belief that sexual abuse may be less common in some other societies. It is not uncommon to find very formal behaviour between senior relatives and children of the opposite sex once they are past a very young age. They are often forbidden to sleep in the same house as anyone they refer to as a parent (and there may be several of these); in such cases, children are sent to sleep with a grandmother or elderly female neighbour instead. Sometimes these close relatives must not speak directly to each other or share the same food bowl. All such customs reduce the intimacy between adults and children and this distant relationship is balanced by warmer, more intimate relationships with others who have not the same coercive power over a child. In addition, where the climate permits, much domestic life is lived outdoors. This means that 'family' behaviour is much more open to public scrutiny so that any deviations will be quickly spotted. (Ironically it is the more spacious, more solid houses of Western societies that provide the separate rooms and privacy for illicit sexual activities.) It is also in societies where members of a household have little real privacy that serious departures from public morality in sexual matters are believed to affect everyone, since such acts are polluting and may bring down disaster on the whole community. In such circumstances, community action against incest is also quite common. Even if neighbours do not intervene, relatives other than the parents have an interest in and rights over children that justify their interceding and makes them a possible refuge for an abused child. Public gossip and opprobrium may have a powerful effect on an offender; one of the earliest recorded cases of incest in a culturally very different society came to Malinowski's attention when the young man concerned committed suicide.[4] In her consideration of the comparative material on the abuse and neglect of children, Jill Korbin concludes that 'a network of concerned individuals acts in many ways to reduce the likelihood of child maltreatment.'[5] A wider set of kin and the presence of neighbours who consider themselves involved may thus offset the power of men and male adolescents.

In the pattern of other deviant acts such as murder or suicide societies differ from one another; thus one may expect them to differ in the amount of incest that occurs and the relationships that are most often incestuous, as well as in the nature and prevalence of the sexual abuse of children. In Japan, as I have already noted, the public sees mother–son incest as its most serious problem; the typical son is believed to be an adolescent who is just beginning to take an interest in girls.[6] However, until the studies are done, we cannot be sure whether children in other societies also suffer sexual abuse.

Acts which Westerners might call sexually abusive do occur as part of normal behaviour in other societies. In the eyes of Turkish women who admire and touch the genitals of small children, this is an appropriate way to convey affection, although it also may be a form of teasing.[7] What is relevant is that no child is particularly singled out, the practice is not secret or furtive. In societies where girls are married young, it may cause them grief to leave home but since most girls must suffer in this way it is endured as part of the lot of women. The more extreme practices of initiation are believed to be necessary to ensure normal maturation, much as Westerners would regard the pain of innoculations or medical treatment to be necessary evils that children must bear.[8] In none of these practices is the sexual gratification of the adult(s) the primary motivation for them. Finkelhor and Korbin found it possible to construct an internationally valid definition of sexual abuse: it is 'proscribed, proximate [i.e. it involves contact] and preventable.'[9] In their opinion, which I share, there are no societies in which incest or the sexual abuse of children is a normal, that is common and acceptable, pattern.

The Protection of Children

Children are easily victimized: they are physically weaker than adults, accept what they are told, and are easily coerced. Children are also completely dependent on adults, not merely for their emotional needs but financially and socially; once past a very early age, they know it. If they try to disclose what is happening their chances of being believed are not good; an adult's denial is more readily believed than a child's story, especially if the allegations concern a parent. Children know this too. If they run away from home they have little chance of earning a living and will be returned home if they are found; small children cannot even contemplate such an action. Some older children do run away successfully but may have to earn their living by criminal activities; others vanish without trace. It is, in fact, surprising that so many children do find the courage to tell someone of their sexual abuse: given that the adults they know best cannot be trusted, why should they trust any other adult?

The consequences of abuse depend on a number of different factors: the age of the child, the duration of the abuse and the relationship between abuser and victim. Some sexual abuse is violent, in other cases it is a process of slow escalation from a gentle beginning and, although the victims may be coerced, they are not physically abused. In some cases it is clear that the man who committed the offence was angry or antagonistic towards the child; in others there may be an obsessive 'love'. Equally common, though unremarked, is the total indifference to the child or its feelings that some men manifest. The relationships involved are varied and can be ambivalent and complex. There is no clear preponderance of one emotional pattern.

The reactions of victims are also far from uniform. Some hate their abusers and are glad or relieved when they leave the house or die. One mother told the Cleveland inquiry that her daughter, aged eight, had received the news of her abusive father's suicide with relief. One of the survivors who filled in a questionnaire for the BBC wrote: 'the worst memory I have is when my Mum and Dad had another one of their fights and my Mum hit Dad on the head with a big marble ashtray. He was knocked unconscious and my Mum thought she'd killed him. For a while I was so pleased to see him lying there with blood on his head. I thought, thank goodness – he would not be touching me any more.' In other cases, the victim shows great affection for the abuser, despite the suffering caused by the sexual abuse.

Even if the relationship is gentle and affectionate, a sexually abused child may suffer serious harm. The consequences vary according to the circumstances and the particular child; some may be seriously affected by minor incidents, while others apparently survive dreadful abuse over many years. If the sexual abuse is accompanied by physical violence or fear induced by threats then very few children escape undamaged; but a lack of violence is no guarantee that the child will not be harmed. Serious psychological damage may be caused by a child's love for the abuser and the resulting conflict of emotions.

In the short term, there may be physical damage and/or emotional disturbance which is shown in nightmares and truanting, eating disorders and bedwetting. Many of these symptoms are not solely the result of sexual abuse; but they make clear that sexual abuse is damaging. While the long-term effects may vary with individual cases, the commonest, in both Britain and America,[10] is a lasting damage to the individual's self-esteem and sense of worth. Sexual problems are almost equally common; many women who filled in the BBC's postal questionnaire described their aversion to sexual relations and the difficulties this caused in their marriages. Promiscuity and other forms of disapproved behaviour are also common, the former among girls, the latter among boys; there is said to be a high percentage of survivors of sexual abuse in childhood among prostitutes, criminals and drug addicts. Victims may attempt suicide, sometimes successfully. As we have seen, some abused boys abuse their sisters or grow up to be abusing adults. Sexually abusing a child distorts its natural development and prevents it growing up into a normal adult.

The strongest argument for intervention, for taking action when children are abused, is of course their undeserved suffering. The loneliness and misery of these children can be stopped and should not be tolerated. In the second place, however, intervention can offer a chance to improve the likelihood of their becoming adequate parents and help to protect the next generation. Among the possible long-term consequences of sexual abuse in childhood is the inability to be an effective parent. While the study of perpetrators of sexual abuse has barely begun in Britain, there is evidence from the United States that the percentage of those who were either abused themselves or were the brothers of abused sisters is high. Women who have been abused themselves in childhood may become battering mothers or find themselves unable to prevent their husbands or lovers from sexually abusing their children. The repetition of sexual abuse in the next generation is not inevitable but the likelihood is high enough to give us cause for concern. Stopping the abuse does not of itself break the chain of abuse and suffering that links the generations; therapy is needed, as it is, to try and heal the other emotional and psychological wounds that all victims have to bear.

Some men declare that because of the general fear of sexually abusing a child they find it impossible to cuddle or even touch their children in case they are thought abusive. If this is so, the features of children's sexual abuse which make it different from normal physical contact need to be more widely known and talked about explicitly. It is also the case that some of those who work in child protection agencies may themselves be ignorant of what constitutes sexual abuse. This should be an additional argument for ensuring that they are properly trained to understand what is involved and not a reason why they should not be concerned with sexual abuse.

First, it is still as true as it ever was that children need physical contact with those they love; they need to be able to touch them and to be kissed and cuddled. However, they do not need, and do not want, their bodies to be treated as adults' playthings and used for adults' sexual pleasure. There are warning signs which indicate when physical caresses are approaching a dangerous point. If an adult finds himself getting sexual excitement from touching his child, he should find another way of expressing his physical affection. If the child shows distress or dislike of the contact, then (s)he should be allowed the right to be spared that kind of touch. Parents must be able to wash their children's genitals when they are too little to do this for themselves; sexual abuse may start in this way but it always involves more than the fleeting contact which is needed to deal with problems of cleanliness in a brief and practical manner. Children's bodies are sensitive in similar ways to adults' long before they can understand what sex is; but it cannot be emphasized enough that this does not mean they are ready for sexual activity. Children may also excite an adult without knowing it but they should not have to suffer the consequences of their unintentional acts. If a father is accidentally aroused by his child's action, then it is his responsibility to stop it and see that it does not happen again; for example a child wriggling about on a father's lap can be moved to sit on his knee, made to sit still or encouraged to get down.

It is likely that many men have occasional sexual thoughts about children. This is not a cause for serious anxiety in itself, if it is rare; the damage is done when the child is seen as inviting these feelings and they are acted upon. It may not be known, too, that much sexual abuse also involves the child's being asked or made to touch the adult's genitals. There seems no good reason why this should ever happen; it is not appropriate and involves a child in actions whose consequences (s)he cannot foresee. Parental responsibility consists of putting the child's welfare first. All activities which are sexual when undertaken with another adult must be considered abusive when the partner is a child. The likely damage is serious and can be avoided without stopping the physical demonstrations of affection that children need.

The Problem of Diagnosis

There are problems in diagnosing sexual abuse that have been avoided until now. The bulk of this book has been written as though it is possible to establish whether or not a child has been abused. In fact, this is not always the case. One of the main causes of dissension at Cleveland concerned the reliability of the diagnoses. It was possible for some parents to assert that their children had not been abused while the professionals involved, doctors and social workers, felt equally strongly that the children had been, or were at risk. Many of the children concerned had not complained of abuse and some remained silent; the professional view depended on medical evidence. The point should also be made here that in almost all the cases there had been more than one reason why there should have been concern and the fact that the contest focused on the medical evidence was partly because it implied a form of sexual abuse which was particularly shocking. The case claimed against the social services and the doctors was that the technique had been used to accuse innocent parents, that it was not evidence of abuse and that children had been bullied into confirming that they had been abused in order to satisfy professional ambitions or prosecute a campaign against the family. The inquiry showed that these accusations against the professionals were unjust and that there was good cause for concern. Nevertheless there had been hasty action and in some cases there was uncertainty. Lack of certainty was largely accepted as 'proof' that the original suspicion had been unfounded; the children went home with triumphant parents. We shall probably never know how many of the Cleveland children had been abused; all we can be absolutely sure of is that if they had been, *no matter by whom*, there is extra pressure on them now never to say so. It seems likely that many of them were correctly diagnosed, although adequate proof of the diagnosis was lacking. A year later, one mother, who separated from her husband during the crisis without the allegations against him having been confirmed, reported that her daughter had made an allegation against her father after an access visit. The further judicial action in that case has not yet been reported. Others may have been abused by men outside their homes; we shall probably never know.

Children do not always make allegations, either about what they have suffered or against a particular person, that allow no room for queries to be raised. In some cases of sexual abuse, and they are more common than is presently realized, children are too young to make an allegation; they lack both the vocabulary and the understanding to describe the events. (It must be remembered that some victims may be as young as two or three years old.) Small children may use words which are capable of more than one interpretation, or respond equivocally to questions. Those under five are more likely to show injury or behavioural disturbances than to tell. Children a little older, who are capable of using words to tell what has happened to them, may still develop psychosomatic illness, revert to bedwetting or show inappropriate sexualized play with other children. They represent in their action what they cannot or dare not put into words.

Many children of all ages are terrified of what may happen if they tell; the threats that have been made are perceived as a reliable prediction of the consequences of telling. Even adolescents may be too distressed, ashamed or frightened to explain clearly what has happened to them. It may take months of therapy and support before they are able to give all the details of the abuse. A rather high proportion of adults who claimed they had been abused reported that they thought someone knew of their abuse, often their mother, but did nothing. Of course mothers may be unable to understand or 'hear' what is being said, for many reasons, some of which may have to do with their own sexual abuse as children, but children may also think that they have communicated their meaning when they have not. For all these reasons there is no certainty in some cases, either about what happened or as to who was responsible.

In the absence of a clear statement from the victim there are two means of diagnosing sexual abuse. The first involves physical examination. Venereal disease is a sexually transmitted disease; in a child it is a clear indication of sexual abuse.[11] There are also other infections that may give rise to suspicion. Medical techniques can discover injuries which may not be visible to the naked or untrained eye. But medical evidence has limitations. There is much sexual abuse which leaves no physical sign on the victim's body or, if there is forensic evidence, such as traces of semen, it may be washed off. The most important disadvantage of medical examination for sexual abuse is that it cannot yet discover the identity of the abuser, despite the development of genetic finger-printing for forensic purposes. If the identity of the abuser is not known then it is possible for adults to contest the diagnosis altogether.

The second means of diagnosis is the elicitation from the child of the necessary information, either by an interview or by using various aids such as anatomically correct dolls. Recent research in Britain and in the United States has shown that sexually abused children play with the dolls in a manner that differs from children who have not been abused in this way.[12] However, it is worth remembering that a willingness to believe that some children *are* sexually abused is necessary to start with. It is quite easy for doctors and therapists who are unwilling to believe in the possibility of sexual abuse to ignore even quite obvious signs, or give them other explanations.

The disclosure interview, as it is often called, has been the focus of attention because the possibility of uncertainty has facilitated continuing dispute about the scale of the problem. Techniques for eliciting information from children have been attacked as 'putting words into the child's mouth' or described as revictimization. Complaints about methods of inducing disclosure have come from the police and from defence lawyers; these complaints concern the validity of such interviews as evidence in the legal process of the criminal law. They claim that leading questions are asked that bias the evidence against the accused. There *are* differences in the methods used by psychotherapists and the police, since their aims are quite different. It is not always necessary for therapists to know who did it if they can establish that their patient has been sexually abused, but the police aim is to find the criminal. Research has shown that these distinct aims can produce different attitudes to the offence. Furniss's study of three cases sets out in graphic detail the conflict over the management of particular cases that may ensue.[13]

It is a pity that these differences are not more generally recognized; until they are, the conflicts are likely to continue.

It has also been argued that attempts to make a child describe what has happened, or tell who was responsible, are themselves a form of abuse by adults. There were complaints from Cleveland parents that their children had been put through a form of third degree examination with threats and bullying to get them to 'tell'. The Children's Legal Centre has argued that children must be allowed the right not to tell as long as they have been given a chance to understand what the consequences of telling or not telling may be. They are right to draw attention to the fact that an attempt by an untrained person to get a child to reveal what has happened may do further damage. Children should not be forced to talk when they are not ready to, but some of the worst experiences of victims seem to have been the result of the ignorance and lack of consideration of adults as much as the fact of telling. There is plenty of room for improvement in the handling of cases of sexual abuse.

If children are to be believed when they disclose sexual abuse, then are they also to be believed when they declare they have not been abused? There are some cases where a child has coped with the abuse by burying it deep in her or his memory and it is only years later or under therapy that it can be allowed to emerge. There are children who are so traumatized that they cannot speak or are so threatened by the abuser that they dare not. Under circumstances where the child is seriously damaged, emotionally or physically, a child's denial of abuse would not be convincing. This does not mean that a child must be pressured to tell who did it, even if there are grave suspicions.

However skilful techniques of eliciting information from children become, there will probably still be cases where there is uncertainty. Cases where the diagnosis is uncertain or where there are doubts about the identity of the abuser pose serious dilemmas for social workers and others whose role it is to protect children. The suspicion that the child is likely to have been abused at home is supported, as this book has shown, by a great deal of evidence. However, it is also true that in a sizable minority of cases, a child is abused by someone (s)he knows outside the household. The recourse to stereotypes of offenders is unfortunate and common. It risks causing the child more suffering and may make it harder for him or her to say what happened. If the child's father is accused and the abuser is a neighbour, then the parents' absence, their confusion, anger and distress may deprive the child of emotional support at a vital moment. It is true that guilty fathers often react with angry denial and may be supported in this by their wives. It requires training and time to distinguish between the denial of all responsibility which characterizes most sexual abusers and a genuine declaration of innocence. The search for an offender should consider the whole range of persons in the child's world and should consider each case anew, without rule-of-thumb judgements. This is very hard for under-staffed and over-extended social service teams to do. Their task is made no easier when parents, even when they are innocent themselves, are so shocked by what has been revealed that they cannot do anything but say the abuse has not happened.

It is also sometimes said that the child's trauma is caused not so much by sexual abuse as by society's reaction to it. It may be argued that until the child is told that such behaviour is wrong, she or he may be unworried by it. The evidence examined for this book does not support this interpretation. First, there is good evidence that children know it is wrong quite early; the fact that it must be kept a secret raises suspicions and the abuser's behaviour may add to them. Moreover, although some survivors recount that they did not know that what was happening was wrong, they also record clearly that they did not like it. Learning that these activities are wrong may actually support a child by justifying its dislike of what is being done and making it legitimate to tell.

Nevertheless it is certainly true that the consequences of disclosing sexual abuse may be deeply distressing to a child. The procedures for dealing with such cases often leave much to be desired. In particular, adults may become so preoccupied with the problems of ensuring protection or prosecuting those responsible that they ignore the child altogether. This appeared to have been particularly true in Cleveland where the conflicts between different organizations and between particular individuals within them drowned the children's voices.

A large part of the public wants to see abusers severely punished and lets the idea of retribution push the child's needs out of their minds. This may also be true of the police whose aim is to apply the law. The rules of evidence still make it impossible for the police to prosecute on the unsubstantiated word of a child. They are also reluctant to put young children through a cross-examination in court. Some judges have now begun to allow young victims to give their evidence on closed circuit television, which may make it less of an ordeal and enable more victims to testify before the court. However, if there is no prosecution, there is no assurance that a disclosure to the police will bring help to the child concerned. Many policemen appear to consider, as some of those involved in the Cleveland affair did, that if there is no firm evidence against a suspect, then he must be innocent. As a result they do not always consider it necessary to refer the case to the social services so that they can ensure the welfare of the child: Gorry reports that of the cases of incest reported to the Metropolitan Police in five years, only just over a third of them were reported to the social services and 42 per cent were not referred to any other agencies at all.[14] At present children are not sure of getting help and the offender remains free to punish the child for telling, ensuring that it will be silent thereafter, and continue the abuse. Without any other support the child is completely helpless. This would seem like the worst of both worlds.

For the social services, the first aim is to protect the child. Since the social services are not bound by the same rules of evidence as the law, they may act on reasonable suspicion. The lack of certainty in many cases of sexual abuse allows abusers who are not prosecuted to claim that they have been wrongly accused and that the continued involvement of the social services is persecution. In some cases this and their different aims may lead the social services into conflict with the police and/or parents. The Report of the Inquiry into Child Abuse in Cleveland has resulted in efforts being made in some areas to develop better co-ordination between the various agencies concerned in such cases, particularly the police and the social services. All too often the co-operation can become an end in itself and the question of how this can benefit the victim is forgotten.

Parents and the State

Many people are outraged at the idea that children may need protection against their parents; they see this as a slur on parents, whom they regard as by nature the best people to look after 'their' children. However, the material in the book should be an adequate demonstration of the fact that some parents are neither good enough nor capable enough to keep their children from experiences that may damage them for the rest of their lives. The reasons that children suffer are many and varied but in the last analysis there is a failure of responsibility on the part of adults. The argument about where to place the responsibility – on the social services or on doctors, on the abuser alone or as a shared responsibility with his partner – distracts attention from the main issue: that adults are to blame and responsibility for the plight of the children should be a matter of general concern. The problem of protecting children must not disappear from sight in wrangles among adults about who is to blame.

Anxieties about the relation between the family, whatever it is seen to be, and the state have existed since at least the turn of the century.[15] The increasing range of situations in which the state or its employees may exercise control is interpreted as an attack on individual freedom. Yet parents' complete freedom from control by society, or by the state as the instrument of society, logically would include their freedom to treat their children badly, to exploit them sexually, even kill them. Few societies permit their parents such powers of life and death over their children; the restrictions may be those entailed in the rights of the child's other relatives or the belief in retribution by supernatural authority but they are there. British parents do not have complete freedom to do what they like with their children even now; the circumstances under which parents may allow children to work for money or make them do so are limited by law and they must see that they are adequately educated. Failure to comply with these state requirements damages children much less than physical or sexual abuse, but there is only the occasional protest against these laws. The views of those who extol the value of the family as a bulwark of freedom ignore the vulnerability of children as individuals, assuming all parents will make their children's interests the first priority. As the material in this book has shown, on the contrary, children's interests, their physical and emotional health even, may be sacrificed to the interests of those adults who are closest to them. Complete freedom for the individual is no protection for the weak.

What Do Children Want?

If we are not to have children grow up into damaged adults who may themselves harm children, what is to be done? We could start by listening to the victims themselves. What abused children most want, according to survivors, sounds relatively simple to provide: they want to be believed, they want information and they want help to stop the abuse. There is no reason why a child's initial disclosure should not be believed, until clearly disproved. Many survivors have written of the great relief of being believed and also of finding out that there are others like themselves. The problems of coping with subsequent silences and retractions should not be minimized but there is no reason why a child who has retracted an accusation should not be recognized as needing extra support, since there will be good reason for the retraction and almost certainly continuing stress and even risk. Retractions or denials from children have been taken as meaning that the allegation was false; however as chapter 3 showed, very few false allegations are made by children; retractions are often followed by further disclosures when the child is more secure. Even a false allegation is an indication that something is seriously wrong.

Many survivors complained that they were not told what would happen, they were taken here and there without explanation and treated as though they had no right to or need for information. This should not happen; it is probably because adults are themselves so shocked by sexual abuse that they cannot act humanely but this is merely further evidence of the need for training of those who deal with children in need, and the need for education of the public at large. However, even more than the need for information after the abuse has been disclosed, survivors say that they wished they could have had advice and counselling beforehand, so that they would have known what to expect. Again, there seems no reason why children should not be given some understanding of how difficult it is to stop sexual abuse. The establishment of the free telephone service, ChildLine, was a response to the overwhelming request from survivors for advice, information and counselling to be made available to children confidentially. The volume of calls that it has received, 5,865 with problems of sexual abuse in one year alone according to their last report, is an index of the need.[16] It cannot be known how many children who confide in ChildLine that they are being sexually abused do afterwards tell someone else in order to get help; but those who do are probably better prepared for what may then happen. Unfortunately this service cannot reach the very young, who may also be at risk.

ChildLine has the advantage of being able to tailor its advice to the child's age and needs and can help children prepare for the shock of disclosure. Children also need information not directly associated with the crisis itself which may serve to give them more protection against being sexually abused. There are now teaching packs, with videos, which aim to teach children that they have the right to control their own bodies, that they are entitled to say 'no' and to say it loudly. But however well-intentioned and well-prepared these preventative efforts are, they fail to consider an important element in the sexual abuse of children: their physical weakness. Where an abuser is prepared to force a child, and such individuals are quite common, saying 'no' is not enough to protect them; in some circumstances, teaching a child to say 'no' may actually put it in danger of violence or give the impression that if (s)he fails to prevent the abuse then (s)he is to blame.[17] It is absurd to refer to this form of education as 'empowering' children; no mere form of words will alter the balance of power between adults and children. Nevertheless children do need to know that they are entitled to object to sexual activities and where they can go for help if they need it, and what can be done to help them. Some parents object to education of this sort and the organization Parents against Injustice describes it as frightening children unnecessarily. There is no evidence, other than the odd anecdote produced for rhetorical effect, that children are harmed by this information if it is properly presented. Parents should certainly be allowed to assure themselves that the programme used for their child is well designed. It may encourage one or two in a class to disclose that they have been abused, which does throw a rather curious light on the point-blank refusal, usually without discussion, of some parents to let their children attend.

There is also a great need, obvious throughout this book, for education directed at the general public. The continuation of myths about children and of excuses for those who sexually abuse them can only be eradicated by adequate understanding of the problem. It will take time to change the general view of children from one which considers them the property of their parents to a recognition of them as citizens in the making. In particular the parents of the future need to be educated for their responsibilities. Many of them have experiences which make it difficult for them to be good parents. Sex education in schools is often not helpful; it is generally too much concerned with the biology of reproduction and much too little directed toward responsibility to sexual partners and to children. If the next generation of parents are made to understand that in having a baby they are taking on responsibility for another human being and what that entails, that in itself would be an advance – although no one would be naive enough to think that it would solve the problem.

It would be wrong to suppose that it is easy to prevent abusers from repeating their offences or to 'cure' them of the propensity to satisfy themselves sexually with children. More than one person who is involved in programmes of therapy for sexual offenders has made the point to me that it is very difficult to ensure that they will not offend again.[18]

A child who has revealed that it has been sexually abused needs support and encouragement. Unfortunately, the reactions of the child's mother are not always supportive of the child. She may either believe the child or not. Some mothers refuse to believe the allegation and become very angry with the child, rejecting it most cruelly. Others do believe it but are so distressed that they collapse and are unable to be of help to anyone. Many mothers do their best but they face financial difficulties as well as having to cope with a damaged and unhappy child, who moreover may harbour angry feelings about not having been protected. Neighbours and friends of the parents may react in a hostile way to the whole family and some can only find a restored equilibrium by moving house. For mothers to offer their children the support they need, they must be supported as well.

There is no reason for not giving victims of sexual abuse the fullest information they can grasp about what is happening to them and their families, including the fact that it may not be possible for them to stay at home. Encouraging them to voice their opinions is one way to indicate that they have some value, which is particularly necessary when children have been abused and deprived of all feelings of self-worth. There are some children who are comforted by a court's judgement which seems to justify them but some protection is possible without a need to convict an abuser. For all children the legal process is a great additional strain and if there is no conviction they may feel accused or betrayed again.

Intervention

Campaigns for disclosure

A section of the public, alarmed at the prospect that the sexual abuse of children may be very common and distressed at the thought of their suffering alone and in silence, is in favour of extensive campaigns to reveal as much of the sexual abuse as possible. They argue that all those who have charge of children should be put on the alert for signs of sexual abuse and children should be widely encouraged to tell someone of any abuse they are suffering. While such general education will probably be helpful, as long as it is accompanied by training, there are dangers in such a campaign which must be faced. To begin with the resources to deal with the massive increase in reporting that might result are not available and at the time of writing it looks unlikely that they will be. Already it is reported in many areas that children known to be at risk of sexual or physical abuse have not been allocated a social worker. It would be cruel to encourage reporting only to leave the victims who revealed themselves without help. One of the factors leading to the Cleveland crisis was the strain placed on the hospital and social services by the rapid increase in cases. The sheer overwork it caused seems to have made it virtually impossible to treat children and parents sympathetically.

Further, it is generally recognized that cases of sexual abuse arouse strong emotions in those who deal with them and training is required if they are not to become a handicap.[19] The lack of staff in Cleveland who were trained to deal with the sexual abuse of children meant that those who did deal with the parents and children seemed unable to cope with their own feelings sufficiently well to act professionally; they were angry with parents, disgusted, outraged, or embarrassed. Their undisciplined feelings contributed to the mistakes being made. There is an overwhelming case for more national resources to be put aside for the purpose of strengthening and improving the services for children who are abused in any way.

There is a case for legislation to be passed making it mandatory for adults who are informed of a case of sexual abuse to report it. At the moment only social workers are required to do so; teachers, doctors, solicitors or lawyers may keep the information confidential. While many do report cases to the police or social services, others do not wish to take the responsibility for 'breaking up the family' or do not see it as their concern. Some are fearful of the consequences if they have made a mistake and persuade themselves that the suspicions are unfounded or that the abuse will stop once it has been revealed. Still others do not believe that sexual abuse happens or are confused about where their professional responsibility lies: to their client or to the client's child. The result is that they do not report it, the child is denied help and it is virtually certain that the abuse will go on. The child's trust is further betrayed and it will be inhibited from telling another adult for fear that nothing will be done. In the United States, most states have laws making reporting mandatory; in Colorado this extends to members of the public. Such laws make it quite clear where the priority must lie: in helping the child. The result may possibly be a larger number of cases where the suspicions turn out to be unjustified but such laws make it more difficult for adults to disregard suspected abuse because it is too unpleasant to think about.

Keeping the child at home

Once sexual abuse has been established it is important to separate the abuser from the child. In a large number of cases he is very angry with the child, who may be terrified at what will be done in revenge for the disclosure. Violence is not so uncommon that it can be ignored. How the separation is effected may depend on a number of factors which should include the child's own wishes. Some victims are only too glad to leave the family where they have suffered. One survivor recorded on the BBC questionnaire that her 'best memory' was 'fooling the social services that I was mad so I would be taken into care'. But for most children it is an added trauma to be taken away from home and all they know to live in a strange place with strange people; it can be, in effect, a second traumatic experience.

People ask why it is not possible to require a suspected abuser to leave the house while matters are sorted out, rather than punishing the child again by removing the child from its home. Unless he is arrested, this is not easy. It may be argued that to expect a man to leave his home before the allegation against him has been proved in court is to go against the basic principle of British justice which states that a person is innocent until proved guilty. To set aside this legal principle, even for serious crimes against children, is a serious matter and cannot be done lightly. Some abusers positively refuse to leave and there are few statutory powers that can make them do so. Of course if the evidence is good enough or there has been a confession, the police may arrest the alleged abuser and ensure that he lives in a bail hostel. This does not make sure that he does not see the victim alone.

This separation of abuser and victim is necessary because the child may be abused again, threatened or bullied to change her or his statement, or punished for telling the secret. While a mother may take out an injunction preventing a suspected offender from coming to the house or seeing the child, this is an unusual, expensive course for a woman to take and she may be too emotionally upset to attempt it. However in the United States, it is said, a high proportion of fathers and stepfathers do leave home after an accusation of sexual abuse; it would not be impossible to make it easier for that to happen in Britain.

There are, however, other reasons for removing a child who has disclosed sexual abuse. If the child is to remain at home, not only must (s)he be kept away from the abuser but there must be emotional support as well. Mothers do not always believe a child and may react angrily, rejecting the children who have, in their eyes, brought all this trouble on them. Even if she believes the child's story, a woman may not find it possible to withstand her husband's emotional pressure to allow him back into the house. Her reactions or those of the child's siblings may make it too punitive an environment for a hurt and confused child, fearful of blame and punishment.

It is often not possible to ensure a child can be protected at home, unless it is known that the danger lies elsewhere. If the victim cannot say who did it and thereby exonerate the father or stepfather, then they cannot be allowed home in case they will be severely bullied or hurt to ensure they do not tell Although cases where children are killed because they told of their sexual abuse are fortunately not common, the possibility of violent retribution from the abuser must be borne in mind. Unfortunately there is clear evidence that those who abuse children are not stopped by the knowledge that they have been found out. Threats to tell the police may have no effect as the case of Dan Grimshaw demonstrated. Even those who have served a prison sentence for sexually abusing a child may re-offend. This makes it extremely difficult for anyone concerned with an abused child to accept the denial and let the child go home if there is a chance that the person responsible is a member of that household. Each case should be considered according to its own circumstances; the slogan 'keep the child at home' is not the solution in every instance and it may prolong the suffering of the victims.

Deterring the offender

The legal process as it is currently constituted does not appear to act as a deterrent to sexual abuse in the first place or even to deter men from re-offending. Even worse, it encourages a man accused of sexually abusing a child to deny responsibility for the offence. Where the child is very young, and the case is contested, there is unlikely to be a prosecution unless there is evidence to support the child's statement. Some people may think these are the most serious cases of all, yet they are the ones least likely to end in the conviction of an offender. Even where a child is old enough and able to give evidence courts may choose to believe the adult's denial. As Gorry, an experienced police officer, pointed out, the chances of a successful prosecution are not high. A solicitor may well encourage his client to plead not guilty, which has the effect of encouraging him to deny his accountability. Gorry gives the proportion of convictions in London over a five-year period as 56 per cent, but the proportion of those imprisoned was just about a third.[20] There was no police charge in 43 per cent of cases. Since many of those who abuse children sexually are not being imprisoned it seems arguable that the law is not the best instrument for dealing with this offence.

The prospects of imprisonment for an offender also encourage denial. It is widely known that sexual offenders have more to fear from prison than most criminals, since they will have to bear the hostility of other prisoners. Some abusers tell their victims this in order to paint a grimmer picture of what will happen if they tell. This indicates that, even so, a prison sentence is not a deterrent, but may merely cause an additional load of blame to be shifted on to the victim. A follow-up of cases involving children treated at Great Ormond Street Hospital two to five years later found that 69 per cent of abusers denied that there had been sexual abuse. Over 60 per cent of these men had been sent for trial, but very few of them (8 per cent) had been acquitted, so that it seems likely that most of those who were still refusing to admit the abuse had already been found guilty of their crime and two-thirds had served a prison sentence for it.[21]

The public puts a high priority on the punishment of offenders. The motive behind the pressure for a campaign to reveal sexual abuse may be the desire to catch and punish offenders. While the general anger against those who do such harm to children is quite intelligible, vengeance does not solve any problems. A prison sentence does not change the offender, who is likely to re-offend once released, even if he chooses a different victim. A study of the rate of recidivism among sexual offenders by Gibbens, Soothill and Way found a 30 per cent rate of reconviction among older offenders.[22] There are therapeutic programmes in some prisons but resources are inadequate and there has been no research yet to try and find out how effective they are. All that may happen is that a man leaves prison determined never to be found out again.

If punishment does not ensure that an offender will not re-offend after leaving prison, this does not mean that nothing should be done about perpetrators of sexual abuse. It would be possible to impose a term of probation with the requirement that an offender undergo treatment. This is done in other countries: Holland is an example. Most treatment programmes are not easy; they require an offender to face up to what he has done and what he is like, something that most are very unwilling to do. They cannot be called soft options and some of them have achieved encouraging results. The results of some American therapeutic programmes, particularly those associated with the name of Giaretto in California, do appear to be preventing recurrence. There is less optimism in Britain, but this work has only just begun here.

It is important to be clear what the success of therapy means and

establish a priority of aims. Is it improved psychological health for
the victim? Preventing the abuser from repeating his abuse?
Keeping the victim at home? Enabling the family to stay together?
Sometimes it appears as though those who refer cases for therapy
expect it to result in the household staying intact with better
relationships established among its members: a miracle. This can
happen but it is very rare. The numbers of 'families' amenable to
treatment are few; one of the team at Great Ormond Street
Hospital for Sick Children estimated that most fell into the
'Doubtful' category.[23] Even those that are treated may not stay
together. In the study of their work on the sexual abuse of
children, the team at Great Ormond Street Hospital also collected
information retrospectively on the people they had seen in the years
between 1981 and 1984. They asked social workers for their views
and also administered a questionnaire to members of the family (it
was not specified whether they filled in one jointly or one per
member). In under a quarter of the cases the composition of the
household was the same as it had been at intake. In all the others,
either the victim or the perpetrator had left and it is important to
note that it was much more often the victim. Only 14 per cent of the
victims and a third of their siblings were still with both parents;
another third of the victims were living with their mother on her
own. A few of these children might have left home anyway in the
normal course of events, but it is not likely that 86 per cent would
be separated from both parents when many were very young when
they were referred. The perpetrators had suffered much less
disruption; 42 per cent had stayed in their homes.[24] We are not told
what outcomes are specifically associated with domestic abuse. In a
number of these cases the abuser was not a member of the
household; one would not expect the consequences to be the same
in such cases. Nevertheless, these facts are a salutary reminder of
who suffers most from children's sexual abuse.

The breakdown of these households cannot easily be attributed
solely to interventions by the state. The report from which the facts
above are quoted does not indicate how these people separated and
on whose initiative. There are a number of possible reasons for
these changes in household membership. Case histories indicate
that often the marriage breaks down; the relations of husband and
wife do not recover from the shock of the abuse's disclosure. The
largest number of victims still living with a parent are living with

their mother alone. Sometimes the abused child runs away or chooses to leave home; some abusers may not return home when they are released from jail. It is worth reminding ourselves too that the real cause of the upheaval and the ultimate reason for the separation and the unhappiness is not the action of the authorities, but the sexual abuse which made that action necessary.

The Best We Have to Give?

In 1959 the United Nations Declaration of the Rights of the Child contained the statement of a universal principle: 'Whereas mankind owes to the child the best it has to give.'[25] In November 1989 the United Nations at last ratified a Declaration of the Rights of the Child and member governments will be asked to sign it. We must hope that the British Government will do so without reservation. Its provisions provide a statement of the standard of care and concern that children should have, that governments should try to ensure for all our children.

Yet we cannot expect governments and professionals to give children's needs the highest priority if the general public continues to ignore them. The man quoted at the head of this chapter remarked: 'children compose a third of the population and yet they have no civil rights and no protection against exploitation by adults.' His statement is particularly telling since he has been both abused and abuser: he was abandoned at nine months old and brought up in a children's home, where he was abused by some of the older boys; he also reported himself as having abused several children. Histories of child care refer to the modern family as child-centred; this often appears to mean not much more than considering children as expensive pets.

This victim is of the opinion that children are treated as property. There is no great difference between pets and property; certainly they are not taken to have the same rights as people. This attitude continues to be held even when the community is outraged at what those parents do. One national newspaper reported that news of group sexual activities among some related adults and a number of children, their own and others, leaked out into the estate where they lived. They were attacked in various ways by their neighbours.[26] Obviously those who did that believed that children were being sexually abused; yet they apparently told no one who could do something about it, leaving the children to go on suffering physical and sexual abuse of the most extreme kind, until one child broke down and told his teacher. Their indignation was reported but none of the quotes printed mentioned helping the children. The attacks the neighbours seem to have mounted on the households concerned would certainly not have encouraged any of the victims to think of these people as a source of support.

It is time that the nation really learned to see children apart from their parents and to put the children first. It is not necessary to abandon the way we organize domestic life to do this. All it takes is the recognition that parents, like any other people with rights over other people, may sometimes abuse their rights and neglect those responsibilities. If it is true that the involvement of other relatives and the community is a protection for children against the abuse of parental powers, and there is evidence from other societies that this is so, then public concern and readiness to watch for and report suspicions of sexual abuse may do a great deal of good. We also need to ensure that our legal procedures protect children and spare them unnecessary suffering. We need teams of social workers who are sufficient in numbers and well enough trained to shoulder the responsibilities that they carry and make informed, considered judgements as to the appropriate action in each case. All this will require public expenditure and pressure may have to be put on successive governments to make funds available. But we cannot rely on the state alone. Until we all abandon the dogma of parents' natural infallibility, children will continue to be sexually abused and despair of getting help.

Notes

1 E. A. Olson, 'Socio-economic and psycho-cultural context of child abuse and neglect in Turkey', in J. E. Korbin (ed.), *Child Abuse and Neglect: Cross Cultural Perspectives* (University of California Press, Berkeley, 1981), p. 108; and see p. 106 this volume.
2 See La Fontaine, 'Preliminary remarks'.
3 Ennew, *Sexual Exploitation*.
4 B. Malinowski, *Crime and Custom in Savage Society* (Routledge Kegan Paul, London, 1926).

5 J. E. Korbin, 'Conclusions', in Korbin (ed.), *Child Abuse and Neglect*, p. 208.

6 Dr Margaret Lock, personal communication.

7 Olson, 'Socio-economic and psycho-cultural context', p. 108.

8 L. L. Langness, 'Child abuse and cultural values: the case of New Guinea', in Korbin (ed.), *Child Abuse and Neglect*, pp. 21–30, discusses the whole issue of cultural relativities.

9 D. Finkelhor and J. E. Korbin, 'Child abuse as an international issue', *Child Abuse and Neglect*, 12(1) (1988), pp. 3–23.

10 A. Bentovim and P. Boston, 'Sexual abuse – basic issues', in Bentovim et al., *Child Sexual Abuse*; A. A. Cavarola and M. Scheff, 'Behavioural sequelae of physical and/or sexual abuse', *Child Abuse and Neglect*, 12(2) (1988), pp. 181–8. Similar reports have been made from Australia, Canada and New Zealand.

11 Some doctors may still be reluctant to recognize venereal disease in children, particularly if they are young; if they do, they may shy away from accepting the mode of transmission and suggest ways in which the disease might have been caught which they would think ludicrous if the patient were an adult.

12 E. Vizard and M. Tranter, 'Helping young children to describe experiences of child sexual abuse – general issues', in Bentovim et al., *Child Sexual Abuse*; also D. Glaser and C. Collins, Department of Child Psychiatry, Guy's Hospital, London: 'The response of young, non-sexually abused children to anatomically correct dolls', ms, March 1988. For America, L. Jampole and M. Weber, 'An assessment of the behaviour of sexually abused children and non-sexually abused children with anatomically correct dolls', *Child Abuse and Neglect*, 11(2), 1987, pp. 187–92; these authors point out that in a few cases the sexualized behaviour was only shown when adults were out of the room (and observing behaviour through one-way glass).

13 E. J. Saunders, 'A comparative study of attitudes towards child sexual abuse among social work and judicial system professionals', *Child Abuse and Neglect*, 12(1) (1988); Finkelhor, *Child Sexual Abuse*, chapter 13, written in collaboration with B. Gomez-Schwartz and J. Horowitz; T. Furniss, 'Mutual influence'.

14 Gorry, 'Incest', p. 35.

15 J. Lewis, 'Anxieties about the family and the relationships between parents, children and the state in twentieth-century England', in Light and Richards (eds), *Children of Social Worlds*. See also R. Dingwall, J. Eekelaar and T. Murray, *The Protection of Children* (Basil Blackwell, Oxford, 1983), and F. Mount, *The Subversive Family: An Alternative History of Love and Marriage* (George Allen and Unwin, London, 1982).

16 This appears to be the number of children calling rather than the number of calls; but a child may call more than once before revealing his or her name so that it is hard to be sure of the numbers.

17 B. Trudell and M. H. Whateley, 'School sexual abuse prevention: unintended consequences and effects', *Child Abuse and Neglect*, 12(1) (1988), pp. 115–17.

18 See also T. C. Gibbens, K. L. Soothill and C. K. Way, 'Sibling and parent–child incest offenders: a long-term follow-up', *British Journal of Criminology*, 18(1), (1978).

19 Tranter and Vizard, 'The professional network', p. 141.

20 Gorry, 'Incest', p. 41.

21 Bentovim, van Elburg and Boston, 'The results of treatment', in Bentovim et al. (eds), *Child Sexual Abuse*, p. 262.

22 Note that this refers only to reconvictions, not to further offences; there may have been many of these that were not discovered. Even so, the fact that one in three of these convicted men were convicted of offending again strongly suggest that prison sentences are not effective deterrents. Gibbens, Soothill and Way, 'Sex offences'.

23 A. Elton, 'Assessment of families for treatment', in Bentovim et al. (eds), *Child Sexual Abuse*, p. 176.

24 A. Bentovim, A. van Elburg and P. Boston, 'The results of treatment', in Bentovim et al. (eds), *Child Sexual Abuse*, p. 261.

25 United Nations Declaration of the Rights of the Child, 20 November 1959.

26 *Sunday Mirror*, 20 November 1988.

Bibliography

Arens, W., *The Original Sin: Incest and its Meaning*, Oxford University Press, Oxford and New York, 1986.

Bailey, V. and McCabe, S., 'Reforming the law of incest', *Criminal Law Review*, 1979, pp. 749–64.

Baker, A. and Duncan, S., 'Child sexual abuse: a study of prevalence in Great Britain', *Child Abuse and Neglect*, 9 (4), 1985.

Barnes, J. A., 'Genetrix: genitor::nature: culture?', in J. Goody (ed.), *The Contexts of Kinship: Essays in Honour of Meyer Fortes*, Cambridge University Press, Cambridge, 1975.

Bender, L. and Blau, A., 'The reaction of children to sexual relations with adults', *American Journal of Orthopsychiatry*, no. 7, 1936, pp. 825–37.

Bentovim, A., 'Understanding the phenomenon of sexual abuse – a family systems view of causation', in Bentovim et al. (eds), *Child Sexual Abuse*.

Bentovim, A. and Boston, P., 'Sexual abuse: basic issues: characteristics of children and families', in Bentovim et al. (eds), *Child Sexual Abuse*.

Bentovim, A., van Elburg, A. and Boston, P., 'The results of treatment', in Bentovim et al. (eds), *Child Sexual Abuse*.

Bentovim, A., Elton, A., Hildebrand, J., Tranter, M. and Vizard, E. (eds), *Child Sexual Abuse within the Family: Assessment and Treatment. The Work of the Great Ormond Street Team*, Wright, London, 1988.

Bentovim, A. and Vizard, E., 'Sexual abuse, sexuality and childhood', in Bentovim et al. (eds), *Child Sexual Abuse*.

Brake, M. (ed.), *Human Sexual Relations: A Reader*, Penguin, Harmondsworth, 1982.

Brandes, S., 'Like wounded stags: male sexual ideology in an Andalusian town', in S. B. Ortner and H. Whitehead (eds), *Sexual Meanings*, Cambridge University Press, Cambridge, 1981.

Browne, L. and Holder, W., 'The nature and extent of child abuse in contemporary American society', in *Sexual Abuse of Children* American Humane Association, Denver, 1980.

Burgoyne, J. and Clark, D., 'From father to stepfather', in McKee and O'Brien (eds), *The Father Figure*.

Burgoyne, J., Ormrod, R. and Richards, M. (eds), *Divorce Matters*, Penguin, Harmondsworth, 1987.

Butler-Sloss, Lord Justice E., *Report of the Inquiry into Child Abuse in Cleveland 1987*, HMSO, London, 1988 (Cleveland Report).

Campbell, B., *Unofficial Secrets*, Virago, London, 1988.

Caplan, P. (ed.), *The Cultural Construction of Sexuality*, Tavistock, London, 1987.

Carter, R., 'ChildWatch, November 1986', overview of 2,530 self-completion questionnaires, BBC Broadcasting Research Special Projects Report, 1986, unpublished.

Cavarola, A. A. and Scheff, M., 'Behavioural sequelae of physical and/or sexual abuse', *Child Abuse and Neglect*, 12, 1988, pp. 181–8.

Chesser, E., *The Sexual, Marital and Family Relationships of the English Woman*, Hutchinson, Watford, 1956.

ChildLine: 'The first year', report for 1987 issued by ChildLine, London, unpublished.

Coggeshall, J. M., 'Ladies behind bars: a liminal gender as cultural mirror', *Anthropology Today*, 4 (4), 1988.

Creighton, S., *Trends in Child Abuse*, National Society for the Prevention of Cruelty to Children, London, 1984.

Dingwall, R., Eekelaar, J. and Murray, T., *The Protection of Children: State Intervention and Family Life*, Blackwell, Oxford, 1983.

Durkheim, E., 'Le problème de l'inceste et ses origines', *Année Sociologique*, 1, 1896–7.

Elias, J. and Gebhard, P., 'Sexuality and sexual learning in children', in R. S. Rogers (ed.), *Sexual Education – Rationale and Reaction*, Cambridge University Press, Cambridge, 1969.

Elton, A., 'Assessment of families for treatment' and 'Treatment methods and techniques', in Bentovim et al. (eds), *Child Sexual Abuse*.

Ennew, J., *The Sexual Exploitation of Children*, Polity, Cambridge, 1986.

Finkelhor, D., *Sexually Victimised Children*, Free Press, New York, 1979.

—— *Child Sexual Abuse: New Theory and Research*, Free Press, New York, 1984.

Finkelhor, D. and Korbin, J. E., 'Child abuse as an international issue', *Child Abuse and Neglect*, 12(1), 1988, pp. 3–23.

Finkelhor, D. and Russell, D., 'Women as perpetrator', in Finkelhor, *Child Sexual Abuse*, pp. 171–87.

Fortes, M., 'Ritual and office', in M. Gluckman (ed.), *Essays on the Ritual of Social Relations*, Manchester University Press, Manchester, 1956.

—— *Rules and the Emergence of Society*, Occasional Paper 39, Royal Anthropological Institute, London, 1983.

Fox, R., 'Sibling incest', *British Journal of Sociology*, 13, 1962.

—— *The Red Lamp of Incest*, Hutchinson, London, 1980.

Frazer, J. G., *Totemism and Exogamy*, Macmillan, London, 1910.

Freeman, M. D. A., 'Legal ideologies, patriarchal precedents, and domestic violence', in Freeman (ed.), *State, Law and the Family*.

—— (ed.), *State, Law and the Family: Critical Perspectives*, Tavistock, London, 1984.

Freud, S., 'The aetiology of hysteria', 1896, reproduced in Masson, *Freud: The Assault on Truth*.

—— *Totem and Taboo*, W. W. Norton, New York, 1950.

Furniss, T., 'Mutual influence and interlocking professional–family processes in the treatment of child sexual abuse and incest', *Child Abuse and Neglect*, 7, 1983.

—— 'Conflict-avoiding and conflict-regulating patterns in incest and child sexual abuse', *Acta Paediatrica Scandinavica*, 50, 1984.

Gagnon, J. H. and Simon, W., *Sexual Conduct: The Social Sources of Human Sexuality*, Aldine, Chicago, 1973, excerpted in Brake (ed.), *Human Sexual Relations*.

Gibbens, T. C. N., 'Sibling and parent–child incest offenders: a long-term follow-up', *British Journal of Criminology*, 18 (1), 1978.

Gibbens, T. C. N., Soothill, K. L. and Way, C. K., 'Sex offences against young girls: a long-term record study', *Psychological Medicine*, 2, 1981, pp. 351–7.

Goody, E., 'Why must might be right? Reflections on sexual Herrschaft', *Cambridge Anthropology*, January 1987.

Goody, J., 'A comparative approach to incest and adultery', *British Journal of Sociology*, 7, 1956.

—— *The Development of the Family and Marriage in Europe*, Cambridge University Press, Cambridge, 1983.

—— (ed.), *The Developmental Cycle in Domestic Groups*, Cambridge Papers in Social Anthropology 1, Cambridge University Press, Cambridge, 1958.

Gorry, P. J., 'Incest – the offence and police investigation', M.Phil. thesis in Criminology, University of Cambridge, 1986.

Haskey, J., 'Social class and socio-economic differentials in divorce in England and Wales', *Population Studies*, 38, 1984.

Heider, Karl G., 'Dani sexuality: a low energy system', *Man*, 11(2), 1976.

Henderson, D. J., 'Incest', in A. M. Freedman, H. I. Kaplan and B. J. Sadock (eds), *Comprehensive Textbook of Psychiatry*, Williams and Wilkins, Baltimore, 1975, p. 1532.

Henshall, C. and McGuire, J., 'Gender development', in Light and Richards (eds), *Children of Social Worlds*.

Herman, J., *Father–Daughter Incest*, Harvard University Press, Cambridge, Mass. and London, 1981.

Hildebrand, J., 'Working with mothers of abused children', in Bentovim et al. (eds), *Child Sexual Abuse*.

Hopkins, K., 'Brother–sister marriage in Roman Egypt', *Comparative Studies in Society and History*, 22, 1980.

Houlbrook, R. A., *The English Family, 1450–1700*, Longmans, Harlow, 1984.

Howard League for Penal Reform, *Unlawful Sex: Offences, Victims and Offenders in the Criminal Justice System of England and Wales*, report of a Howard League working party, Waterlow, 1985.

Jampole, L. and Weber, M., 'An assessment of the behaviour of sexually abused children and non-sexually abused children with anatomically correct dolls', *Child Abuse and Neglect* 11(2), 1987, pp. 187–92.

Jones, D. and McCraw, E. M., 'Reliable and fictitious accounts of sexual abuse to children', *Journal of Interpersonal Violence*, 2(1), 1987, pp. 27–45.

Jones, D. and Seig, A., 'Child sexual abuse allegations in custody or visitation disputes', in E. B. Nicholson (ed.), *Sexual Abuse Allegations in Custody and Visitation Cases*, American Bar Association, Washington DC, 1988.

Kempe, C. H., Silverman, F. N., Steele, B. F., Droegmuller, W. and Silver, H. K., 'The battered child syndrome', *Journal of the American Medical Association*, 181, 1962.

Kempe, R. S. and Kempe, C. H., *Child Abuse*, Fontana, Glasgow, 1978.

Kendall-Tackett, K. A. and Simon, A. F., 'Molestation and the onset of puberty', *Child Abuse and Neglect*, 12(1), 1988.

Kinsey, A., Pomeroy, W. B. and Martin, C. E., *Sexual Behaviour in the Human Male*, Saunders, Philadelphia, 1948.

Kinsey, A., Pomeroy, W. B., Martin, C. E. and Gebhard, P. H., *Sexual Behaviour in the Human Female*, Saunders, Philadelphia, 1953.

Korbin, J. E., (ed.), *Child Abuse and Neglect: Cross-Cultural Perspectives*, University of California, Berkeley, 1981.

Koshal, N., 'An audience analysis on *ChildWatch*', BBC Broadcasting Research, Information Section, 1986, unpublished.

La Fontaine, J. S., 'The domestication of the savage male', *Man*, new series, 16(3), 1980.

—— 'Anthropological perspectives on the family and social change', *Journal of the Economic and Social Science Research Council*, 1(1), 1985.

—— 'An anthropological perspective on children in social worlds', in Light and Richards (eds), *Children of Social Worlds*.

—— 'Preliminary remarks on a study of incest in London', in Scheper-Hughes (ed.), *Child Survival*.

—— 'Child sexual abuse and the incest taboo: practical problems and theoretical issues', *Man*, new series, 23(1), 1988.

—— 'Public or private? The constitution of the family in anthropological perspective', *International Journal of Moral and Social Studies*, 3(3), Autumn 1988.

Langness, L. L., 'Child abuse and cultural values: the case of New Guinea', in Korbin (ed.), *Child Abuse and Neglect*.

Leach, E. R., *Political Systems of Highland Burma*, G. Bell, London, 1954.

Levin, J. (ed.), *Family Law by His Honour Judge Brian Grant*, 3rd edn, Sweet and Maxwell, London, 1977.

Lewis, J., 'Anxieties about the family and the relationships between parents, children and the state in twentieth-century England', in Light and Richards (eds), *Children of Social Worlds*.

Light, P. and Richards, M. (eds), *Children of Social Worlds*, Polity, Cambridge, 1986.

Lowe, N. V., 'The legal status of fathers: past and present', in McKee and O'Brien (eds), *The Father Figure*.

Lukianowicz, N., 'Incest', *British Journal of Psychiatry*, 120, 1972, pp. 301–13.

Maddox, B., *The Half-Parent*, M. Evans, New York, 1975.

Mair, L. P., *Marriage*, Penguin, Harmondsworth, 1971.

Maisch, H., *Incest*, Andre Deutsch, London, 1973.

Malinowski, B., *Crime and Custom in Savage Society*, Routledge and Kegan Paul, London, 1926.

—— 'A sociological study of the rationale of the prohibited degrees of marriage', in *Kindred and Affinity as Impediments to Marriage*, as appendix 3, Church of England Commission, London, 1940.

Masson, J. M., *Freud: The Assault on Truth*, Faber and Faber, London, 1984.

McCron, R. and Carter, R., 'ChildWatch national opinion survey', BBC Broadcasting Research Special Projects Report, 1987, unpublished.

—— 'Researching socially sensitive subjects: the case of child abuse', BBC Broadcasting Research, unpublished, n.d.

McKee, L., 'Fathers' participation in infant care: a critique', in McKee and O'Brien (eds), *Father Figure*.

McKee, L. and O'Brien, M. (eds), *The Father Figure*, Tavistock, London, 1982.

Meiselman, K. C., *Incest: A Psychological Study of Causes and Effects with Treatment Recommendations*, Jossey-Bass, San Francisco, 1984.

Mount, F., *The Subversive Family: An Alternative History of Love and Marriage*, Allen and Unwin, London, 1982.

Mrazek, P. and Kempe, C. (eds), *Sexually Abused Children and Their Families*, Pergamon, Oxford, 1981.

Mrazek, P. B., Lynch, M. and Bentovim, A., 'Recognition of child sexual abuse in the United Kingdom', in Mrazek and Kempe (eds), *Sexually Abused Children*.

Mrazek, P. B. and Mrazek, D. A., 'Definition and recognition of sexual child abuse: historical and cultural perspectives', in Mrazek and Kempe (eds), *Sexually Abused Children*.

Murdock, G. P., *Social Structure*, Macmillan, New York, 1949.

Nash, C. and West, D., 'Victimisation of young girls', in D. West (ed.), *Sexual Victimisation*, Gower, Aldershot, 1985.

Nelson, S., *Incest: Fact and Myth*, Stramullion Co operative, Edinburgh, 1988.

Olson, E. A., 'Socio-economic and psycho-cultural context of child abuse and neglect in Turkey', in Korbin (ed.), *Child Abuse and Neglect*.

Ortner, S. B. and Whitehead, H. (eds), *Sexual Meanings*, Cambridge University Press, Cambridge, 1981.

Pahl, J., 'The allocation of money within the household', in Freeman (ed.), *State, Law, and the Family*.

Parker, S. and Parker, H., 'Father–daughter sexual abuse: an emerging perspective', *American Journal of Orthopsychiatry*, 56(4), 1986.

Parsons, T. C., 'The incest taboo in relation to social structure and the socialization of the child', *British Journal of Sociology*, 5, 1954.

Radcliffe-Brown, A. R., *African Systems of Kinship and Marriage*, International African Institute, Oxford University Press, London, 1950.

Reid, I., *Social Class Differences in Britain*, 2nd edn, Grant McIntyre, London, 1981.

Renvoize, J., *Incest: a Family Pattern*, Routledge and Kegan Paul, London, 1982.

Richards, M., introduction to Light and Richards (eds), *Children of Social Worlds*.

Runcie, J., 'Tips from a wicked stepfather', *Observer*, 3 April 1988.

Russell, D. E. H., *Sexual Exploitation: Rape, Child Sexual Abuse and Workplace Harassment*, Sage, Beverly Hills, 1984.

—— *The Secret Trauma: Incest in the Lives of Girls and Women*, Basic Books, New York, 1986.

Sanders, D., *The Woman Book of Love and Sex*, Sphere, London, 1985.

—— *The Woman Book on Men*, Sphere, London, 1985.

Scheper-Hughes, N., *Child Survival*, Reidel, Holland, 1987.

Schildkrout, E., 'Children's roles in urban Kano', in J. S. La Fontaine (ed.), *Sex and Age as Principles of Social Differentiation*, ASA Monographs 17, Academic Press, London, 1978.

Schneider, D. M., 'The meaning of incest', *Journal of the Polynesian Society*, 85, 1976, pp. 149–69.

Seidler, V. J., 'Reason, desire and male sexuality', in Caplan (ed.), *Cultural Construction*.

Sgroi, S., 'Kids with clap – gonorrhea as an indicator of child sexual assault', *Victimology*, 2, 1977, pp. 251–67.

Shepherd, G., 'Rank, gender and homosexuality: Mombasa as a key to understanding sexual options', in Caplan (ed.), *Cultural Construction*.

Smith, H. and Israel, E., 'Sibling incest: the study of the dynamics of 25 cases', *Child Abuse and Neglect*, 2(1), 1987.

Tardieu, A., *Étude médico-légale sur les attentats au moeurs*, Ballière et fils, Paris and London.

Tong, L., Oates, K. and McDowell, M., 'Personality developments following sexual abuse', *Child Abuse and Neglect*, 2(3), 1987, pp. 371–83.

Tranter, M. and Vizard, E., 'The professional network and management of disclosure', in Bentovim et al. (eds), *Child Sexual Abuse*.

Trudell, B. and Whately, M. H., 'School sexual abuse prevention: unintended consequences and effects', *Child Abuse and Neglect*, 12(1), 1988.

Tylor, E. B., 'On a method of investigating the development of institutions: applied to laws of marriage and descent', *Journal of the Royal Anthropological Institute*, 18, 1889, pp. 245–69.

Vizard, E. and Tranter, M., 'Helping young children to describe experiences of child sexual abuse – general issues', in Bentovim et al. (eds), *Child Sexual Abuse*.

Walmsley, R. and White K., Supplementary Information on Sexual Offences and Sentencing, Research Unit Paper No. 2, Home Office, 1980.

Weeks, J., 'Questions of identity', in Caplan (ed.), *Cultural Construction*.

Weinberg, K., *Incest Behaviour*, Citadel, New York, 1955.

Wells, N. H., 'Sexual offences as seen by a woman police surgeon', *British Medical Journal*, 2, 1958 (cited in Howard League, *Unlawful Sex*).

Whitehead, A., ' "I'm hungry, Mum." The politics of domestic budgeting', in K. Young, C. Wolkowitz and R. McCullagh (eds), *Of Marriage and the Market*, CSE Book, London, 1981.

Wilner, D., 'Definition and violation: incest and the incest taboo', *Man*, new series, 18(1), 1983, pp. 134–59.

Wolfram, S., 'Eugenics and the Punishment of Incest Act 1908', *Criminal Law Review*, 1983, pp. 508–18.

—— *In-Laws and Outlaws: Kinship and Marriage in England*, Croom Helm, London and Sydney, 1986.

Wyatt, G. E. and Peters, S. D., 'Issues in the definition of child sexual abuse in prevalence research', *Child Abuse and Neglect*, 10, 1986, pp. 231–40.

—— 'Methodological considerations in research on the prevalence of child sexual abuse', *Child Abuse and Neglect*, 10, 1986, pp. 241–51.

Yanagisako, S., 'Family and household: the analysis of domestic groups', *Annual Review of Anthropology*, 8, 1979.

Index

abuse
    definition of 16, 41, 45, 61, 65,
        111–12
    nature of 81, 83
abusers 9, 12, 50, 51, 53, 67,
    72–3, 74, 79, 88, 99–124,
    137, 149–50, 196, 219,
    225–7, 229; see also offen-
    ders; perpetrators
addiction 199; see also alcohol
adopted children 24–5, 133
adultery 30, 36
Age of Marriage Act 89
age of victims 23, 41, 62, 83,
    88–93, 133, 157, 172, 176,
    178, 184, 189, 212
alcohol 26, 100–1, 108
all-male institutions 86
allegations 216; see also disclosure;
    false allegations
altruism 187
American Humane Association 70,
    101
Amphlett, Mrs 11
anal dilatation 5, 10, 40
anal intercourse 5, 50, 81, 117,
    135–6, 175, 200; see also
    buggery
anatomically correct dolls 217,
    233
antecedents of abuse 146–7, 173,
    177
Arens, W. 43
aunts 24
authority 153, 187, 208–9
    parental 8
aversion, human

to inbreeding 158
to incest 33, 37, 136

Bailey, V. and McCabe, S. 42
Baker, A. and Duncan, S. 69, 111
Barnes, J. A. 205
BBC national survey 59, 61–2, 66,
    75, 87, 104, 119, 120–1, 133,
    134–5, 168, 171, 177, 199
BBC volunteer survey 66, 77, 213
Bell, Mr S. 2, 4, 6, 10–11, 75
Bentovim, A. 205
    and Boston, P. 98, 206, 233
    and Vizard 159–60, 180
    van Elburg, A. and Boston, P.
        234
bias 46, 56, 58–61, 120, 217
biological relationship 136–7; see
    also blood relations
Bishop, Mr 10
blame 71; see also denial; guilt
blood relations 126, 129, 141,
        185; see also biological rela-
        tionships
bonding 137–9
Bowlby, J. 137
boys, abuse of 85, 128, 135, 172,
    213
    compared with girls 84–8, 93,
        159, 162–3
Brake, M. 181
Brandes, S. 206
brothers 17, 28, 88, 128
brother/sister incest 29, 50,
    156–80
    theories of 151–8
buggery 50, 200

Burgoyne and Clark 154–5
Butler-Sloss, Lord Justice E. 2, 13, 42, 70

Campbell, B. 143, 199
Caplan, P. 206–7
Cavarola, A. A. and Scheff, M. 233
Chesser, E. 147, 154, 197, 206
child molesters 21; *see also* abusers
child pornography 65, 72, 102, 105
child prostitution 39, 102, 115, 209
child protection 2, 45, 58, 94, 114, 120, 122–3
ChildLine 107, 168, 181, 222–3
Children's Legal Centre 218
children's rights 8, 40
ChildWatch 3, 7, 64, 75, 92, 116, 168
Clark, D. and Burgoyne, J. 153, 154
class 58–60, 62, 135
Cleveland affair 1–13, 27, 42, 65, 74–5, 94, 110, 142, 143, 200, 215, 218–20, 225
Cleveland Inquiry 79, 212
Cleveland Parents Support Group 4, 6, 11
Cleveland Report, 10, 13, 42, 220
coercion 74, 143, 162, 169, 177
Coggeshall, J. M. 97
comparisons
  with other societies 27, 36–7, 138, 197, 209–11
  with USA 39, 60, 70, 75, 87, 136–8
competition, sexual 35, 195
consent 22, 30, 71, 73–4, 156, 177
consequences
  of disclosure 219
  of sexual abuse, 78, 83, 84, 212–13
cousins 28, 29
Creighton, S. 69
criminal offences 21, 22, 26

CSA Unit 14–15, 57, 95, 117, 134–5, 147, 149, 167

daughters 25, 32, 71, 80, 103, 142
Declaration of the Rights of the Child 231
definitions
  of incest 24–6
  of incestuous abuse 26
  of sexual abuse 16, 45, 61, 65, 111–12
denial 71, 211, 218–19, 228
dependence 35, 79, 111, 126, 144, 188, 189, 208
deterring the offender 228
diagnosis 3, 5–6, 10, 40, 53, 101, 216–18
digital penetration 81
Dingwall, R., Eekelaar, J. and Murray, T. 233
disclosure 217, 222–3, 226, 230
divorce 105, 131, 135, 142, 144, 145–6, 169, 187, 197
doctors 1, 4–6, 48, 53, 60, 63, 215
domestic organization 208; *see also* household
dominance 100, 160, 175, 189
Durkheim, E. 35, 195, 206

Elias, J. and Gebhard, P. 159, 180
Elton, A. 181, 234
Ennew, J. 102, 124, 207, 232
equality, 35, 156–7, 189
ethnic origin 104
exhibitionism 41, 61, 81, 111

false allegations 11, 51, 75–6, 222
family 8, 10, 17, 20–1, 24, 30–1, 34, 36–7, 51, 104, 110, 142, 147, 156, 178–9, 183–4, 186, 209, 221
fantasies 33–4, 71, 77, 99; *see also* false allegations
fathers 1, 17, 33–4, 71, 73, 88, 89, 104, 110, 115, 126–53, 189
female relatives 24, 73, 80, 106,

108, 210; *see also* daughters;
mothers; sisters
Finkelhor, D. 39, 70, 87, 88–9,
92, 101, 104–5, 109, 146,
154, 168–9, 181, 198, 201,
206–7, 233
and Korbin, J. E. 211, 233
and Russell, D. 107, 124, 125
fondling 41, 81
Fortes, M. 155, 192, 206–7
fostering 77, 133, 145
Fox, R. 156, 157, 163–4, 167,
180
Frazer, Sir J. 32, 33, 38
Freeman, M. D. A. 205
Freud, S. 32–4, 37, 99
friends of the family 87, 108, 114,
121, 123, 127, 134
Frosh, S. 207
Furniss, T. 18, 205, 217, 233

Gagnon, J. H. and Simon, W.
181–2
gender 10, 62, 105, 157, 160, 172,
187, 189
General Household Survey 133
generation 27, 35, 84, 187
genital fondling 81
Giaretto 229
Gibbens, T. C. N., Soothill, K. L.
and Way, C. K. 229, 234
girls' abuse compared with boys'
84–8, 93, 159, 162–3
Goody, E. 205
Goody, J. 42, 205
Gorry, P. J. 30, 50–1, 59, 69, 89,
103, 165–6, 181, 220, 228,
233, 234
granddaughter 24, 73
grandfather 115, 128
grandmother 5, 80, 106, 210
Great Ormond Street Hospital
229, 230
Groth 198, 207
guilt 80, 96, 131, 193; *see also*
blame; consequences

Harris, C. 204

Haskey, J. 153
Heider, K. G. 207
Henderson, D. J. 43
Henshall, C. and McGuire, J. 181,
205
Herman, J. 101, 153, 182, 198,
206
Higgs, Dr M. 1, 4, 6, 10–11, 74
Hildebrand, J. 194, 206
Hobbs, Dr C. 10
and Wynne, J. 18
homosexuality 21, 35–6, 85–6,
88, 195–6, 200
Houlbrook, R. A. 153, 154, 205
household 17, 36–7, 56, 113, 114,
117, 149, 150–3, 180, 187,
208, 230
Howard League for Penal Reform
42, 51, 69

ignorance 26, 79, 109
illegitimate daughter 25
inbreeding 31–2, 33, 38, 158,
183; *see also* aversion, human
incest 14, 16, 23–31, 36, 38, 39,
41, 49–51, 59–60, 86, 89,
100, 104, 128, 130, 131–8,
150, 156, 183–4, 190, 192,
195, 209–10
concern over 39
paternal 126–53
sibling 156–80
Incest Crisis Line 48, 59
incest survivors' groups 48
incest taboo 23, 28, 30–1, 131–8,
180, 192, 209
theories of 31–8
incestuous abuse 26, 130–2, 138,
166, 168, 171, 177
incestuous adultery 27, 30, 94
incidence of abuse, 47, 51, 52
Independent, the 182
indicators of damage 83; *see also*
disclosure; physical signs
inequality, of persons 35, 167,
172, 190, 202
innocence 23, 72, 164, 189,
227

intercourse, sexual 21–3, 24–5, 28, 81, 89, 131, 158, 165
anal 21, 26, 41, 88, 132, 200
heterosexual 21, 23, 41
homosexual 23
oral 26, 41, 88, 132
unlawful sexual 23, 49
with penetration 24–6, 89
intervention 8, 225–32; *see also* protection of children
Irvine, Dr 4, 10

Jampole, L. and Weber, M. 233
Jones, D.
and McCraw, E. M. 75, 97
and Seig, A. 97, 154, 194, 206

Kempe, R. S. 40
and Kempe, C. H. 109, 206
Kendall-Tackett, K. A. and Simon, A. F. 98
Kinsey, A., Pomeroy, W. B., Martin, C. E. and Gebhard, P. H. 160–2, 181
Korbin, J. E. 106, 210, 233
Koshal, N. 18

La Fontaine, J. S. 70, 154, 204, 232
Langness, L. L. 233
legal aspects 22, 24–5, 27, 40, 48, 75, 77, 144, 183, 219, 221, 228
Levin, J. 97
Lewis, J. 233
lies 71, 74–5, 99; *see also* denial; false accusations; unfounded accusations
Light, P. and Richards, M. 181, 205
Lock, Dr Margaret 233
love affair 27, 30, 94
Lowe, N. V. 153
Lukianowicz, N. 26, 104

Maddox, B. 154
magazine survey 161–2, 181
magazines 164, 196

Mair, L. 206
Maisch, H. 100–1, 154
male relatives 24, 30, 87–8, 115, 128, 145, 208; *see also* brothers; fathers; sons
Malinowski 176, 195, 206, 210, 232
mandatory reporting, 48, 60, 226
marriage 25, 194
prohibitions on 24, 29, 30
masculinity 8, 20, 83, 86–7, 89, 96, 99, 176, 190, 195, 207; *see also* dominance; gender; paternity
Masson, J. 39
masturbation 81, 88, 159–60, 162
maternity 106, 191
McKee, L. 153
and O'Brien, M. 153
media *see* magazines; newspapers; television
medical evidence 23, 215, 217; *see also* physical signs
Meiselman, K. 154
methods of research 61, 68, 103, 124
mother–son incest 106, 211
mothers 17, 33–4, 72, 78, 104, 146, 189, 224
motivation 100, 191–2, 198, 199
Mount, F. 233
Mrazek, P. B. 83, 124
Lynch, M. and Bentovim, A. 43
and Mrazek, D. A. 12, 97
multiple abuse 116, 118
abusers 115, 173
victims 57, 66, 115, 118–19, 173
Murdock, G. P. 204

Nash, C. L. and West C. D. 63, 65, 69, 111
National Society for the Prevention of Cruelty to Children (NSPCC) 40, 48, 51–2, 69
neighbours 67, 87, 108, 115, 121, 123, 127, 134–5, 208, 210, 224

Nelson, S. 182, 206
nephews 25
newspapers 1–2, 7, 9, 27, 163, 173, 199
niece 24, 25, 30
nightmares 84, 213; *see also* consequences, of sexual abuse

Observer, the 69, 181
offenders 17, 48, 51, 101–2, 110, 139, 148, 210, 220, 229; *see also* abusers; perpetrators
Olson, E. A. 232–3
oral sex 81, 200

Paedophile Information Exchange, British 22, 102
paedophilia 35, 74, 99, 124
parental authority 9–11, 34, 77, 143, 172, 176
parental power 77
parental rights 8, 9, 11, 141
parenthood 20, 31, 45, 187, 189
parents 1, 4–6, 8, 22, 28, 40, 45, 78, 84–5, 102, 120, 122–3, 126, 156, 170, 172, 188, 215, 220
Parents Against Injustice (PAIN) 4, 9, 11, 75, 110, 223
Parker S. and Parker H. 101, 136–7, 139, 153
Parsons, T. 204
paternity 141–2, 144, 191
perpetrators 22, 50, 56, 61, 78, 95, 107, 110, 121, 168, 175, 213, 229–30; *see also* abusers; offenders
physical signs 5; *see also* medical evidence
police 3–4, 12, 48, 52, 59, 105, 115, 219
police surgeons 6, 10
pornography, child 21
Post Traumatic Stress Disorder 92; *see* trauma
power 77, 144, 178, 180, 208, 210, 223

masculine 86, 176
prevalence
  of sexual abuse 3, 46–7, 52, 61–4, 66–7
  of sexual interest in children 102
privacy 150, 208, 210
promiscuity 84, 213
prostitution 65, 67, 172
protection of children 8, 225–32
psychological abnormalities of abusers 99, 101
punishment 21, 79, 100, 143, 188, 227, 229
Punishment of Incest Act, 1908 24, 40

questionnaires 3, 15, 60, 61, 63

Radcliffe-Brown, A. R. 183
Rantzen, Esther 3, 64
rape 35–6, 49–50, 73, 169, 195, 200–1
rates of sexual abuse 46, 52, 168; *see also* prevalence
referrals to the CSA Unit 55, 57
  from Essex 56–7
reflex anal dilatation 5
Reid, I. 153
relations by marriage 25; *see* stepfathers
relatives 23–5, 28, 30, 32, 33, 85, 88, 121, 123, 127, 128, 135, 210
Report of the Inquiry into Child Abuse in Cleveland 10, 13, 42, 220
representative survey 15, 59, 61–2, 66, 75, 87, 104, 119, 120–1, 133, 134–5, 168, 171, 177, 199
research 2, 5, 41, 44, 48, 54, 61, 63, 64, 68, 85, 101, 111, 217
Richards, M. 153
Richardson, S. 1, 4, 10
rights 9, 77, 208, 234
rights of children 9, 234
Roberts, Dr R. 11

Russell, D. 4, 62, 64, 68, 92, 182, 206

Sanders, D. 42, 70, 80, 181
Sarsby, J. 181
Saunders, E. J. 233
Schneider, D. 37, 183–4, 204
secrets 45, 67, 122, 211, 219
seductive children, 71–2
self-esteem 84, 100, 213
Seidler, V. J. 206
sexual
    abuse by women *see* women
    aversion 138
    competition 33, 197
    experimentation 156, 161, 166, 184; *see also* play *below*
    gratification 41
    intercourse *see* intercourse
    needs 195, 196
    offenders 100
    play 157–8, 162–4, 167
    powers 89, 96, 99
    problems 197, 213
    relationships 159, 195
sexuality 20, 83, 195
sexualized behaviour 72, 84, 117, 148, 166, 176, 216
Sgroi, Dr S. 20
sibling incest 27, 156–80; *see also* brother/sister incest
silence 77–9, 85, 92, 96, 145, 215, 222
sisters 28, 32, 33
Smith, H. and Israel, E. 173, 182
social and cultural factors 103, 106
social characteristics of offenders 108
social life of children 126
social services 1–4, 6, 7, 12, 45, 53, 56, 57, 59, 77, 86, 89, 92–3, 94, 103, 123, 215, 220
sons 33, 136
South London Press 181
state, role of the 1, 8, 21, 40, 141, 185, 194, 220–1, 230
statistics 23, 46, 48, 51, 58, 60, 68
step-child 25, 28, 72, 96, 103

step-relations 25, 28, 29
stepfathers 1, 17, 76, 88, 114–15, 128
stereotypes 177, 218
strangers 108–10, 111–13, 127–8, 134, 135, 200
suicide 84, 213
Sunday Mirror, the 206, 234
Sunday Times, the 74, 97
survey 3, 15–16, 22, 38–9, 46, 51, 58–63, 64, 66–7, 75, 85, 87, 108, 113, 115, 119, 136, 168, 171
survivors 110, 114, 136, 219, 222

Tardieu, A. 39
teachers 86, 127, 156, 208
television 1, 3, 59–61, 64, 123
threats 78, 96, 212, 216, 228
Tranter, M. and Vizard, E. 23, 234
trauma 39, 84, 218, 226; *see also* Post Traumatic Stress Disorder
Trudell, B. and Whateley, M. H. 234
Tylor, E. B. 32

uncle 24, 30, 87–8, 128, 145
Underwager, Dr R. 11
unfounded accusations, 76; *see also* false allegations
United Nations Declaration of the Rights of the Child 234

victims 6, 17, 48, 51–3, 56, 72, 86, 95, 107–8, 114, 123, 136, 168, 198, 201
violence 74, 78–9, 132, 143, 144, 169, 176, 212, 223, 226
    paternal 175
    sibling 167–71
Vizard, E. and Tranter, M. 233

Walmsley, R. and White, K. 69
wards of court 3
Weeks, J. 206
Weinberg, S. K. 157, 163, 165, 180, 181

248

Wells, N. H. 69
Westermarck, E. 32, 33
    158
Wolf, A. 138
Wolfram, S. 29, 4?
women 24, 28, ?
    104, 105-
    192-4,
women as

13, 114, 118, 121, 211
, Rev. M. 4, 10
Dr G. 10-11
G. E. and Peters, S. D. 70
Dr J. ?0

207